Shays' Rebellion

THE UNIVERSITY OF MASSACHUSETTS PRESS
AMHERST, 1980

SHAYS' REBELLION

The Making of an Agrarian Insurrection

DAVID P. SZATMARY

Printed in the United States of America
Library of Congress Cataloging in Publication Data
Szatmary, David, 1951–
Shays' Rebellion.
Includes index.
1. Shays' Rebellion, 1786–1787. I. Title.
F69.S99   974.4'03   79–22522
ISBN 0–87023–295–9

To Mary

Acknowledgments

I have many people to thank for this book. Sidney Kaplan graciously allowed me to look at his notes, gave me substantive and masterful editorial suggestions, let me stay at his home, and became my friend during the writing of the manuscript (so, too, Emma Kaplan). Mary C. Wright, Rudolph Bell, and Larry Henry painstakingly read the manuscript many times and gave me encouragement to finish the project. I thank my dissertation advisor, James Kirby Martin, as well as Wayne Cooper, Joel Shufro, Allen Kaufman, George Billias, Thomas Forstenzer, Dick Kohn, and the readers of the University of Massachusetts Press for their many careful readings of the manuscript and their helpful comments. Richard Martin of the University of Massachusetts Press gave me an immeasurable amount of assistance, while Mary and John Wideman, through the help of Susan Tracy, allowed me to stay in their Whately home as I completed the research for this book. I wish to thank Wendell B. Cook, Jr., of the University of Massachusetts library for his help in making the Badlam Papers of the Dorchester Historical Society accessible. Most of all, I want to thank my parents, Peter and Eunice, for giving me an interest in history and the chance to pursue it, and my wife, Mary, for her understanding during the trauma of writing this book.

Contents

Preface

Shays' Rebellion has been a topic of historical debate for almost two hundred years. In 1788, a year after the insurrection had ended, George Richards Minot wrote *The History of the Insurrections in Massachusetts*. Trained in Boston as a lawyer, Minot served as clerk of the Massachusetts House during the Rebellion and personally deprecated Shaysite activity, calling for the punishment of leading rebels. "Daniel Shays's decapitation," he suggested on June 9, 1787, "would have dissolved a common tie, or prevented [the rebels] engrafting their several oppositions upon his: and so rendered their opinions harmless speculations."[1] Minot carried his anti-Shaysism into his *History*, calling the troubles an "unfortunate rebellion" and castigating "those deluded citizens who were concerned in the insurrections or rebellion."[2]

Concern for foreign opinion, however, moderated Minot's progovernment bias in his *History*. Writing at least partly "to preserve the reputation of my country" against European criticism, Minot sought to avoid the impression of fundamental differences between competing groups in Shays' Rebellion. Through such an approach, he wrote,

> many misconceived ideas, tending to the discredit of the country, may be removed; and the public reputation vindicated; as the causes which led to the late national difficulties, when rightly understood, operate as an apology for them; and the manner in which these difficulties were suppressed, does honor to the government, and displays the strongest marks of reflection and wisdom in the people.[3]

As a result, his treatment of the insurrection became an only moderately progovernment study. As historian David Ramsey contended after its publication, the *History* had "the air of impartiality."[4]

Nineteenth-century historians, not as concerned as Minot about European opinion, reflected the nationalism of their day and came out strongly against the insurgents. "When the materials of the rebellion are taken into consideration," Josiah Holland, the founder and editor of *Scribner's Monthly,* wrote in his *History of Western Massachusetts* (1855), "their entire lack of moral power, their utter cowardice, their boastings and their threatenings, their insolence and malice, their outrages and robberies—apology for them stammers with awkward qualifications and justification stumbles with the weight it carries." For Holland, the Shaysite troubles "taught a lesson, and let that lesson be remembered: That the rebellion of a people against a government established by themselves is not justifiable, even in an extreme case, and can only result in dishonor to the state, and calamity and disgrace to those who participate in it."[5] John Fiske, writing in 1888, similarly deprecated "the delicious *naiveté*" of the "craze for paper money" and concluded that the Massachusetts "rebels had behaved shamefully."[6] Andrew McLaughlin in 1905 assessed the Shaysites even more harshly than Fiske, calling them "the vicious, the restless, the ignorant, the foolish," who "were advocating measures which if given free opportunity for development would have undermined government and liberty together."[7]

As the application of scientific methods to American history became more prevalent during the early twentieth century, some historians tried to correct the unbalanced treatment of Shays' Rebellion. Jonathan Smith, for example, felt that previous narratives were, "for the most part, strongly colored with the opinions of those actively engaged in its suppression, and also of the conservative classes, who had no sympathy with the movement." He consequently sought to present "an impartial examination of the facts."[8] Joseph P. Warren also attempted to deal with the Shaysites impartially: "Many conservative and influential persons believed that the insurgents desired to overthrow the state government, and to establish some purely democratic or even communistic system in its place. The present writer believes that this interpretation of the aims of the rebellion was unjust to most of the participants."[9]

Following the lead of Charles Beard, historians soon began to characterize the Shaysites even more favorably, laying blame for the insurrection upon government supporters. Placing the Shaysite attacks in the "age-long struggle between debtor and creditor, the agrarian and commercial classes," Albert Farnsworth argued that the rebels generally were "farmers and mechanics and the ex-Revolutionary soldiers, and the ex-Revolutionary soldiers formed a considerable part of Shays' Army. On the other side were the conservative groups, the professional classes and the commercial classes along the seaboard." The farmers attacked the debtor courts, he concluded, due to "economic discontent and social inequality."[10] Robert East similarly placed the blame for the Massachusetts insurrection upon "the conservative fiscal and social policies which were pursued in that state after 1780."[11] Millard Hansen also saw the uprising as a reaction of "impoverished" farmers in the "Populist Party" against the social program of the "Massachusetts conservatives."[12]

Some historians viewed conservative government policies in terms of class. Richard B. Morris believed that such "tension as had existed between classes and sections was in considerable measure suspended during the military conflict" but resurfaced after the Revolution as the state elites consolidated their power. To Morris, Shays' Rebellion represented an example of postwar class conflict.[13] Sidney Kaplan hinted at the same interpretation, contending that many prominent government supporters during the uprising "were class conscious."[14] In his *Western Massachusetts in the Revolution,* Robert Taylor argued that "Shays' Rebellion separated the citizens of Massachusetts into two class-conscious groups—debtors and creditors."[15] In the same vein, Marion Starkey thought "Shays' Rebellion did bear some resemblance to a class war."[16]

As the McCarthy era developed, however, historians started to downplay the differences between the conflicting groups in the insurrection. Because they seemed like "small capitalists in the American backwoods," reasoned Louis Hartz, the Shaysites "frightened the nation" in "the mood of unhappy kindred spirits, not in the mood of wholesale antagonists. They were inside, rather than outside, the liberal process of American politics."[17] Robert Feer also believed that the insurrection "was not so great or so deeply rooted as to constitute anything approaching 'class war' or a fundamental disagreement over values or goals."[18] Pauline Maier forced Shays' Rebellion into a similar "consensus" interpretation. "So often considered a class uprising," she contended, the postwar disturbances of the Shaysites in New England "proved *extra-institutional* in character more often than they were anti-institutional; they served the community where no law existed, or intervened beyond what magistrates thought they could do officially to cope with a local problem."[19] The Shaysites, added Alden Vaughan, "demanded evolution, not revolution."[20] As late as 1972, Van Beck Hall continued to minimize the disagreement between the New England rebels and their governments: "These Regulators who blocked the courts had no intention of destroying the social and political institutions of their commonwealth."[21]

Some recent scholars have questioned the consensus model and have asked for a fresh look at the uprising. Alfred Young, for example, believed that "we need a fuller picture of the radicalism of the 1780s—of Shaysism, and not only Daniel Shays's rebellion in Massachusetts."[22] Thus, this study will attempt to provide an interpretation of Shaysite activity in all of New England. Following in the path of such American scholars as Jackson Turner Main, Edward Countryman, and Barbara Karsky and of such English historians as E. P. Thompson and Eric Hobsbawm, it will locate the roots of the insurrection in a clash between a traditional, agrarian way of life and an ever-encroaching commercial society.[23] The rebellion represented a dynamic process that had its basis in the continuing struggle between a largely subsistence, family-based, community-oriented culture of independent farmers and an acquisitive, individualistic way of life dominated by merchants, professionals, speculators, and commercial farmers. In the larger context of American social development, the insurrection illustrated the tumultuous effects of the transition from traditional society to merchant capitalism.

*The insurrections of the year 1786 form one of the
most instructive periods in the history of our country . . . [and] will give [citizens] a deeper insight into
the character of this people, a more extensive view of
our social organization, and its internal operations
at critical times, than they could obtain by years of
personal observation. . . .*

*John Quincy Adams, May 28, 1802,
in a eulogy of George Richards Minot*

State Vermont

Gen. Lincoln left
this with 3000
y Feb. 3. sunset
& reached Petersham
& Morng Feb. 4. at IX
& routed Shays

Amherst New Hampshire
y Jany. Feb. 8. left &

Hadly

G. Patterson
& took 80 at
Stockb.

Shays joyn
Feb 27

Day routed +
y Feb 27. Springfd

Shays & 12

G. Lincoln here with
3500. y Jany 27

*From the Ezra Stiles Papers, The Literary Diary, February, 1787,
Beinecke Rare Book and Manuscript Library.*

State New Hampshire

State Line

Petersham Shays here night Feb 3, 1787 with 2000.

Flight

Here G. Lincoln overtook Shays Feb. 4. at X in maine and put him to Flight

Shays left his X Feb. 3

Pelham

Day 2000

repulsed Janr 25 H Sheperd 900.

Gen. Worcester

Gen. LINCOLN and 3000

Janr 23 1787 Court sitting

BOSTON

1
The Two Worlds of New England

POSTWAR NEW ENGLAND, in the aftermath of the American Revolution, was a society and culture in which rural tradition and commercial expansion came into conflict. During the 1780s, the vast majority of New Englanders lived in a largely subsistence culture. As Jackson Turner Main has pointed out, "the subsistence farm society was the most common type throughout New England and perhaps the entire North." Although some New Englanders in market towns of Massachusetts such as Springfield, Deerfield, Northampton, Stockbridge, and Worcester were becoming more commercially oriented than they had been in the colonial period, the overwhelming majority of the citizenry labored in a relative subsistence economy and followed a way of life defined by subsistence production.[1]

In rural New England, three basic occupational types predominated—yeomen, artisans, and agricultural laborers. Yeomen, comprising about 70 percent of the agrarian population, grew crops primarily for survival. In the words of a typical Massachusetts yeoman, a farm provided "me and my whole family a good living on the produce of it. Nothing to wear, eat or drink was purchased, as my farm provided all." [2] But, as Rodney Loehr has shown, farmers did not grow crops for home consumption only. Most yeomen produced a small amount of surplus crops to exchange for such needed manufactured articles as glass, gunpowder, iron, and medicine.[3] One

Bay State farmer spent about "$10 a year, which was for salt, nails, and the like." Other New England farms, observed the author of *American Husbandry* in 1775, yielded "food—much of clothing—most of the articles of building—with a surplus sufficient to buy such foreign luxuries as are necessary to make life comfortable; there is very little elegance among them, but more of the necessaries."[4] Yet the subsidiary role of such surplus production must be emphasized. As *American Husbandry* concluded, farmers in the North produced mainly for home consumption and only secondarily for exchange. One historian accurately describes the "subsistence surpluses" as constituting "the residue remaining after the farmers had fulfilled their principle responsibility of feeding themselves and their dependents." Thus, the surplus formed only a small part of an overall economy defined by production for subsistence.[5]

Farm production in Whately, Massachusetts, demonstrates such subsistence-oriented goals. In 1784, twenty-nine-year-old farmer Paul Smith had three dependents and owned fifty-six acres of land, an ox, two cows, and six swine. To feed himself and his family for a full year, he needed roughly 60 bushels of flour, 500 pounds of pork, 200 pounds of beef, flax for making clothes, and small amounts of peas, turnips, potatoes, fruit, and carrots to round out his family's diet. In addition, he needed grain for seed to be planted the following year, another 16 bushels of corn to feed the cows, some grain to pay the cost of milling grain into flour, and about 5 tons of hay for the ox and the cows.[6]

Paul Smith utilized only enough land to meet these immediate needs. Although he had the chance to grow more surplus crops for market, given his fifty-six acres of land, the labor of himself and his wife, and the close proximity of Whately to the Connecticut River, he generally used only the land and labor necessary for short-range requirements. Smith set aside 3.6 acres of pastureland for his ox and two cows, cultivated another 3.6 acres for the needed five tons of hay, and grew hemp and flax on 2 acres. He utilized a small plot for diversified crops necessary for home consumption and set aside about an acre for an apple orchard. Probably most important, he sowed only 3.8 acres of land with the commonly grown Indian corn or wheat.[7] His crops would have varied with the weather and soil, of course, but the tillage yielded about 102 bushels of Indian corn or 68 bushels of wheat.[8] After he fed his family and animals, he was left with 12.6 bushels of Indian corn and 250 pounds of beef for the market. Smith's wife sometimes supplemented this surplusage by spinning wool to exchange for extra food and manufactured goods.[9] All told, this farm family had an annual surplus of about £3 2s. 6d. that barely covered the cost of commodities needed from the country retailer.[10] Although he held in reserve forty-two acres of uncultivated land, or 73.2 percent of his total acreage, Smith did not till this extra land but continued to produce diversified crops for subsistence and a small surplus.

Farmers in other inland Massachusetts towns followed the same pattern of land utilization. In Brookfield, the average yeoman tilled only 5 percent of his total acreage and left 82 percent of the land unimproved or in woodland.[11] The 250 landholders in Amherst showed a similar proclivity in 1779, tilling only 9 percent of their land and leaving more than 60 percent unimproved, with the rest in pasture, mowing, or meadowland.[12] As in other New England villages, yeomen cultivated a mere fraction of their land and decided against further land development for large-scale production. "What need has the man who possesses 300 acres, to destroy the wood, or clear the land, as they call it, any faster than he can make use of the soil?" argued some farmers.[13]

The traditional economic mentality of New England yeomen can also be seen in crop selection. Farmers invariably produced Indian corn as a major crop, although it brought little return on the market in contrast to alternate crops such as hemp and flax, the production of which merchants encouraged since the two plant fibers were used to make sailcloth. In addition, noted the author of *American Husbandry,* maize depleted the soil quickly: "scarce anything exhausts the land more."[14] Yet most farmers continued to raise Indian corn despite alternatives. Indian corn, grown initially by settlers because it could be ground into flour more easily than wheat, seemed more desirable than flax or wheat. Given the option, farmers chose the crop planted by their forefathers rather than more marketable staples. At the same time, yeomen grew diversified crops. Besides Indian corn, they produced small yields of peas, turnips, beets, cabbages, potatoes, and carrots for home consumption. Such diversification, like the production of maize, exemplified the subsistence rationale in land cultivation and the absence of a strong commercial orientation among most husbandmen.[15]

During the 1780s, the persistence of traditional farming methods further disclosed the traditional attitudes of New England yeomen. Knowledge of fertilizers, the Norfolk system of crop rotation, purposeful breeding, and other agricultural innovations had reached farmers in the northern colonies as early as the 1760s, but many of them continued the customary methods of their ancestors. "Farmers do many things for which they can assign no other reason than custom. They usually give themselves little or no trouble in thinking, or in examining their methods of agriculture, which have been handed down from father to son, from time immemorial," lamented agricultural reformer Samuel Deane in 1790.[16] A year earlier, geographer Jedediah Morse had observed the same adherence to traditional farming techniques among northern farmers: "Annual improvements are made in agriculture chiefly by gentlemen of fortune. The common husbandmen in the country, generally choose to continue in the old track of their forefathers."[17]

Choosing a traditional life-style, New England farmers usually intensified cultivation of land only when they were driven by necessity. In the inland areas, necessity most often took the form of an increase in family size. Again, farmers in Whately provide an example. There, yeomen in their fifties, with families of six or seven, had more land and animals, but more needs, than their younger counterparts. On the average, they had six human dependents, two cows, two horses, fourteen swine, and two oxen. To feed himself, his family, and his animals and provide for the next year's planting, the farmer needed roughly 294 bushels of grain, 330 pounds of beef, and 700 pounds of pork. Once again, the yeoman rose to the occasion but produced little more than the necessities. He set aside 6.8 acres for pastureland, 8.8 acres for hay, 2 acres for hemp and flax, and only 13.5 acres for crop production. Like the younger Whately farmer, the older, more established yeoman left 66 percent of his land unimproved or in woodland. The land actually tilled by the older man, usually sown with Indian corn, produced relatively small surplus crops. After the family and animals had been fed, he was left with 104 bushels of Indian corn in addition to the 100 extra pounds of beef and 300 pounds of surplus pork. The total market commodities probably gave this yeoman just enough to buy necessities for a large family.[18] Increased crop production, then, seldom stemmed from the lure of the market; rather, it resulted from the size of a family. A. V. Chayanov's characterization of nineteenth-century Russian peasants seems applicable to New England farmers in the 1780s. The measure of land and labor utilization depended "to the greatest degree on how heavily the worker is burdened by the consumer demands of his family."[19] For subsistence-oriented yeomen, kinship ties largely determined the extent of crop production and human toil.

The New England subsistence culture, besides emphasizing traditional attitudes toward crop production, involved a sense of independence. In late eighteenth-century New England, most men owned their land. "Any man who is able to procure a capital of 500 or 600 livres [£25] of our money, and who has strength and inclination to work, may go into the woods and purchase a tract of land," wrote French traveler Marquis de Chastellux in 1781 as he toured the northern states.[20] The relative abundance of land, especially in central and western New England, allowed most farmers to till their own soil. Although found in scattered areas throughout Massachusetts and Rhode Island, tenantry did not represent a primary form of agricultural production.[21]

Many yeomen entertained a sense of self-mastery that stemmed in part from the ownership of their soil. The landed property held by "the yeomen of the country," observed Bostonian George Richards Minot in the 1780s, "had always been held of a higher and more valuable nature than any personal estate." The "possession of it seems to be a greater gratification to the pride and independence of men."[22] Owning land and tools and therefore controlling their labor, some farmers were understandably anxious to guard the autonomy gained through landed property.

Rural New Englanders revealed a consciousness of their independence through the labels they fashioned for themselves. Living in a traditional culture, they seem to resemble "peasants." "The peasant," wrote Eric Wolf, "does not operate an enterprise in the economic sense; he runs a household, and not a business concern." In contrast, Wolf equated an agricultural entrepreneur with a producer of chiefly marketable commodities. The entrepreneur runs "primarily a business enterprise, combining factors of production purchased in a market to obtain a profit by selling advantageously in a products market."[23] In relation to these commonly used definitions, New England farmers would appear to have been peasants rather than rural businessmen. Recently, two anthropologists, Joel Halpern and John Brode, have suggested as much. "If it is possible to overlook the pejorative use of the term, might not the North American farmers also be called peasants?" they asked about yeomen of the revolutionary era. "After all, many of them are only a generation or two removed from the European countryside."[24]

Yet, Yankee farmers seldom applied the continental European term *peasant to* themselves, feeling that it connoted "the idea of one who hires a farm to cultivate." Emphasizing their independent status within a largely subsistence economy, they usually preferred *yeoman,* a term that included all "property freeholders who cultivate their own land." Referring to the care of animals as well as the cultivation of crops, *husbandman* was "commonly used as if it were perfectly synonymous with agriculture" and the yeomanry.[25] Rural New Englanders sometimes equated *farmer* with both yeoman and husbandman and characterized themselves with one of these labels. Stressing the independence inherent in land ownership, they normally eschewed the peasant label despite the many similarities between the European and the American social and economic experiences.

But a feeling of independence did not necessarily lead to individualism. Although priding themselves on their autonomy, yeomen lived in a community-directed culture. To ease their backbreaking work during planting and harvesting, they asked family and friends for help. The independent status of yeomen, then, resulted in neither self-sufficiency nor a basically competitive society but led, rather, to cooperative, community-oriented interchanges.[26]

The work patterns of many yeomen reflected such communal action. In a typical situation, everyone within the immediate family contributed to agricultural production during the hectic times of planting and harvest. In a relative subsistence economy centered around the household, women labored in the fields along with the men. Daughters "Jean and Sarah helped us the 6th and 7th to rake and hay," Matthew Patten of Bedford, New Hampshire, noted in his diary on August 7, 1784. During the last harvest in October, 1785, "the Girls digged potatoes" while Patten "finished pulling beans between the barn." The members of the extended family similarly helped one another, exchanging labor during peak periods. On June 20, 1785, Patten's sons James and Alexander went with their father and helped their uncle "to hoe at his corn." Joseph Patten returned the favor a few days later: "My brother Joseph and their boy and their horses helped us and we hoed the corn," Patten wrote on June 22.[27]

Neighbors also traded labor and animals. On May 26, 1785, Matthew Patten "had the same team of my brother's today that we had yesterday and John McLaughlin came with his four oxen and helped us and we finished plowing between meadow and harrowed." Neighbor Simeon Chubbuck arrived with his horse and toiled in Patten's fields a few days later. To repay their friends, the Patten family gave their own time and energy to neighbors. Alexander Patten "hoed for John McLaughlin which paid for what they helped us." In addition, he helped "Simeon Chubbuck to mow most of the afternoon which I suppose will pay for his horse we had yesterday" and "worked for James Wallace towards his helping us frame at the barn." [28] Throughout the busiest seasons, family and neighbors worked with one another for common survival.

Community help even extended to the new farmer in a village. "In America a man is never alone, never an isolated being," observed Marquis de Chastellux in 1781. "The neigh-

bors, for they are every where to be found, make it a point
of hospitality to aid the new farmer. A cask of cider drank
in common, and with gaiety, or a gallon of rum, are the only
recompense for these services." [29] During the 1780s, community cornhuskings, barn raisings, logrollings, and quilting bees
symbolized the overall cooperation among rural New Englanders.[30]

The system of barter similarly points to the community
orientation of yeomen. In most cases, farmers directly exchanged small amounts of surplus produce for needed items
and seldom sold extra crops for money. Some entered into
barter relations with neighbors. James Patten, for instance,
received four bushels of grain from Lieutenant Orr during an
especially poor harvest and a year later "took four bushels of
the rye to Lt. Orr that he owed him." In the fall of 1784,
James's father Matthew similarly made a "swap of oxen" with
James Marrs and later made many other trades with neighbors.[31] When a farmer entered into barter transactions with
country retailers, it was within a framework of subsistence
production. He offered a small amount of surplus crops to the
store owner and received needed articles such as iron and
medicine. If the deal was an investment for market to the
storekeeper, it nevertheless involved a direct exchange of one
product for another to the husbandman. Farmers occasionally
sold extra crops to neighbors and retailers for cash. But even
when one yeoman sold goods to another and recorded "the
obligation in money terms," James Henretta has observed,
"it was assumed that the debt would continue (usually without
interest) until it was balanced in a subsequent barter transaction." [32] New England farmers, like the rural villagers described by Ferdinand Tönnies, generally based their exchanges
"not on contracts, but, like those [agreements] within the
family, upon understanding and reciprocal obligation." [33] The
many quarrels between farmers over unfulfilled agreements,
some ending in court, existed within such a traditional framework.

The community orientation of the yeoman in work and
exchange encompassed both the agricultural laborer and the
country artisan. During the 1780s about 10 percent of male

New Englanders in rural areas worked as agricultural laborers and helped nearby farm families daily or seasonally during planting and harvest.[34] These workers, although laboring for others, did not form a fledgling rural proletariat in a rationalized wage economy. Usually men in their twenties or early thirties, they often owned a modest tract of land themselves. Young Abner Sanger, a day laborer in Keene, New Hampshire, during the revolutionary era, had a small plot sown with corn, string beans, and potatoes.[35] Sanger toiled for family and neighbors in exchange for additional land, services, and a supplemental crop. Along with his brother-in-law William Stanwood, he worked "down in ye low land heaping and burning, raking, burning leaves and other trash" for his brother Eleazer on October 1, 1774. The Keene laborer pulled Eleazer's "white beans till time to go to court" four days later and continued to work for his brother throughout the rest of the year. In return for his labor, Sanger received a small plot of cleared land.[36]

Abner Sanger sometimes labored for others in exchange for services. On December 1, 1774, for example, he traveled to the home of neighbor Benjamin Carpenter "to get him to come and plow at ye South end at ye little new bridge." Sanger shoveled wood chips "by said Carpenter's door for him till near noon" in return for his neighbor's plow and team. But, most commonly, the Keene laborer worked for supplemental crops. Early in 1775, he went "to a week's work at A. Partridge's" in exchange for grain, and on July 1 he journeyed "over to Captain Wyman's to see if they want me to work for them and let me take ye pay in grain." Two days later Isaac Wyman decided "to let me have grain and employ me three or four days to work."[37] Although some agricultural workers, especially in towns near major markets, may have worked for wages, laborers such as Abner Sanger received payment in goods, services, and land. Such agricultural work aided the labor-short farm family in its immediate needs and eased the struggling young yeoman past the first few years of land ownership.

As did the day laborers, country artisans lived within a community-oriented culture. Many craftsmen owned small

farms and engaged in the collaborative social relations of other
yeomen, bartering crops and labor with family and neighbors.
Thus, a consciousness of community carried over into their
artisanal work. Rather than producing large numbers of items
for market, rural craftsmen, in most cases, limited production
to goods specifically requested by their neighbors. "In rural
villages," argues Carl Bridenbaugh, "nearly every craftsman
restricted his work to spoken goods." [38] Inland craftsmen also
traded finished products for supplemental crops. On January
13, 1787, shoemaker William Nutting of Groton, Massachusetts, "received two bushels of wheat for one pair calf-skin
pumps." The same day, he got "four bushels of corn from
Abel for one pair thick shoes sold to Timothy Holden" and
"received two and one-fourth bushels wheat of Captain Bur-
lingham for one pair large shoes." [39] Clockmaker Jonathan
Hartwell of Shirley, Massachusetts, conducted his trade in the
same manner. On July 1, 1786, for example, he gave farmer
James Parker a new clock in exchange for a cow and a calf.[40]
Jackson Turner Main, summarizing the barter practice of
country artisans, found that in the northern countryside artisans exchanged goods for crops and services: "The blacksmith
shoed the doctor's horse in return for medical care. Farmers
and their oxen ploughed the land and harvested the crop and
were credited accordingly. The rural artisan's life was much
like that of the small farmer." [41]

While most yeomen and country artisans followed a traditional way of life in the 1780s, most New Englanders along
the coast and in inland market towns lived in a largely commercial culture. Their market-oriented way of life included
the drive toward acquisition and accumulation and emphasized
the individual over the community. Merchants, shopkeepers,
professionals, commercial farmers, urban artisans, sailors, and
fishermen formed the most important economic groups in
this society. New England merchants, residing in large port
towns such as Boston, Newport, and Providence, dominated
and represented the most successful sector in the commercial
culture. Handling and transporting farm goods, manufactured
commodities, and, at times, human cargoes, they primarily
sought personal wealth. Such middlemen, although they

worked at a slower pace than modern industrialists, had the accumulation of money as their primary goal.[42]

Once these merchants made initial gains, they funneled earnings back into business enterprises. Many reinvested profits in new trading ventures in hopes of yet greater gains. Some relatively large wholesalers—Bostonians James Bowdoin, Samuel Breck, Christopher Gore, and Samuel Otis—funded the Massachusetts First National Bank, hoping the large reserve of money centered in the bank would soften any sudden commercial setbacks and yield sizable interest on loans.[43] Other merchants reinvested in the enterprises of an emerging industrial capitalism. During the 1780s, a group of Salem merchants, for example, built the first American cotton mill, and some Connecticut wholesalers constructed a glassworks and a snuff-making factory.[44] Still other successful merchant capitalists put profits into land. In the late 1780s, for instance, New England and New York wholesalers spearheaded the formation of the Ohio Land Company. The merchants did not plan to farm, however, but intended to profit from their purchases through quick sales to incoming settlers.[45] Finally, some wholesalers such as James Bowdoin, Samuel Adams, and Benjamin Lincoln speculated in continental and state securities, buying cheaply and hoping for profits after the government backed the currency with gold.[46] In early 1785, noted Boston lawyer James Warren pointed out the rationale for such ventures: "Money is the only object attended to, and the only acquisition that commands respect." [47]

The mercantile desire to accumulate money engendered an ethic of competitive individualism. Boston wholesaler Thomas Hancock revealed an attitude common among coastal traders in a letter to a failing business associate: "As to the profit you get on your goods its your look out, not mine. I expect my money of you when it's due," he told Connecticut retailer Seth Osborne in February 1755.[48]

Competing with one another, merchants tended to downplay the importance of community. "Community and society," a political theorist has observed about New England traders, "meant little more than the ground upon which each challenged or used others for his own gain. Others were accepted

insofar as they were useful to one in his search for self-sufficiency." [49] Although not precluding the existence of familial
ties, individualism sometimes hampered strong friendships. As
Massachusetts trader Samuel Collins told his brother in a dis-
pute over a transaction, "it is a common saying business before
friends." [50]

Country retailers—a second element of the commercial society—similarly viewed social relations from the perspective of
businessmen, even though they lived in the midst of a largely
subsistence, community-oriented culture. Every year they
bought significant quantities of such goods as glass, iron, and
rum from coastal wholesalers and sold them to inland farmers.
Storekeepers, usually situated in inland market towns such as
Worcester, Springfield, and Great Barrington, accepted small
amounts of crops from yeomen for payment and then sold
them to large wholesalers in New York and on the Connecticut River. As did the larger coastal merchants, country middlemen bought and sold goods in order to accumulate cash profits.
The shopkeepers, according to Main, usually "accumulated,
over the years, considerably more property than other men in
their community, and had a higher standard of living." Retailer Isaac Thomas of Hardwick, Massachusetts, for instance,
possessed clothing worth twenty-five pounds, an expensive
riding carriage, livestock worth fifty-five pounds, and had
investments in an iron factory, a potash works, a sawmill, and
land at the time of his death.[51]

Their desire for profit tied country shopkeepers to coastal
wholesalers. Although they often opposed the eastern merchants on specific political issues, inland traders largely identi-
fied their interests with those of coastal wholesalers out of
economic necessity. Relying upon the sale of commodities,
country store owners needed harmonious relations with coastal
traders to stay in business. They depended upon seacoast merchants for extensions of credit and constant supplies of European goods. A sudden change in credit or distribution policies
on the part of eastern wholesalers could be disastrous to the
small-scale enterprises of country retailers. While they needed
friendly relations with their agrarian customers for a contin-
uous flow of farm goods, shopkeepers many times drew farmers

into credit relations during a bad harvest and thus had more leverage in their dealings with local yeomen. The store owners' dealings with the wholesaler consequently assumed greater importance and usually determined their allegiance during political crises.[52]

Lawyers bolstered the position of seacoast and inland merchants, forming another element of the commercial society. Before the Revolution, New England law largely dealt with religious concerns outlined most fully by seventeenth-century Puritans. But by the 1780s, contends legal historian William Nelson, the "criminal was no longer envisioned as a sinner against God but rather one who preyed on the property of his fellow citizens."[53] Law increasingly supported the sanctity of contract and provided a means for the regular collection of debts and loans. As political theorist C. B. MacPherson has noted, the law became "a calculated device for the protection of property and for the maintenance of an orderly relation of exchange."[54] By enforcing contract law, members of the bar guarded the bases of a commercially oriented way of life. Moreover, most Massachusetts lawyers practiced in towns along the coast, four-fifths of them in port towns "where they prospered by handling cases for merchants, traders, and other members of the most commercial interest group."[55]

During the 1780s, many clergymen similarly collaborated with the mercantile elite. Initially, the Puritan clergy held both symbolic and real positions of power in a basically religious community. But as a commercial culture slowly replaced a religious ethos in major coastal towns during the early eighteenth century, the function of the ministry changed somewhat. Clergymen no longer simply influenced religious matters but began to uphold the secular order from the pulpit, many times legitimizing merchant capitalism with the word of God.[56] The Reverend Mr. Johnes, for instance, "preached a sermon from Matthew 22 to 27 render to Caesar the things that are Caesar's, and to God the things that are God's." In "the discourse he said the payment of taxes as well as debts was to be included as meant and intended in the comment of rendering to Caesar the things that are Caesar's."[57] The tax-exempt status of New England ministers, coupled with the payment of their salaries mostly in specie from tax funds, probably prompted their rigid attitude toward the enforcement of contracts and tied them to the commercial society.[58]

Besides merchants and professionals, market farmers formed part of the New England commercial elite. A number of gentlemen farmers owned large tracts of land near Boston. In addition, "the most ancient, settled parts of the province, which are Rhode Island, Connecticut, and the Southern part of New Hampshire," as the author of *American Husbandry* wrote in 1775, contained "considerable landed estates, upon which the owners live in much the style of country gentlemen in England." Commercial farmers in these areas generally "cultivated all or part of their estates; and if they are small, the whole; this they do by means of their stewards, who are generally called overseers; the rest is let to tenants." [59] Utilizing their entire land area through some form of hired labor, the country squires produced cash crops for sale at coastal markets. Probably comprising no more than 5 percent of the entire New England population, these agricultural entrepreneurs, offering a stark contrast to inland yeomen, fell squarely within the commercial culture.[60]

Not usually accepted in elite social circles, many urban artisans nevertheless found themselves within a commercial economy. During the 1780s, mercantile business provided much work for coastal craftsmen. Wholesaler Nathaniel Tracy found "ship carpenters and carpenters of every denomination principally, rope walk men also, and sailmakers" forming the majority of the Boston artisan population.[61] Unlike their rural counterparts, some of these artisans worked for wages. Blacksmiths who toiled in the New Haven shipyards, for example, received two shillings and twopence per hour of labor.[62] In addition, the production of some urban artisans differentiated them from rural craftsmen. For example, Boston tallow maker Gideon French, rather than just producing wares needed by family and neighbors, made candles, rushlights, and soap day after day for sale in the marketplace.[63] In Salem and Lynn during the 1780s, shoemakers likewise produced in bulk, making barrels of shoes for sale in Philadelphia and other faraway places.[64] Cordwainer James Weston of Reading, Massachusetts, "sold Mr. Joseph Bexter 85 pair of shoes." [65] Furniture makers in Rhode Island also produced for market, selling chairs, desks, and tables in the American South and the British West Indies.[66]

Often producing for market, coastal artisans sought an accumulation of profits. "If I were to single out any quality of urban craftsmen for particular comment," writes Carl Bridenbaugh, "it would be their driving desire to get ahead in the world. They were men of ambition; they were consciously on the make." [67] Price controls, a carry-over from colonial times, sometimes moderated the artisans' acquisitive bent. But during the revolutionary era, master craftsmen such as the Boston hatters organized against price regulation and gained a relatively free hand in modest capital accumulation.[68] Some town craftsmen even passed commercial values on to their children. As Bernard Farber has noticed, Salem artisans "inculcated in children the drive and skills needed for upward social mobility." [69] In this context, the various alliances of artisans with merchants, such as in the acceptance of the federal Constitution in Massachusetts during 1788, should hardly seem surprising.

As with urban artisans, sailors relied upon mercantile businesses for their livelihood. They depended upon merchants for work and were affected by fluctuations in trade. In addition, the types of payments that seamen received bound them to commercial enterprises. Some sailors, such as the seamen in New Haven, worked for wages, getting a maximum of forty shillings per month. Others were paid part of the voyage's profits, which made the success or failure of a trading venture a personal concern. Although periodically uniting and lashing out in defense of their own interests, seamen remained tied to the commercial economy.[70]

Fishermen also worked for the mercantile elite. In 1775, reported wholesaler Stephen Higginson, Salem and Marblehead merchants employed about 3,600 cod fishermen. Another 1,800 laborers cured the fish on shore, and about 2,800 sailors transported it. Other merchants hired over 540 young men to fish for mackerel, shad, and alewives. Centered in Nantucket, Boston, and Dartmouth, still other merchants gave work to over 8,000 whalemen.[71] In Seth Jenkins' hometown of Nantucket, there were "between 5 and 6,000 inhabitants there, men and boys, employed in the whale fishery; they have no other employment there." [72] Moreover, some of these fishermen received part of their catch as payment. According to merchant Brook Watson, "the cod fishery is fitted out on shares; their men have a share in what they take home." Others got money for their services. Like the sailors, the fishermen earned livelihoods from merchant-operated enterprises and formed part of the commercial society.[73]

These different occupational groups did not play equal parts in the commercial culture. As one historian has contended, "there was a hierarchy of function which also determined social relations" within market towns. "One's place within the complex social structure of the port town was fixed by one's relation to the market." Nevertheless, these groups found themselves tied to the common "culture of a market place, the way of life among the men and women who assisted in the transfer of goods that was the primary task of the merchant," and would act in concert during Shays' Rebellion. This common response to crisis showed the "vast difference between life in these towns and that in the [farm] villages, a difference that in some cases was tantamount to different stages of social development." [74]

Despite the existence of two different cultures in postwar New England, commercial leaders steadily penetrated the more traditional world of the yeoman. Coastal and inland merchants, seeking expanded markets, persuaded farmers to consume a few manufactured items. Because most farmers possessed little money, merchants offered these articles on short-term credit and accepted surplus farm goods on a seasonal basis for payment. If the farmer experienced a poor crop, shopkeepers usually extended credit and thereby tied the farmer to their businesses on a yearly basis. Such exchanges, although delayed barter transactions from a traditional perspective, encouraged the production of surplus crops and inescapably drew farmers into the market economy. During a credit crisis, the gradual disintegration of the traditional culture became more apparent. During hard times, merchants in need of ready cash withdrew credit from their yeomen customers and called for the repayment of loans in hard money. Such demands demonstrated the growing power of the commercial elite over the inland farmers.

Market penetration into the backcountry created a continuum of commercial and subsistence social relations within the inland areas. Some yeomen in the most westerly reaches of New England had few commercial links. On the other hand, farmers in developing market centers such as Northampton, Springfield, and Worcester were gradually drawn toward the market and either accepted, however reluctantly, a commercial orientation or moved to uninhabited land in the West. Between these extremes stood the subsistence farmers, who were increasingly being dragged into the marketplace by small exchanges with country retailers. During the revolutionary era, this group probably accounted for the mass of yeomen in New England. In the words of James Henretta, most husbandmen felt "the tension between the demands of the market and the expectations stemming from traditional social relationships." [75] Like the English farmers analyzed by E. P. Thompson, they found themselves caught between "the breakdown of the old moral economy" and "the breakthrough of the new political economy of the free market." [76]

Some yeomen resisted market penetration and the social relations it embodied. As Robert Brenner has written about French rural freeholders in the late eighteenth century, they often rejected competitive, acquisitive values and tenaciously clung to a more traditional life-style.[77] Shays' Rebellion, spreading across New England during 1786 and 1787, may be viewed in this context of cultural resistance. By and large, the Rebellion represented the reaction of subsistence farmers against an intruding commercial society. Shaysite sympathizer William Whiting outlined the basis of the conflict in late 1786. On the one hand stood the "most laborious part of the people," including many yeomen and "a large body of reputable mechanics" from the countryside. Opponents of the Rebellion were "composed principally of lawyers, sheriffs, commutationers, impost and excise collectors and their respectable creatures, servants, and dependents; brokers, jobbers, jockeys, little shopkeepers." [78]

A few historians have interpreted this confrontation as a class conflict in purely economic terms. Such a position, however, may be misleading. Undeniably, the rebellion became primarily a contest between two economic classes: yeomen who faced the loss of their properties, and merchants, lawyers and speculators who stood to gain from these losses. But without neglecting the economic base of the turmoil, it seems clear that Shays' Rebellion can be more fully understood as an economic conflict exacerbated by a cultural clash between a commercial society and a rural, subsistence-oriented way of life. This work attempts to explore the dynamics and consequences of such an encounter.

2
New England Merchants and the Chain of Debt

SHAYS' REBELLION AROSE within a specific economic context. Immediately after the war, many New England merchants unsuccessfully sought profits through expanded commercial relations. Unable to trade with the Baltic states, the Mediterranean area, and France, they soon turned to merchants in their former mother country for large-scale commerce. The renewed economic relationship, however, proved unprofitable for many coastal wholesalers. British officials, now viewing the United States as another foreign nation, excluded New England importers from the lucrative British West Indies market and left the Americans with few means to repay English merchants for the commodities they had purchased.

This retributive West India policy helped to generate a chain of debt collections in New England. The British demanded specie for their exports to the United States and discontinued credit to their American counterparts. Some coastal wholesalers, seeking an extension of English credit for continued business activity, passed the demand for hard money to their own clients—the retail shopkeepers in the inland regions. Also struggling for financial survival, country store owners in turn tried to collect loans made to farmers. Accustomed to the payment in crops of debts owed to shopkeepers, some farmers quickly felt the effects of the mercantile intrusion upon their traditional world. Many found themselves dragged into debtor court and threatened with loss of their land. Others ended in jail for unpaid debts. In both cases, economic conditions after the war heightened an already existing antagonism between merchants and yeomen and provided a context for Shays' Rebellion.

In the postwar era, New England merchants in great part did not foresee the pitfalls of commercial expansion as they sought new markets and the reopening of trade with Great Britain. As English commentator George Chalmers wrote in 1784, the Americans claimed "the *right of free trade* with the transatlantic settlements of Spain, Portugal, and France, as much as with the plantations of Britain."[1] New England wholesalers did not necessarily endorse free trade doctrines for an unlimited period of time. "In spite of the clamor and enthusiasm Americans affect for general freedom of commerce when such liberty is favorable to them," noticed French minister Louis Guillaume Otto in 1785, "they will be equally warm for an exclusive system when they can apply it advantageously to their commerce. They share this way of thinking with all merchants, alternately zealous for a monopoly and for free trade according to the interest of the moment."[2] But plans for trade monopolies lay in the future. Many New England traders, sensing the precarious position of the newly independent, agricultural nation among the eighteenth-century economic giants, wanted first to put their states on a solid foundation in the postwar world economy through free trade.

To that end, New England entrepreneurs made overtures to European merchants in the major eighteenth-century trading areas located near the great seas—the Baltic, the Mediterranean, and the Atlantic.[3] Certain economic and political factors, however, hampered their efforts. In the Baltic, the problem revolved around marketable commodities. New England generally sent surplus grains, fish, and lumber abroad; from 1768 to 1772, these three items comprised half of all exports from the northern colonies.[4] But Baltic exporters usually offered similar goods for sale and had little need for massive imports of these commodities. Moreover, beef, another major New England export, tended to spoil on the long voyage to the Baltic region.[5] Possessing few exchangeable articles, only a handful of New England merchants did business in the Baltic. From 1783 to 1786, only twenty-two Yankee ships sailed into Baltic ports, carrying cargoes that comprised less than 1 percent of the total Baltic commerce.[6]

Political sanctions retarded commercial relations in the Mediterranean. Although they had exported large quantities of fish, lumber, and grain to the Spanish states before the war, New England merchants were now blocked from the Mediterranean by Barbary pirates.[7] As Salem merchant Stephen Higginson lamented in late 1785, the New England states "used to send fish, wheat, flour, and sometimes the West-India Produce" to Malaga, Leghorn, and Barcelona, but for "want of a treaty with those piratical states we are deprived of carrying our own exports and those of the other states to those markets." In the postwar era, the "danger of seizure by the Algerines" crippled trade possibilities in the region.[8]

Some New England merchants also complained about the difficulties connected with possible French commerce. Even though trade with France was championed by such American leaders as Thomas Jefferson, John Jay, and Benjamin Franklin, it foundered upon postwar credit problems.[9] According to Marechal de Castries, French minister of marine, the American wholesaler was "often obliged to make his arrangements rather with the Englishman, who gives him credit, than with the Frenchman, who can give him less credit, but who would furnish him the same goods at a better price." [10]

Such postwar economic realities drew American merchants toward British exporters. Having traded almost exclusively within the British Empire network before the war, coastal merchants looked to their English counterparts for credit after the Revolution.[11] The resulting loans helped to cement mercantile relations between the United States and Great Britain. England supplied America with manufactured commodities such as glass, iron, and medicine on credit. In exchange, American merchants seasonally exported foodstuffs, lumber, and fish to Britain. As with modern-day "underdeveloped nations," the United States remained an agricultural satellite of an industrializing England despite a successful political revolution.[12]

This mercantile relationship resumed soon after the war. On

the advice of some influential London merchants in late 1783, British officials permitted the duty-free export of British goods to America and the import of American unmanufactured materials into the British Isles. New England merchants reacted quickly. During the last month of 1783 they bought £199,558 worth of British commodities; during the next year, the first full year of peace, wholesalers purchased almost triple that amount. The total roughly equaled the average yearly importation of British wares in the decade before the Revolution.[13] As D. A. Farnie has observed, "the United States thus remained an economic frontier of Europe, dependent especially on England."[14]

By importing vast quantities of goods into postwar New England, merchants glutted the market as they had done in 1745 and 1763.[15] "The importation of European goods has been so considerable, within the last six months that the exportable produce of the states probably will not equal it in less than three years," grumbled merchant Edward Bancroft in late 1783.[16] By the autumn of 1784, Jonathan Amory of Boston completely halted the importation of English goods and offered remaining commodities at 2 or 3 percent over cost and charges.[17] Merchant Christian Febiger aptly characterized the New England market in the summer of 1785, finding "in Connecticut, Rhode Island, and Boston such an amazing superfluity of all kinds of European goods," while Portsmouth to his "great surprise" was "equally stuffed with goods without a purchaser." Although they blamed the postwar recession upon "the people at large" who "have for several years lived in a manner much more expensive and luxurious than they have been able to support," some wholesalers still complained of a variety of unsold wares in their storehouses.[18]

An exclusionary British West Indies policy increased the problems of New England merchants. Although American commerce with the British mainland was resumed after late 1783, English officials nonetheless barred all American vessels from the British West Indies and permitted only British bottoms to carry American produce into the islands. At the same time, they encouraged the duty-free exportation of West Indian coffee, pimento, rum, sugar, and molasses to the United States.

Seeking maximal exports and minimal imports, British leaders hoped for the best of both economic worlds.

Postwar British policy on the West Indies originated from a variety of factors. Some English policy makers attributed past success in trade to the exclusionary Navigation Acts, which prohibited foreign trade with British possessions and seemingly formed the "basis of our great power at sea, gave us the trade of the world." As Prime Minister Lord John Sheffield remarked, Englar.d had "nothing to do but remain quiet, maintain the spirit of her navigation and commercial laws and all must go right with her."[19] After heated parliamentary debate, British officials accepted Sheffield's reasoning and extended the Navigation Acts to the newly independent United States. In the words of George Chalmers, "Great Britain allowed her laws to operate on the American states, as foreign countries."[20]

The extension of the Navigation Acts to the United States, however, may have been only a means to an end. The resentment of both British officials and the English people in general over their defeat in the American Revolution probably accounted for British West Indies policy as much as anything else. "The present exasperated temper—the loss of America," wrote Rufus King in late 1785, irritated Englishmen "to an extreme degree" and made some form of retribution against the former colonies seem necessary. The exclusionary West Indies policy may have given Britain the economic means to punish the triumphant American rebels.[21]

British officials who hoped for revenge partly achieved their design, for the West Indies policy caused financial hardship for at least three types of New England merchants. Before the war, some wholesalers around Portsmouth, New Hampshire, and Newburyport, Massachusetts, shipped lumber, fish, and hemp to the islands. There the produce "was exchanged for rum and sugar which they carried to London principally and took back British commodities." Another segment of the mercantile elite relied upon the carrying trade. They bought large quantities of southern rice and farm goods, shipped the produce to the British West Indies, and returned with rum and sugar for home consumption.[22] Finally, some merchants, especially those in Rhode Island, sent ships to Africa in search of slave cargoes. They exchanged the enslaved Africans in a labor-short West Indies market for molasses and sugar, then sold the West Indian goods at home or abroad. As with other trading patterns, this famous triangle of trade centered around the British West Indies.[23] The islands provided the market and commodities for a reexport trade as well as for more direct, localized shipments, giving some wholesalers the opportunity to repay British merchants for manufactured goods.[24] As John Adams noted in 1783, "the commerce of the West India Islands is part of the American system of commerce. They can neither do without us, nor we without them. The Creator ... had placed us on the globe in such a situation that we have occasion for each other."[25]

Blocked from the Indies trade in the 1780s, coastal New Englanders complained of hard times. In April 1785 Boston wholesalers formally protested their exclusion from the British-held islands. "Our carrying trade that great nursery of seamen and one of the principle sources of national strength and opulence is menaced with annihilation" by English commercial policy, they lamented. A few Providence merchants described the same "embarrassments of trade" by restrictions "in the ports of Britain."[26] Because shipbuilding declined dramatically in the postwar era, Boston artisans tied to that industry voiced a similar protest over British economic policy. "The restrictions of the *British Government* on all *American vessels,* and the shipping of goods from England to America in *British bottoms,* must operate to the destruction of *shipbuilding* among ourselves," wrote an association of artisans from twenty-two different crafts in May 1785: "The consequence must be an entire ruin of our *shipbuilders; blacksmiths; rope makers; riggers; block makers; sail makers; with other branches of business connected with the equipment of vessels.*"[27]

Some Connecticut River valley merchants suffered along with coastal merchants and craftsmen by exclusion from the British West Indies. Following the course of the river, the trade network started in upper Vermont, ran through the most fertile valleys of Massachusetts, swung through Hartford, Connecticut, and ended in Saybrook. Although the New York market siphoned off some trade from western Massachusetts, the river provided a main outlet for farm goods coming from inland New England. As one observer in Hartford noted, "the *natural* course of trade from this country is down the Connecticut River." [28]

Retailers situated along the river managed the valley trade. Generally, they bought British manufactured goods from Boston and New York wholesalers and exchanged them with inland farmers for crops.[29] In Northampton, Massachusetts, shopkeeper Stephen Hubbard traded English glass and iron for agricultural goods with hundreds of yeomen across the countryside. Levi Shepard, another prominent Northampton retailer, likewise sold British medicines on credit to farmers in nearby villages and later accepted farm commodities for payment.[30] Store owners such as Hubbard and Shepard then shipped the produce down the Connecticut River to Hartford where such wholesalers as Jeremiah Wadsworth bought the goods and sent them to the West Indies. After selling their cargoes, the merchants purchased rum, coffee, sugar, and salt in the British islands, sailed home, and sold the imports to inland yeomen. Thus, importation and exportation in the valley focused on the British West Indies. As a few Connecticut merchants reported in mid-1784, this trade "was the only commerce which produced a balance in our favor, yielding a small but almost certain profit, which was continually increasing" in the years before the Revolution.[31]

In the postwar era, a few valley merchants may have successfully smuggled goods into the English islands or redirected trade to the French West Indies and the southern United States, but most middlemen in the region relied to a great extent upon legitimate trade with the British West Indies and felt the crippling effects of English policy. "Our West Indies trade is much against us, being shut out from the English Islands and closely restricted amongst the French," complained Connecticut wholesaler Barnabas Deane in October 1785. Another merchant echoed Deane's feelings a few months later: "Our West Indies business is ten times worse than it was before the *war* and God only knows that was bad enough then. Trade and commerce is almost at a stand." "The West India traders have been the great losers in the last year," added

Connecticut merchant Jacob Sebor in mid-1785.[32] As with coastal merchants and artisans, middlemen of the Connecticut valley complained about the decline of business under an independent United States.

The poor commercial climate partially stemmed from overtrading. Banned from the British West Indies, New England merchants imported great quantities of manufactured goods from England and helped to create a serious imbalance of trade. In 1783, the value of New England exports to the British mainland and English possessions covered the cost of only 13.2 percent of British imports into the northern states. The next year the figure dropped to 9.4 percent, leveling off slightly the next year. By 1786, a huge trade deficit had become apparent to virtually every merchant along the coast.[33]

Merchants who had been sending specie abroad for English imports but receiving little hard money from the export trade soon lamented the shortage of specie. From the "importation of foreign merchandise" into Massachusetts "since the peace," wrote Stephen Higginson on August 8, 1785, "our cash of necessity has been exported in great quantities ... and we are now from that cause almost drained of money." In late 1785, former loyalist Martin Gay recorded the same talk among traders in Boston. "Such a scarcity of money they say was never known amongst them, which together with the restrictions the British Acts of Parliament lay on their navigation, deprive them of the benefit they vainly boasted they should obtain by their glorious independence," he noted sarcastically.[34] Boston merchants accurately assessed the situation. By July 1784 only £150,000 in specie still circulated in Massachusetts.[35]

The overtrading of New England merchants and the subsequent drain of hard money led to a credit crisis and a strangling chain of debt collection. The demands of British wholesalers formed the first link in this chain. Immediately after the war, British tradesmen continued the prewar practice of offering large cargoes to American merchants on credit. Many of these merchants, who had hoped for specie from sales in the lucrative West Indies market but in fact did not get a chance for legitimate trade in the area, defaulted on postwar obligations owed to British creditors. Merchants "who have imported largely from the British are generally in distressed circumstances. They have incurred debts they will never be able to discharge," Stephen Higginson told a friend in December 1785. From London, Abigail Adams reported that some New England merchants similarly had so "shackled and hampered themselves that they cannot extricate themselves [from] a credit they cannot support." [36]

The insolvency of some New England wholesalers soon caused problems for merchants on the other side of the Atlantic. "Those who have given credit here have already suffered and must suffer still more," wrote exiled American Silas Deane from London. "Complaints of failures of remittances from America, are general and loud on all hands." Especially prevalent during the 1780s, the bankruptcies of British merchants illustrated Deane's point.[37]

Reeling from the effects of a liberal credit program, many British merchants followed a course taken in 1745, 1763, and 1772 and withdrew loans from New England traders. In July 1784, five well-known London merchant houses closed their doors to American business. One had a deficit of £140,000 while three others had taken £400,000 in losses.[38] Despite "numberless" applications "made to us to ship goods to different parts of America," the Bristol firm of Protheroe and Claxton also "declined executing a single order, knowing the difficulty people there must labor under of making their remittances." [39] Moreover, some British merchants demanded immediate, hard-money payments for past exports given on credit. In the midst of economic hardship, they felt that "to send goods abroad without having effects in hand for payment thereof, is not a reciprocal advantage between nations, but a species of speculative quixotism and mercantile insanity." By the middle of 1785, some English wholesalers consequently started "numerous collections" of their loans in New England.[40]

The demands of British creditors threw many New England merchants into dire economic straits. Ethan Allen, Vermont trader of Green Mountain Boy fame, outlined his financial distress resulting from foreign debts in late 1786: he had "not a copper to save" himself "from the devil. We are rich poor cursed rascals, by God," he explained to his brother Levi. The debt collections of British traders reduced some New England merchants to bankruptcy. "Many failures have already happened and many more must happen," predicted Stephen Higginson. On July 8, 1786, David Spear, Jr., son of a wealthy Boston merchant, had the same news for his fiancée: "There has been many more failed in business since I last wrote you about it." [41]

The economic difficulties of New England traders revolved around liquid capital. In 1786, few merchants lacked assets. Despite his complaints, Ethan Allen owned a 1,000-acre farm in New Burlington and at least £100 in goods for sale.[42] During the previous year, Boston merchants as a whole had reported £225,262 in stock and trade and another £7,315 in factories. But while wholesalers possessed goods, many needed specie to pay British debts. Boston merchants collectively admitted to over £80,000 in foreign debts, yet had on hand only £24,225 in hard money. They lacked the liquid capital necessary in a cash economy.[43]

Although they were in desperate need of specie, many New England merchants nonetheless escaped financial ruin. Some troubled merchants received support from wealthy kin during the postwar recession. Others continued to make profits in spite of the economic downturn. In 1785 alone, Boston wholesalers sold over $6 million in merchandise. Still other coastal merchants such as Samuel A. Otis avoided disaster through the benefits of political office.[44] Probably most important, merchants had no legal obligation to discharge postwar debts owed to foreign creditors.

Despite the absence of legal sanctions, some New England merchants felt compelled to fulfill their obligations to British creditors out of economic necessity. Throughout the colonial era, most wholesalers relied almost solely upon British capital for business operations. Aaron Lopez of Providence, for example, ran his mercantile business with £12,000 from the British merchant house of Hayley and Hopkins.[45] Needing British capital for postwar economic prosperity and feeling that only the payment of English debts would lead to a resumption of British credit, merchants sought some means of acquiring hard money.

To satisfy British creditors, New England wholesalers tried

to collect their own outstanding loans. "Most of the commercial interest have been very unsuccessful abroad since the war; and many of them seem now to be turning their attention to the estates of their debtors to make their fortunes at home," Connecticut minister John Tyler told a friend on April 20, 1786. Some found loan collection difficult. In late 1786, Aaron Cleveland traveled to Norwich, Connecticut, to secure payment on his loans but met with frustration. "I have been trying to make a collection of debts, but my attempts are nearly in vain for money is scarcer if possible than at Wyoming [Pennsylvania]," he reported. Boston merchant James Swan experienced the same problem. "In consequence of the scarcity of money," he was unable to "collect money on principle or interest of my old bonds or from debts contracted personally a few years since."[46]

Having difficulty with debt collections, merchants increasingly chose legal action that contributed to a great increase in debt suits. In Hampshire County, Massachusetts, the Court of Common Pleas prosecuted 2,977 debt cases between August 1784 and August 1786—a 262 percent increase over the 1770–72 period. Perhaps more significant, debt cases from 1784 to 1786 involved 31.4 percent of the county's male citizenry over sixteen as compared with 12.5 percent from 1770 to 1772.[47]

Other counties in Massachusetts followed the same pattern. In Worcester from 1770 to 1772, creditors took about 1,200 debtors to court. Debt suits jumped to 4,789 in the 1784 to 1786 period and involved 32.8 percent of adult males. The Essex County court similarly heard a large number of lawsuits; in the single session of April 1785, creditors initiated over 300 debt actions.[48] And in Bristol County from 1770 to 1772, about 500 creditors dragged debtors to court. Debt cases climbed to 1,429 from March 1784 to September 1786, representing about 18 percent of the adult males.[49] Berkshire County also experienced a dramatic rise in court actions against debtors.[50]

Judges in other states likewise heard a multiplicity of debt cases. During 1786, Connecticut creditors initiated more than 6,000 actions, taking over 20 percent of state taxpayers to court.[51] In Vermont, observed Governor Thomas Chittenden in 1786, "law suits become so numerous that there is hardly money sufficient to pay for entering the actions, not to mention the debts."[52] New Hampshire citizens also "were much involved in debt suits," according to Representative William Plumer.[53]

Some of these debt suits had originated during the prewar period. In New England during the Revolution, most provisional governments had suspended debt prosecutions, forcing most creditors to wait until the end of the war. When the courts finally resumed business in 1780, wrote Massachusetts retailer Timothy Edwards, "the general disposition [was] to settle estates, at least partially."[54] In the Hampshire County court from August 1785 to August 1786, roughly 17 percent of the debt cases had been initiated before 1780; and in Bristol County at the March 1784 session, the figure was about 11 percent.[55]

It seems clear that most debt suits resulted from the postwar credit crisis. New England wholesalers initiated some of these many court actions, prosecuting inland retailers for large sums. From 1784 to 1786 in the Hampshire County court, they claimed an average debt of almost thirty-eight pounds—a larger amount than in over 85 percent of all other debt cases and a considerable sum for the postwar era. More crucial, in 10 percent of all Hampshire County suits from 1784 to 1786, a wholesaler sued a retailer. Connecticut merchant Joseph Webb, for example, took to court Hatfield store owner Jonathan Pierce. Another Connecticut wholesaler, Jabez Bacon, took action at the same session for £188 against retailers Simeon Smith and Charles Dibbert of Lenox, as did wholesalers Robert Henry and Robert McClellen against shopkeeper James Perry of Easton for a £555 debt. In Hampshire County as a whole, 79.5 percent of all prosecuting wholesalers took retailers to court. From wholesalers, then, the chain of debt extended to country shop owners.[56]

Fighting for solvency, these shop owners tried to collect their own debts. Some of them, who had been selling manufactured goods to farmers on credit, had amassed a great number of small debts owed by local yeomen. Badgered by their own creditors and seeking good relations with wholesalers in order to preserve their economic stability and ongoing profits, some retailers sought to force collection of these debts during the mid-1780s. In Hampshire County from 1784 to 1786, over 58 percent of all debt suits originated in the western market towns of Northampton, Springfield, Westfield, Deerfield, Hatfield, and Hadley. Although retailers did not initiate all of these suits, they were responsible for a vast majority of them. Moreover, a few Hampshire shopkeepers repeatedly undertook legal action for the recovery of debts. From 1784 to 1786, thirty-one middling and prominent retailers, such as Warham Parks of Westfield and Springfield's "River God," John Worthington, initiated at least 35 percent of all debt suits. In every case involving a known retailer, the debtor earned his livelihood through farming and usually owed country shopkeepers less than twenty pounds for a few British imports. Country retailers, it appears, hoped to pay their debts to wholesalers by collecting small debts from yeomen.[57]

The demands of store owners thrust some yeomen into a difficult position. Farmers usually paid their debts to country retailers in crops and work on a seasonal basis. During the early 1780s, for example, over 72 percent of the customers at Oliver Dickinson's store in Amherst, Massachusetts, paid their bills in goods and labor. The situation changed rapidly during the postwar credit crisis. In 1786, retailers such as Dickinson often rejected payment in produce and demanded specie.[58] Although some farmers continued to pay bills in farm goods and labor, the nature of the credit crisis usually made such barter untenable. Pressed by wholesalers for hard money, country shopkeepers needed specie from rural debtors to stay in business.

The various state governments, pressured by speculating interests, compounded the difficulties of New England yeomen with stringent taxation programs. Massachusetts leaders, many of them Boston merchants, formulated the most oppressive policy. From 1774 to 1778, the most trying years of the Revolution, officials levied £408,976 in taxes. Tax assessments then jumped to £662,476 for the 1783–86 period and nearly equaled "one-third part the rents, or incomes of the estates of all the inhabitants."[59] Moreover, the Massachusetts government called for this extravagant sum in specie. Hoping to pay the Revolutionary War debt and to promote commerce, legislators in

Boston demanded hard money from Massachusetts taxpayers.

Just as burdensome was the decision of state leaders to weight taxation in favor of the mercantile interest and against the yeomanry, levying one-third of the tax on polls and the remaining two-thirds on land. Because most of their assets were in stock, merchants paid little tax compared to landholders. "In 1784," wrote Van Beck Hall, "the ten leading shipowning towns contained only 12 percent of the total taxpaying males who held two-thirds of the state's inventory, 72 percent of her vessel tonnage, and 87 percent of her wharfage facilities, but were assessed for only 14 percent of the state's total tax bill." [60] The remainder of the burden fell largely upon the yeomanry.

Farmers who had little hard money found it difficult to pay the state taxes. As early as 1784, yeomen in Conway described "the great difficulty we labor under in regard to paying our taxes"; and the "great scarcity of a circulating medium" in the backcountry made it difficult for the inhabitants of Palmer "to pay their taxes." Around 1785, tax collector Peter Wood wrote about the same distress. He had to exact over £1,000 from one-quarter of the farmers in Marlborough. They were already "behind in settling with the preceding collector," and it appeared to Wood that "there was not then the money in possession or at command among the people in my quarter of the town, to discharge taxes." Wood's problem exemplified overall conditions in rural Massachusetts. From 1784 to 1786, at least twenty-nine towns in the inland areas remonstrated against the heavy load of taxes payable only in specie.[61]

Legislators in other states, though enacting more moderate tax laws, also heard complaints from backcountry taxpayers. In Rhode Island, Baptist minister James Manning reported that "money is become so scarce that our people in the country, although possessed of property, cannot command sufficient to pay their taxes." [62] In Tinmouth, Vermont, yeomen likewise contended that "the present mode of taxation appears to us a great and real grievance." [63] In Connecticut, noted Anglican minister John Tyler, "the taxes that have already been laid, are a burden that daily crushes the estates of many of the people by its weight." [64] "Several thousands" of the "middling class of farmers" actually left the state for unoccupied lands to the west due to the heavy "weight of taxation." Only New Hampshire farmers, whose taxes were reduced from £110,000 in 1782 to £22,000 in 1785, failed to complain. Although generally paying local taxes with labor—almost 90 percent of Springfield farmers paid these taxes in this way—many yeomen felt burdened by the collection of state taxes in hard money.[65]

Deprived of specie for the payment of state taxes and personal debts, New England farmers faced the tough realities of the marketplace. Creditors tore some yeomen from their land and movable property. "The constables are daily venduing our property both real and personal, our land after it is appraised by the best judges under oath is sold for about one-third of the value of it, our cattle about one-half the value," angrily petitioned the townsmen of Greenwich, Massachusetts, in January 1786.[66] Common Pleas Judge William Whiting found the same practice in nearby Berkshire County. "Great numbers of farmers," he observed, "have been constantly stripped of whatever little stocks they possessed, and those often sold at public auction for a mere trifling."[67] "In the small state of Connecticut alone," added French minister Louis Guillaume Otto, "more than 500 farms have been offered for sale to pay the arrears of taxes. As these sales take place only for cash, they are made at the very lowest price, and the proprietors often receive not more than one-tenth of the value."[68]

Seizures of property infuriated the farmers. Living in a community-oriented society, they were indignant at the plight of friends and relatives. "To see a collector distrain upon one of their neighbors, and carry off a hog, or his colt, for the payment of his taxes, this startles them exceedingly," wrote one commentator in the *Independent Chronicle*.[69] Property seizures also created a fear of tenantry. As they watched the property of their friends auctioned for debt, the farmers feared the loss of their own land and stock. Many of them, like panic-stricken people of our own time, started to entertain "the belief or feeling of *possible* entrapment." The "*mortgage of our farms,*—we cannot think of, with any degree of complacency," declared the yeomen of Conway, Massachusetts. "To be *tenants* to *landlords,* we know not who, and pay rents for lands, *purchased with our money,* and converted from howl-ing *wilderness,* into fruitful fields, by the *sweat of our brow,* seems to carry with it in its nature truly shocking" conse-quences.[70] Although few farmers in Conway actually lost land through indebtedness during the postwar period, the vivid apprehension of possible tenantry made the farmers dread the calls of their creditors.

Some yeomen feared another possible consequence of in-debtedness—the debtor's cell. During the revolutionary era, a small landholder without sufficient property for settling his debts faced an indefinite jail sentence. According to the law in Connecticut, a creditor could "levy the execution of the debtor's body, and commit him to the common gaol in the county in which the execution is levied, where the debtor shall remain until he shall pay the debt and charges." Con-sidering the horrible state of New England jails during the eighteenth century, incarceration for indebtedness represented an extreme punishment. The Worcester County jail in Mas-sachusetts, disclosed newspaper editor Isaiah Thomas in 1785, operated in a "prejudicial manner" on the health of the in-mates from the "peculiar disagreeable condition which it is in." Some even died "by means of being confined in a place which disgraces humanity."[71] A Massachusetts House committee inspecting the jail a year later found the prison in just such a state: twenty-six prisoners languished without proper food or ventilation in one small cell.[72] Other New England inmates suffered the same abject conditions. Samuel Ely, a prisoner in the Bristol County, Massachusetts, jail during March 1783, was "alive and that is all as I am full of boils and putrified sores all over my body and they make me stink alive, besides having some of my feet froze which makes it difficult to walk."[73]

During the postwar credit crisis, Massachusetts retailers did not hesitate to throw indebted yeomen into prison. In Hamp-shire County from July 1784 to December 1786, they sent to jail, for an average two-month term, seventy-three men with relatively small debts. Of the total number of prisoners at that time, about 70 percent called themselves yeomen or husband-men. Another 22 percent aspired to a higher status and labeled themselves gentlemen farmers, while a blacksmith, cordwainer, carpenter, and some laborers rounded out the prison population. Significantly, no retailer sat in a Hampshire jail cell.[74] Inmates in the Worcester County prison told a similar story. Before and during the war, creditors had jailed only a handful of people for debt. In 1784, the situation began to change. At Worcester from September 1784 to February 1786, sheriffs confined 169 persons for crimes ranging from fighting to fornication. As with inmates of the Hampshire jail, 145 of them—the vast majority—were confined in the Worcester prison for small debts. Yeomen, husbandmen, day laborers, and rural craftsmen comprised 91 percent of these debtors while no prominent retailer and only four petty "traders" were behind bars.[75]

The jailing of debtors generated anxiety among farmers. Although few farmers were jailed for debt, their imprisonment alerted other yeomen to the possibility of such a jail sentence. The well-publicized case of Timothy Bigelow, an indebted Massachusetts farmer and Revolutionary War veteran who died in a damp cell of the Worcester County prison, along with the efforts of Worcester printer Isaiah Thomas for prison reform, further heightened agrarian fears. Fear of being jailed, as well as anxiety over possible tenantry, polarized debtors and creditors. Often setting retailers and farmers against one another, debt suits helped to push the two groups more rapidly into opposing camps.

To some farmers, their economic problems seemed especially burdensome because they came at the end of the Revolution. In Hampshire County, some yeomen felt "that it cost them much to maintain the *Great Men* under George the 3rd, but vastly more under the Commonwealth and Congress." It seemed that *"they were miserably deceived by Hutchinson's opposers,* who were the men who brought all their burdens upon them which, they are told, they should have been ever free from . . . *that they would take care how they were catched again."* [76]

In 1786, then, the scene had been set for a confrontation. Larger merchants, badgered by British creditors, asked for specie from country retailers, and shopkeepers passed the de-

mand on to yeomen. Either feeling the actual effects or fearing
the consequences of the call for hard money, some farmers
came to a bitter assessment of the newly won independence
from Great Britain. "What are the present state of facts as
they represent the yeomanry of this Commonwealth?" grumbled one Massachusetts farmer in 1786. "Our taxes are so high,
together with calls of a private nature, that our stock and
cattle are greatly diminished.... the greater part then of those
who gloriously supported our independence now find their
moveables vanishing like empty shades, their lands sinking
under their feet."[77] Perceiving themselves as trapped, many
farmers would soon protest against the demands of more commercially minded New Englanders.

3
Protest and Government Response

NEW ENGLAND YEOMEN responded to the postwar demands of their creditors with reformist measures before embarking upon a more forceful course of action. In the first stage of a dynamic process to be known as Shays' Rebellion, they proposed, in town meetings and county conventions, state-issued paper money and tender laws as panaceas for their troubles. As with the reformers analyzed by Eric Hobsbawm, the Shaysites accepted the "general framework of an institution or social arrangement, but considered it capable of improvement or, where abuses have crept in, reform." Working through the existing legislative process, they hoped for the security of a "traditional world in which men are justly dealt with, not a perfect world."[1] The situation would soon change. As Henry Knox, secretary at war for the Confederation, understood in 1786, "this business must and will progress from one stage to another until it amounts to a pretty formidable rebellion."[2] The Shaysite troubles, as with the North Carolina insurgency of 1766–76 described by Marvin Michael Kay, started with peaceful protest, proceeded to armed regulation, and ended in rebellion.[3] The fundamental nature of the clash between a traditional society and a developing commercial culture made the progression almost inevitable. But between early 1784 and August 1786, violent conflict did not emerge. Farmers still trusted the existing political systems in New England and made reformist demands in a nonviolent way.

Despite the nonviolent nature of these demands, the New England commercial sector almost universally condemned suggestions of paper money and tender laws. During the postwar credit crisis, it perceived mercantile expansion of credit in the backcountry as both financially unsound and socially disruptive. Most New England legislators, situated in major coastal ports, supported the economic interest and social vision of the mercantile community. Except for assemblymen in Rhode Island, they rejected proposals for paper money and tender laws in 1785 and 1786, allowing antagonisms between yeomen and the commercial interest to reach a stage of incipient violence by late 1786.

Agrarian Protest: The First Stage of Shaysite Activity

Before turning to clubs and muskets, New England farmers pleaded peacefully for relief. Between 1784 and 1787, yeomen in seventy-three rural Massachusetts towns—more than 30 percent of all communities in the state—sent petitions to the General Court in Boston.[4] Small landholders in New Hampshire matched the record of the Massachusetts farmers: from January 1784 to late September 1786, yeomen in forty-one towns forwarded complaints to the state assembly.[5] Similarly, the Vermont Assembly received petitions from farmers in ten western settlements during the October session alone, while Connecticut yeomen also handed their legislators numerous petitions.[6]

Simultaneously, many of these farmers, relying upon their revolutionary heritage, clamored for relief in county conventions. In 1774, patriots had organized committees of correspondence on the county level under the Continental Association to govern the emerging states during the war. New England farmers would later use conventions to expose their economic grievances. In March 1781, farmers in Worcester County, Massachusetts, called a convention "to remonstrate to the General Court against the repeal of the tender act."[7] Bay State yeomen held conventions in the western towns of Hadley, Hatfield, and Pittsfield the next year. According to Van Beck Hall, they "advocated reforms that would ease the payment of debts, reduce taxes, publicize the expenditure of state funds, and pare down the powers of the court of common pleas." [8] In 1783, agrarian unrest and reformism spurred new conventions in Hatfield, Hadley, and Deerfield. A year later, farmers in Wells, Vermont, hosted a county convention to ameliorate economic ills.[9]

During the postwar credit crisis, farmers continued to protest through county conventions. In Rutland County, Vermont, they held assemblies on August 15, 1786, at Rutland and on September 26, 1786, at Middletown.[10] Rhode Island farmers called for conventions at Scituate on August 10, 1786, and at East Greenwich two weeks later.[11] New Hampshire landholders similarly organized county conventions. By the late summer of 1786, wrote an observer in the *Massachusetts Gazette,* meetings "were held in most of the towns of this state, appointing members to meet in convention" for "relieving the alarming distresses of the people at large." Assemblies subsequently met at Concord, New Hampshire, in June, at Londonderry, Rockingham, and Chester during July and August, and at Rochester in September.[12]

In Massachusetts also during the summer of 1786, conventions were the order of the day. Yeomen in fifty of the sixty towns in Hampshire County attended the August 22 convention at Hatfield. On August 17, farmers in forty-one of the fifty Worcester County villages met at Leicester, even though voters in the market town of Worcester sent no delegate. In the same month, a majority of the farming communities in Bristol, Middlesex, and Berkshire counties formed popular assemblies. By September 1786, commented one observer in the *Worcester Magazine,* "county conventions [became] the general topic of the times." [13]

Both town petitions and county conventions illustrated the reformist nature of agrarian dissent. Rather than confronting New England governments with armed demands for a revolutionary change of the state, farmers sought to protect a traditional way of life through existing legislative channels. Although assuming limited legislative authority in county conventions, yeomen never formulated measures against established governments in the meetings. All identifiable conventioneers, such as the yeomen in the Hampshire County

convention, believed that the assemblies were "constitutional."
And they had a basis for their claim. According to the Massachusetts Constitution of 1780:

> the people have a right, in an orderly and peaceful manner,
> to assemble and consult upon the common good; give in-
> struction to their representatives, and to request of the leg-
> islative body, by way of address, petitions or remonstrances,
> redress of wrongs done them, and of the grievances they
> suffer.

In this light, as J. R. Pole has observed, "the conventions were
the only mode of collective protest or the concerting of policies,
which the dissidents could hit on before the rise of the organized political party." [14]

Through county and town petitions, yeomen proposed rem-
edies to neutralize the demands of creditors. Paper money became the most popular suggestion. In Massachusetts, over half
of all town petitions and every county convention specifically
asked for a paper currency. [15] Landholders in twenty-seven
Rhode Island towns argued for a paper medium, and every
town petition framed in New Hampshire between 1784 and
1786 did the same. [16] Communities such as Sharon, Connecticut,
likewise expressed the hope "that a paper currency be struck." [17]
Throughout New England during the mid-1780s, reported the
New Hampshire Gazette, "three-quarters at least, and more
likely seven-eighths of the people" wished that "paper money on
loan be made by government." [18]

Remembering their wartime experience, most yeomen who
asked for paper money wanted a depreciating currency. During the Revolution, New England state governments had
enacted a number of paper emissions to finance wartime operations, and in almost every state the paper rapidly depreciated. The value of a 1777 Massachusetts paper dollar, for
instance, fell to thirty-two cents in only one year. After another
year, the currency had a specie worth of fourteen cents, and
by 1779 it hit a low of four cents. [19] In the 1780s, some farmers
may have sensed the implications of such depreciation. Cornered by retailers with calls for specie, they could have more
easily paid their debts with soft currency. While it would have

eventually taken them closer to a market economy, paper money nonetheless would have given immediate relief and eased their fears over the possible consequences of unpaid debts.

On January 2, 1786, small landholders in Middleboro, Massachusetts, requested a £1,300,000 "bank of paper money" for a "legal tender in all payments throughout this state." Through "depreciation" of the proposed currency, farmers believed that they could escape the "most pressing demands" of the "wealthy and overbearing sets of men who can build up their fortunes on the ruins of the country in its present distressed situation." [20] Yeomen in Marlborough presented the same rationale for paper money. "Greatly distressed, while the merchants may riot in grandeur and luxury," they proposed a depreciating paper "medium to pay our debts or taxes." [21] In Windham, Connecticut, farmers similarly advocated "a paper currency depreciating 5 percent annually for twenty years" to meet the demands of their creditors.[22] The petition of the Hampshire County convention, a model for other New England county meetings, recommended the same solution. Conventioneers hoped to "have emitted a bank of paper money, subject to a depreciation; making it tender in all payments, equal to silver and gold." [23]

Yeomen also hoped to discharge their obligations through tender laws. These laws, passed by some states for limited periods of time during the revolutionary era, allowed farmers legally to discharge specie debts through payments in goods. Permitting yeomen to exchange crops for manufactured articles received in the past, the arrangement legalized a form of barter. During the postwar era, some yeomen sought tender laws to pay taxes and personal debts owed in specie. The farmers of Dracut, Massachusetts, epitomized the view: "Unless debtors are permitted to pay their private debts with property, both real and personal," it would "be out of the power of a great part of the community, as well as the inhabitants of this town, to extricate themselves from the labyrinth of debt" and to satisfy "those who have a greater love to their own interest than they have to that of their neighbors." [24]

Other farmers, such as those attending the Hampshire County convention at Hatfield, outlined other ways to neutralize the pressures of creditors. They called "the existence of the Courts of Common Pleas and General Sessions" a "grievance" and demanded their abolition. Offering creditors one easy way to collect debts, the two courts seemed a burden to subsistence-oriented farmers. Yeomen in over thirty rural Massachusetts towns echoed the plea for an abolition or restructuring of the debtor courts.[25] Some of these husbandmen also urged that the work of the probate court and the Registry of Deeds be given to town clerks and that the Court of Common Pleas be replaced with committees of arbitration staffed by elected rather than appointed justices of the peace.[26]

In addition, farmers in the Hampshire County convention complained about "the present mode of taxation as it operates unequally between polls and estates, and between landed and mercantile interests." Along with townsmen in at least seventeen other New England farming communities, they wanted a more equitable balance between inland and coastal areas. Since it appeared that "the General Court sitting in the town of *Boston*" gave the mercantile interest an undue influence in governmental affairs, they proposed moving the capital to a town closer to the Massachusetts backcountry. Twenty-nine towns in the inland counties put forth the same proposal.[27]

Still other petitioners in town meetings and county conventions of inland communities attacked the profession of the law. As early as 1774, reported Massachusetts legislator Theodore Sedgwick, lawyers had been, "almost universally, represented as the pests of society" by backcountry farmers.[28] Some western yeomen, mobilized by revolutionary sentiment, had even forced a few inland lawyers to sign agreements promising not to practice during the war. When the courts reopened in 1780, an anti-lawyer sentiment reemerged in rural areas, gaining momentum from newspaper attacks upon lawyers penned by Benjamin Austin, Jr., under the name of "Honestus." Feeling the pressure from creditors, farmers looked "with disgust and aversion" at the lawyers' "great appearances of wealth by their splendid tables, rich furniture, sitting up chariots, and the like," and blamed them for the ruin of "many good, worthy families." The members of the bar, they believed, were "an altogether useless order," and they hoped "to crush or at least put a

proper check or restraint on that order of gentlemen denomin-
ated laywers." [29]

A few farmers in Massachusetts did more than complain
about the mercantile elite. In January 1782 Samuel Ely, an
itinerant minister, exhorted Hampshire County yeomen to rise
against retailers such as John Worthington, Moses Bliss, and
John Chester Williams. The merchants, he suggested, "should
be made a sacrifice of and should be given to the fouls of the
air and to the beasts of the field." Two months later, Ely rallied
yeomen in Northampton for an attack against the Hampshire
County debtor court: "Come on, my brave boys, we'll go to
the woodpile and get clubs enough and knock their grey wigs
off and send them out of the world in an instant." In April
1782, farmers followed the minister to Northampton and
clashed with the militia on the courthouse green. During the
melee, militiamen arrested Ely. In June, however, about 130
farmers, headed by future Shaysite Reuben Dickinson, rode
into the town to rescue Ely. In the ensuing confusion, Ely escaped and government men jailed yeomen Abel Dinsmore,
John Bardwell, and Paul King, all future Shaysites. Hearing
that the three would be transferred to the Boston jail, over 500
husbandmen descended upon the Northampton jail on June 17
and convinced the authorities to release the prisoners.[30] In
October, New Hampshire yeomen closed down the Cheshire
County court.[31]

Crowds of New Englanders continued to assemble after the
Ely incident. The next year in Massachusetts, yeomen in Douglas and Sutton attacked tax collectors as they passed through
their towns while Hampshire County farmers marched into
Springfield and unsuccessfully tried to prevent the debtor court
from sitting. In Middlesex County, Job Shattuck, later prominent in the Shaysite troubles, organized fellow farmers and
manhandled local tax collectors.[32]

Despite these occasional assaults, most yeomen showed a
decided moderation in their proposals for change. From 1784
to late 1786, no town meeting or convention suggested a redistribution of property or an overthrow of government in
theory or in act. Most farmers only sought some form of paying their debts compatible with an agricultural society. Paper

money and tender laws represented their major recommendations to gain relief.

The Response of the Commercial Interest

Merchants and speculators generally rejected postwar proposals for paper money and tender laws, although in the
colonial era some traders had backed schemes for a paper
medium. In 1740, Boston wholesalers such as John Coleman,
Samuel Adams, Sr., and Peter Chardon had successfully
headed a movement for paper currency based upon a land
bank as they sought an expansion of capital for business
growth. Through paper currency, they hoped to buy and to
sell more goods in domestic and foreign trade.[33]

By the 1780s, however, the economic climate had changed,
making paper money undesirable to most New England merchants. Laden with British imports, wholesalers and retailers
no longer wanted paper money for an expansion of business
enterprises. They saw little prospect for commercial growth in
an area flooded with unsold wares. Some merchants also felt
that paper currency would not significantly increase the sale of
their goods. Noticing that "country people furnished themselves principally with cotton, and linen clothes" as well as
"their own shoes, hats, and stockings," they believed that paper
money would not generate greater consumption.[34]

At the same time, it was clear that a paper medium would
allow yeomen to pay for past purchases in inflated currency
and thus to pass a portion of the postwar economic burden
to the mercantile elite. According to Dedham lawyer Fisher
Ames, a new paper currency would result "in the transfer of
my property to my debtor ... a confiscation of my estate, and
a breach of that compact under which I thought I had secured
protection." Ames warned that inflated paper would bring an
end to "the legal protection" of his property under "fair contracts made under the due regulation of law."[35]

Some merchants decried in terms of morality the possible
breakdown of contracts. During early colonial times, a theo-
logically oriented system of law had protected a traditional,
religious community in New England. In the late seventeenth
and early eighteenth centuries, however, the New England

populace slowly became secularized, and as commercial relations increased, contractual law soon assumed a religious aura. "Bargains, conveyances, and voluntary grants, where two parties are concerned, are *sacred things*," young Connecticut lawyer and lexicographer Noah Webster wrote in 1788. "They should be religiously observed." [36] The contractual "right of property is a sacred right," agreed Newburyport merchant Jonathan Jackson in the same year, "and one most religiously to be respected by every society, that in these modern times wishes to flourish." [37] As C. B. MacPherson has noted about the secularization of English society, "all morality tended to be the morality of the market." [38]

Viewing morality from such a perspective, merchants condemned paper money as immoral. William Pynchon, Thomas Stebbins, and Reuben Bliss, three retailers from Springfield, exemplified this view: a paper medium was "iniquitous in itself, pregnant with innumerable evils, both political and moral . . . contrary to the spirit of our constitution, and inconsistent with the rights of mankind." [39] Believing that it favored "dishonest members of society" at the expense of "honest and industrious creditors," most merchants rejected postwar proposals for paper currency.[40] Speculators showed a similar disdain. During the postwar era, poor economic conditions forced revolutionary war veterans to sell their Continental and state certificates. Large speculators, many of them coastal merchants, bought this paper for a fraction of its stated value. "A very few men in each state," complained "Oliver" in the *Massachusetts Centinel,* "have monopolized these obligations to such an immense amount, and originally on so easy terms, that there are now some fortunes among us which would tolerably well support the expenses of an Earldom." Many of these speculators lived in New England. "We have a large proportion of the Continental securities in our state on which the Southern states complain they are paying us interest," wrote Massachusetts legislator Nathan Dane in January 1786. Among them were James Bowdoin with over £1,000 in securities and Benjamin Lincoln with £104. Seeking quick profits, speculators hoped the Confederation and state governments would refund the full value of the depreciated bonds in specie. Emissions of depreciating paper, they feared, would allow American governments to pay wartime debts in cheap money and to offer a depreciating paper for already depreciated Continental and state certificates. As Boston merchant J. J. Amory cautioned in October of the same year, a paper currency would "be the utter ruin of a great number of people who have invested their whole property in public securities which will be of no value." [41]

Tender laws likewise tended to undermine the financial growth of the mercantile elite. For most rural New Englanders, they offered a means to institutionalize barter, allowing farmers to give some of their crops to other farmers or country artisans in exchange for goods or services that they had provided, establishing traditional justice between neighbors. Merchants approached tender laws from a different cultural perspective. Because they sold manufactured goods and crops for profit, they were primarily interested in produce for its market value. Unable to ship goods to the West Indies during the 1780s, most wholesalers and retailers had little need of surplus crops and rejected proposals for tender laws. For them, acceptance of goods instead of cash spelled only economic loss.

Economic interest led to mercantile repudiation of other agrarian proposals. Some New England tax programs favored the seaboard, so schemes for a greater equalization of the tax burden between landed and commercial interests generally met with coastal disapproval. The coastal populace, enjoying a preponderant influence over New England governments due to their location, also dismissed proposals for the removal of capitals from the seaboard. As with the major recommendations of paper money and tender laws, such suggestions impinged upon the commercial interest and met with a firm rebuff.

Some merchants and lawyers even condemned a method used to implement rural demands for change—the county convention. To Maine wholesaler David Sewell, "these conventions of counties are seeds of sedition" that "ought always to be opposed." [42] A "Citizen" in the *Worcester Magazine* shared this point of view: "Instead of cheerfully paying, as far as they are able, their own private debts, retrenching their idle, unnecessary expenses, and contributing their portion to support a government of their own making," farmers in convention apparently performed acts "treasonable to the state" and concerted "measures to defraud their own and public creditors." [43] As another observer added, the assemblies ultimately subverted the principles of "free and rational government." [44] Although they had spearheaded a movement for conventions during the Revolution, the coastal elite vigorously criticized postwar county meetings. A "Freeman" in the *Worcester Magazine* captured the irony in 1786: "When we had other *rulers,* committees and conventions of the people were lawful—they were then necessary; but since I *myself* became a ruler, they cease to be lawful—the people have no right to examine my conduct." [45]

Spurning county conventions and the measures they generated, some merchants and professionals recommended instead industry, frugality, and saving to indebted farmers. These three traits, stressed by the American Puritans in a religious context, had been emphasized throughout the late colonial period. In 1749, for example, one letter writer instructed the readers of the *Boston Gazette to* "live frugally and spend no more than we can pay for, and encourage industry." [46] Although ultimately damaging to the interests of merchants who sought consumers, such arguments were now designed to overcome traditional notions of justice and work in the formative stages of a market society. Merchants and professionals, dreading the possible consequences of paper money and tender laws, stressed these traits during the 1780s. "Industry, economy, and honest principles, with the aid of a little patience and performance," would certainly insure the observance of contractual relations, argued Isaiah Thomas in August 1786.[47] During the same month, Noah Webster offered a more specific route to the same end. "The best way to redress grievances," he wrote to Timothy Pickering, "is for every man, when he gets an expense, instead of purchasing a pint of rum or two ounces of tea, to deposit his pence in a desk until he has accumulated enough to answer the calls of the collector." The practice,

Webster hoped, would diminish agrarian resistance to the demands of creditors and make paper money and tender laws unnecessary.[48]

New England Legislatures and a Commercial Society

New England legislators generally backed the commercial interest, supporting it for a number of reasons—for one, the location of state assembly houses in commercial centers. Massachusetts had its capital in the port of Boston; Connecticut lawmakers assembled in Hartford, the nexus of the Connecticut River valley trade; the port of Providence became the meetingplace of Rhode Island legislators; and the New Hampshire General Court met on the coast at Exeter. Only Vermont, a newly settled inland territory sandwiched between New Hampshire, Massachusetts, and New York, had its legislative seat in a noncommercial area.

The location of most capitals in or near major trading centers gave the commercial elite several advantages in state politics. For one thing, it offered the delegates of mercantile towns a chance to interact regularly with one another. As J. R. Pole has observed, the geographical position of Massachusetts legislators from the seaboard "gave them the opportunity of seeing each other and conferring in ways denied the interior." [49] The seaport sites of New England governments further allowed merchants and lawyers to directly influence political leaders. Close to the scenes of legislative debate, they could personally present their views at the statehouse, thereby exercising a direct voice in government that was inaccessible to inland yeomen. Finally, the location of New England capitals made it economically feasible for most coastal voters to send delegates to state assemblies. In contrast, wrote one contemporary, some rural villages "neglected to send representatives in order to save the cost of travel to a distant seat of government." [50] Attendance at the May 1786 session of the Massachusetts Assembly provides an example. Of the 130 towns in the most westerly areas of the state, only 67 communities, or 51.5 percent, sent delegates to the General Court. On the other hand, over 72 percent of the 40 towns in the eastern counties of Suffolk and Essex sent delegates to the legislature. The high cost of sending delegates from the inland areas, together with the apathy or hostility of relatively self-contained rural communities toward state government, probably accounted for the difference and often resulted in a slim majority for the mercantile interest in the Massachusetts House.[51]

The constitutions of many New England governments further enhanced the position of the commercial elite. Framed largely by lawyer John Adams and merchant James Bowdoin, Jr., the Massachusetts Constitution of 1780 raised provincial property qualifications for officeholding by 50 percent. Although extending the franchise to most males, it limited the senatorial post to men with a freehold of £300 or a personal estate of £600, restricted the representative office to males having a freehold of £100 or £200 in personal estate, and established a £1,000 qualification for governors. Obviously, the mercantile elite had the best chance for political office under this plan.[52] Some yeomen complained that "the landage interest have not a proper weight" compared to the "mercantile towns," but as Samuel Eliot Morison has written, merchants pushed the constitution through convention with a "manufactured" two-thirds majority. "The Constitution of 1780," he concluded, "was a lawyers' and merchants' constitution, directed toward something like quarterdeck efficiency in government, and the protection of property against democratic pirates." [53]

Most of the other New England constitutions in effect during the postwar era reflected a similar commercial orientation. In 1784, New Hampshire lawmakers modeled a new constitution upon the Massachusetts Constitution of 1780. Almost word for word, it mirrored the Massachusetts document.[54] Connecticut officials never even bothered to change the Royal Charter of 1662, which emphasized a mercantilist relationship between the colony and Britain and stipulated that merchants "ship and transport all and all manner of goods, chattels, merchandizes, and other things whatsoever that are or shall be useful or necessary for the inhabitants," but left the particulars of a political system to proprietors in the colony. Politically flexible within the context of a commercial society, the 1662 charter formed the basis of the postwar Connecticut government.[55] In New England, only the 1786 Vermont Constitution struck a balance between landed and mercantile interests. Patterned after the popularly framed constitution of Pennsylvania, it gave rural Vermonters an influence comparable to the political weight of the merchants and lawyers.[56]

Not only the social structure of the constitutions but also the social composition of the New England leadership favored the commercial interest. In Massachusetts during the 1780s, the speakers of the House and the Senate came from seaboard areas.[57] Governor James Bowdoin, elected in May 1785, by the General Court, likewise had his roots in the mercantile society. Son of James Bowdoin, Sr., one of the largest wholesalers in Boston during the prewar years, Bowdoin engaged in large-scale commercial activity and speculated heavily in Maine lands. Samuel Huntington, governor of Connecticut in 1786, started his career as a lawyer in the town of Norwich, became the king's attorney for Connecticut in 1765, and was appointed chief justice of the Supreme Court in Connecticut in 1784. New Hampshire governor John Sullivan similarly began his rise to power through the ranks of the bar. He eventually became New Hampshire's attorney general before his election to the president's office in 1786.[58]

Thus, the backgrounds of New England leaders, coupled with the location of state capitals and the social intent of New England constitutions, influenced the response of legislators to proposals for reform in 1785 and 1786. Rhode Island proved to be an exception to the overall pattern. In February 1785, Rhode Island legislators repudiated paper money by a two-to-one margin but, a year later, passed a tender law.[59] Farmers in the state, however, wanted further change and, in the spring 1786 elections for state officials, they turned out the Mercantile party headed by merchants William Greene and Jabez Bowen in favor of the Country party, led by sea captain John Collins and blacksmith Daniel Owens, which campaigned under the slogan "To Relieve the Distressed." In the legislature, forty-five new men, mostly from the Country party, won seats in the seventy-man House while five new men entered the ten-man Senate. According to one historian, the change "constituted somewhat of a political revolution, because it transformed the legislature from a merchant-dominated body to one in which the interests of the farmer took precedence." [60] The new Rhode Island leadership almost immediately turned its attention to the paper money issue. "Being persuaded that the opposition made in preceding years in the Legislative Body to this issue depended on the members having been merchants," observed Italian traveler Count Luigi Castiglioni, the Country party was "delighted to topple their influence" and in May 1786 proposed an emission of paper based upon a land-bank scheme. The bill, authorizing £100,000 in paper currency for the payment of all debts, became law at the end of the month with only the market towns of Providence, Newport, Westerly, and Bristol in dissent. [61]

After the law passed, economic conservatives throughout the United States hurled insults at the Rhode Island paper currency. To one trader in Providence, the paper money law was the height of "palpable fraud and dishonesty." [62] "Fraud and injustice have, in the state of *Rogue Island,* not only been encouraged, but even enjoined by solemn law," echoed another. [63] The paper emission even seemed a "daring attack upon the first principles of society" to one Boston gentleman. [64] The Connecticut Wits—satirists David Humphreys, Joel Barlow, John Trumbull, and Lemuel Hopkins—summarized the mercantile attitude:

Oh, roguery! their being end and aim
Fraud, tendry, paper bills, whate'er thy name ...
The crafty knave his creditor besets,
And advertising paper pays his debts;
Bankrupts their creditors with rage pursue,
No stop, no mercy from the debtors crew.
Armed with new tests, the licens'd villain bold,
Presents his bills, and robs them of their gold ...
Where grow'st thou not? If vain the villain's toil,
We ought to blame the culture, not the soil. [65]

Some coastal merchants demanded reprisals. One Boston trader recommended that "Fool-Island" should be given to another state "for care and protection." [66] Boston merchant and diplomat Francis Dana likewise suggested the division of Rhode Island between Massachusetts and Connecticut. Such

a partition, Dana believed, would meet "the general approba-
tion of the commercial part" of Rhode Island and save the
state from ruin.[67]

The general opprobrium cast upon Rhode Island paper
stemmed from a variety of fears. Some New England merchants, looking at the precedent set by Rhode Island, dreaded
emissions of paper money in their own territories. Others
braced themselves for foreign criticism and a subsequent loss
of trade. Still others had a more concrete interest at stake. New
York traders such as Daniel Verplanck, Benjamin Seixas,
Joseph Winter, James Sebor, and Edward Livingston had
speculated in the Rhode Island state debt and feared economic
losses with the issue of depreciating paper. For these reasons,
Rhode Island generally appeared "the one example of political
depravity" to many mercantile leaders.[68]

Reacting defensively to criticism, Rhode Island assemblymen
enacted stiff measures to enforce the paper money law. On
June 26 and August 22, 1786, they passed the Force Acts,
which dictated a £100 fine for creditors who refused the new
currency. If a creditor continued an intransigent posture, he
would be banned from holding office. In October, some assemblymen further recommended a test act according to which
each citizen would be required to take an oath in support of
paper money with disfranchisement as the penalty for refusal.
Merchants who refused to comply also would be prohibited
from sailing a ship from a Rhode Island port. Although the
test bill never became law, its consideration revealed the temper
of the Rhode Island legislature.[69] In September, a pro–paper
money convention in Smithfield proposed an even more radical
measure—a state take-over of all Rhode Island commercial
enterprises. The suggestion apparently gained some favor in
the assembly and created a furor in mercantile communities
along the coast. "A state trade is now proposed and should
it be adopted, would complete the mad system," nervously
wrote Noah Webster from Providence on September 28, 1786.
The scheme never progressed beyond the initial stages, but its
very suggestion disclosed the agrarian sympathies of the Rhode
Island government.[70]

Rhode Island legislators upheld their paper money policy

even in defiance of the courts. On September 13, 1786, John Weeden, a Newport butcher, refused to accept paper currency from cabinetmaker John Trevett. Trevett took the butcher to court a few days later and lost the case. "Whereupon all and singular premises being seen, and by the justices of the court aforesaid fully understood," the judges "considered, adjudged and declared, that the said complaint does not come under the cognizance of the justices here present, and that the same be, and it is, hereby dismissed." Within two weeks, Rhode Island legislators brought the justices before the assembly and charged them with criminal activity. Although criminal charges were dropped, the assembly reversed the court's decision.[71]

Legislators in other states followed a different course. On November 9, 1785, the Massachusetts General Court dismissed a proposal for paper money by a 93-to-23 margin, and a few days later rejected a proposed tender law by a resounding 89-to-35 vote.[72] Some yeomen hoped for a change in legislative policy the next year but met with disappointment. In late May, Massachusetts legislators offered only two minor reforms to their constituents, promising an investigation of supposedly exorbitant court fees and permitting payment of debts owed in other states with the paper currency of those states.[73] Completely sidetracked were the substantive issues of a paper medium and a tender law. In the last days of May 1786, recorded Northampton lawyer Caleb Strong, the General Court rejected "the bill for making all property a tender in satisfaction of executions" by a 90-to-35 vote. "Immediately after, a motion was made for the emission of paper bills and no more than 19 appeared to support it."[74]

A similar antipathy to agrarian reform marked the mood of the Connecticut legislature. Despite repeated pleas from farmers in 1785, assemblymen rejected paper money and tender laws by large majorities. The situation changed little during the next year. By November 1786, Connecticut representative David Humphreys could boast of legislative inaction. "We have done some negative good," the former revolutionary general informed George Washington. "We have prevented an emission of paper money and tender laws from taking place."[75]

More complex situations developed in New Hampshire and

Vermont. In the Granite State, the Senate and House unan-
imously rejected a paper money bill in October 1785 but passed
a two-year tender law by a close vote two weeks later. The
new act represented a compromise between landed and commercial interests. On the one hand, it institutionalized a form
of barter, providing farmers with a much-needed reform; on
the other hand, it gave a creditor "his choice what part of the
said debtor's estate he will take," punishing the yeoman se-
verely for a lack of specie.[76] In 1786, New Hampshire legislators continued a haphazard path toward reform. Assemblymen in the House recognized "the want of a circulating
medium" in June and accepted a plan for a £50,000 emission
of paper in September by a 52-to-12 vote. Conservative senators
such as merchants George Atkinson and Joshua Wentworth
halfheartedly agreed to the emission but rewrote the original
House measure, making the proposed paper good for tax payments only. They then decided to make the paper money issue
a subject for general approval or rejection by towns within
the state rather than a matter for the assembly. Senatorial
tactics thereby transformed the present reality of a paper legal
tender into the distant dream of a paper currency good only
to discharge unpaid taxes.[77]

Vermont conservatives similarly avoided significant conces-
sions to agrarian reformers. In 1785, legislators in the independent territory set aside proposals for paper money and
tender laws, permitting only gold, silver, and copper to be
used for "the legal money of this state." [78] The clamor for
reform throughout the countryside changed the minds of some
assemblymen the next year. In October 1786, the General Court
gave serious attention to a tender law and an emission of paper.
It seemed likely, wrote one representative, that "one or both
of the measures would be adopted by the legislature." Fearing
an enactment of the proposals, Assemblyman Nathaniel Chipman organized the leading economic conservatives in the court
and sought to block the measures by delay tactics. In the end,
the conservative group triumphed. "The whole subject was
postponed until the next session," Chipman exultantly reported.[79] Indebted farmers received no relief from the Ver-

mont government. As with most other New England assemblies, the Vermont General Court backed the mercantile
interest to the detriment of subsistence-minded yeomen. But
these legislative decisions would soon be challenged by agrarian
reformers armed with guns and clubs.

4
From Petitions to Arms:
The Regulation Movement

VERMONT ASTRONOMER Samuel Ellsworth, disturbed by economic troubles in America, looked to the planets for advice in the spring of 1786, and on July 17 he announced his findings: "By the malign influence of the [moon's] eclipses, the United States of America will be troubled with intestine jars, and domestic quarrels, and contentions of every kind." The eclipse of January 1787 would create the most trouble: "It will have much influence on men's tempers and dispositions.... Great tumults and contentions will arise.... several parts of America will suffer great disorders."[1] Ellsworth had read the movements of the heavenly bodies well. Throughout the fall of 1786, New England yeomen abandoned peaceful protest and took up guns. Calling themselves Regulators, they followed the example of their namesakes in North and South Carolina and proposed "moderating government" by planned attacks upon the court system. The Regulation—armed protest to achieve reform—formed the second stage of Shaysite activity.[2]

In late 1786, some farmers, reacting bitterly against legislative opposition to paper money and tender laws, urged stronger action. "When such mushrooms can play with laws, and laugh at the calamities of the people," wrote "Rusticus" about New Hampshire assemblymen in August, "society must unhinge government" or farmers "must be content to live in bondage all the days of their lives.... people cannot bear their burden any longer." George Brock, yeoman from Attleboro, Massachusetts, similarly criticized the policies of his state legislature. The General Court, he wrote, has treated "with supreme contempt our respectful petitions" and stigmatized farmers in convention as "traitors, incendiaries, vile creatures and nearly threatened them with prosecutions for daring to inquire into the present gross mismanagement of our rulers." Rather than responding sympathetically to peaceful protest, assemblymen rejected paper money and tender laws, charging "that they, the people, are luxurious in their diet, idle and profligate in their manners, encouragers of foreign manufacturers." By telling farmers how to live, Brock continued, legislators intended to "drive out that hardy and independent spirit from among us, and forge the chains for our liberties so strong, that the great exertions and convulsions will not break them"; they hoped eventually to reduce yeomen to wage laborers or tenants under "lordships." Brock exhorted fellow yeomen to rise against "all the machinations of those who are aiming to enslave and oppress us" and to strike down "that aristocratical principle too generally prevalent among the wealthy men of the state." [3] As did "Rusticus" in New Hampshire, the Attleboro farmer recommended decisive action to cope with legislative intransigence.

All over New England, except in Rhode Island and Maine, farmers heeded the calls to action. The rural citizenry in Rhode Island had been placated possibly by the emission of paper money, for the sole popular action during 1786 in that state was an urban protest aimed at the illegal actions of merchants. In June embittered wholesalers in Newport and Providence had remonstrated against the new paper currency by closing their stores in an attempt to starve the people into submission. By the end of the month, according to one observer, "this step of the merchants enraged some of the lower class of people in Newport to such a degree, that they proceeded in a riotous manner to distribute among their own adherents all the corn and flour they could violently lay their hands on." This food riot, like many of the eighteenth-century Parisian food disturbances described by George Rudé, ended in bloodshed. "Clubs and fists were liberally made use of for ten or fifteen minutes" before the turmoil subsided and the merchants fled.[4] This clash represented something unique for postwar New England. Unlike most other crowd disturbances, it occurred in an urban area and involved two groups of the commercial society. Moreover, the aims of the urban militants differed from those of the agrarian rebels. The Newport "lower class" wanted food, an item seldom demanded by subsistence-oriented farmers. Finally, the Newport masses gained legitimacy for their action from established authority, as they tried to force Newport merchants to comply with the paper money law.

The farmers of Maine—a part of Massachusetts until 1820—also stayed within the bounds of the law. Although they had organized conventions during the mid-1780s, their primary goal was a clear title to their lands, and to that end a secessionist movement was begun. Maine yeomen, unlike the Shaysites, seldom complained about indebtedness or taxation. As one secessionist wrote, "our difficulties took their rise, from a different source." Moreover, the assembly in Boston made a real effort to meet the demands of the Maine farmers: in March 1786, it awarded each yeoman in Maine 100 acres at a nominal price. The "100 acres of land confirmed to them *gratis* will quiet them," predicted land speculator Rufus Putnam. Despite a few suggestions to the contrary, Putnam proved to be correct; the secessionists postponed any organized attempts to obtain further redress until the close of Shays' Rebellion.[5]

Farmers in the rest of New England followed a very different course. Throughout the late summer, fall, and winter of 1786, they sought reform by launching attacks upon the New England court system. The timing was right for rural armed protest. For a typical farmer, notes historical geographer James Lemon, "the most demanding periods were June and July, when hay was cut and small grains harvested." The yeoman then labored less intensively until the October harvest of Indian corn.[6] New England crowd activity, following this seasonal timetable, started in late August 1786. In Massachusetts, on August 29, almost 1,500 farmers stopped the Court of Common Pleas at Northampton. Over 300 took the same action against the debtor court at Worcester on September 5.

A week later, three more court closings occurred in Massachusetts: more than 300 farmers stopped the debtor court at Concord; 500 militants did the same at Taunton in Bristol County; and 800 Berkshire Regulators closed down the Great Barrington court.

On September 20, discontent spread to New Hampshire. Probably hearing of the disturbances to the south, 200 militants surrounded the state house in New Hampshire and held the governor and the assembly prisoners for over five hours. Trouble meanwhile continued in Massachusetts. From September 25 to September 28, 1,500 Shaysites occupied the Springfield courthouse. A week later, over 200 Regulators again closed the court in Berkshire County, and 150 did the same at Taunton.

Crowd disturbances temporarily came to a halt during the rest of October. Since the judges did not sit in rural areas during this time, farmers had time to harvest their Indian corn. As courts resumed business in inland New England, however, yeomen again armed themselves with clubs and muskets. In Connecticut, plans were made to attack the New Haven court in late October. On the last day of the month, 35 Vermont farmers stopped the Windsor County court and continued to harass the judges throughout November. Three weeks later in Rutland County, more than 150 militants disrupted the proceedings of the court. On November 21, trouble exploded in Massachusetts as 150 Shaysites closed down the Court of Common Pleas in Worcester. By the end of the year, an uprising that involved almost 9,000 militants or about one-quarter of the "fighting men" in rural areas had surfaced in every New England state except Rhode Island.[7]

The seasonal nature of the attacks reveals the agrarian makeup of the crowds. Of the known Massachusetts Regulators, most lived in the counties of the rural West. The analysis of the places of residence of those militants who later took the oath of allegiance shows that over 840 lived in Berkshire; 1,427 in Hampshire; 969 in Worcester; 213 in Middlesex; and only 81 in Bristol. Few Shaysites came from the seaboard counties of Suffolk, Essex, and Plymouth. Moreover, most lived in rural villages rather than market towns. In the farming community of Pelham, about 43 percent of the adult males armed against government, as did over 35 percent in the inland town of Amherst. In contrast, less than 6 percent in the market town of Brookfield and only a few from Worcester, the largest market center in the county of the same name, joined the Shaysites.

Most Regulators, living as they did in rural villages, followed an agrarian way of life. Of 1,151 Shaysites with known occupations, more than 54 percent called themselves yeomen or husbandmen and cultivated small tracts of land. On the average, Regulators in Pelham and Whately owned sixty acres; in Amherst, sixty-two acres; in Barre, fifty-three acres; and in Shirley, sixty-nine acres. Of the known militants, about 22 percent labeled themselves agricultural laborers, and more than 11 percent referred to themselves as country artisans. Significantly, less than 5 percent of the militants claimed the title of gentleman farmer. No wholesaler or retailer admitted to involvement in the uprising. Noah Webster accurately described the majority of the Shaysites as "the yeomanry of the country." [8]

The Shaysites further mirrored the ethnic makeup of rural New England. During the revolutionary era, the vast majority of inland New Englanders had English or Scotch-Irish ancestors, and most Regulators reflected this ethnic composition. Since almost all New England blacks lived on the coast, only black Massachusetts yeomen Moses Sash of Worthington, Tobias Green of Plainfield, and Aaron Carter of Colrain fought with the Shaysites.[9]

Similarly, few women took a direct part in the Regulation. The wife of Shaysite Job Shattuck, who helped a group of women capture prominent Tory Leonard Whiting in 1775, may have been active in the postwar disturbances.[10] Two women from Pelham, writing against government in 1787, also may have furthered the Shaysite cause.[11] But newspaper reports and oaths of allegiance reveal few women who armed against government.

As in race and sex, the militants were homogeneous in religious affiliation. In 1789, over 77 percent of all Massachusetts churches and 80 percent of the population adhered to the

Congregational faith. The Baptists, the other important religious group in postwar Massachusetts, included about 16 percent of the citizenry. Few Shaysites, however, came from the twenty-five towns in western and central Massachusetts that had a Baptist church.[12] Baptist leader Isaac Backus' vitriolic denunciation of the Regulators may have partially accounted for the reluctance of many rural Baptists to side with the Shaysites. While some Baptists undeniably fought against government, most militants probably were Congregationalists. Moreover, splits within the dominant Congregational church apparently had little bearing upon the uprising. Of the known Shaysites in Amherst, for example, 49.6 percent belonged to the First and 50.4 percent to the Second Congregational Church.[13]

The social uniformity of the Regulators enhanced the possibility of unity and facilitated communication between individuals and communities. Although this social uniformity did not cause solidarity, it made concerted action easier by taking ethnic, racial, and religious antagonisms out of the picture.

Family ties gave solidarity to discontented yeomen who had common economic problems and similar social backgrounds. In Hampshire County, Massachusetts, the Regulators included 100 yeomen from Pelham: among them stood eight Johnsons, twelve Greys, and six McMillans. In all, almost 60 percent of the Pelham militants attacked the debtor court with a father or a brother. "Near relations," as Shaysite Timothy Hinds of Pelham pointed out, had induced many yeomen "to take part with them against government."[14] In Amherst, too, families united against government. Nathan Dickinson and John Ingram each had seven sons, who helped their fathers close down the Northampton court. Isaac Goodale and his sons Thomas and David also marched against government. Overall, more than 78 percent of the 118 Amherst militants had sons or brothers at their sides. The ages of the Amherst Shaysites consequently spanned a wide range: seventy-eight-year-old Isaac Hubbard, the oldest Amherst Regulator, walked alongside fifteen-year-old Timothy Green. Farmers from West Springfield organized along similar lines. Among the 150 yeomen and country artisans walked ten Days, seventeen

Leonards, and ten Elys. As with other Hampshire County Regulators, direct family ties linked about two-thirds of the West Springfield Shaysites.

Regulators in other Massachusetts counties also united with their kin. In early September 1786, about twenty husbandmen and country artisans from Oxford helped stop the proceedings of the Worcester County court. Their number included brothers Josiah and Samuel Kingsbury, as well as Thomas, Nahum, and John Pratt. From Palmer came Jesse and Benjamin King, Silvanus Walker and his son Silvanus, Jr., as well as brothers Ephraim and Robert Smith. Direct family ties linked over 60 percent of the forty-one Palmer militants. Kinship also bound together Regulators from Princeton; over 52 percent of the Shaysites from that town marched to Worcester with other members of their immediate families.

In Middlesex County on September 12, 1786, a parallel situation developed as discontented families flocked to Concord. The Shattucks, the Kemps, the Bloods, and the Woods of Groton marched in opposition to the debtor court. From Pepperell came the Parkers, Shattucks, Wrights, and Nuttings, and from Shirley came the Longleys, Pratts, and Campbells. In Berkshire County, the Loomises, Nobles, and Dodges of Egremont helped stop the court at Great Barrington, where they were joined by Isaac Van Burgh and his son Isaac, Jr., brothers Enoch and Stephen Meachum, and Moses Hubbard with his three sons, all from Sheffield. The Loveland and the Morse families of Tyringham also took the side of the Shaysites. In Bristol County, family played a similar role. The three Briggs brothers, Benjamin, Luke, and Asa, and the Bliss family of Rehoboth helped plan the attack upon the Taunton court. The Newcombs and Strongs of Norton as well as the Lincolns and Thayers of nearby Easton lent their assistance. As with court closings in other counties, the incident in Bristol showed the importance of kinship ties in the organization of the Massachusetts Regulators.

In the same way, family united militants of different states. The farmers involved in the incident of October 31, 1786, at Windham, Vermont, provide an example. Among the Vermont militants was Elijah Barnes of Barnard, who on October

17, 1775, had married Margaret Shays, sister of the prominent Massachusetts Regulator Daniel Shays. Barnes undoubtedly lined up against the Windham court with the approval of his brother-in-law. Fellow townsman Abner Perkins had married Polly, another sister of Daniel Shays. In an analogous situation, Barnard farmer Samuel Steward had kin among the Regulators in Hardwick, Massachusetts, and joined his family to stop a Worcester County court. Other Barnard yeomen— Daniel Egery, George Haskell, and Nathaniel Haskell—likewise aided their Hardwick relatives in closing the Worcester court. All told, bonds of family were a significant unifying force in an uprising that extended throughout rural New England.[15]

Neighborhood friendships probably served a like function. Accustomed to helping each other in everyday tasks, neighbors in the inland regions almost naturally concerted their protests. In Massachusetts, virtually every Regulator from Conway came from the south side of town.[16] In Springfield and Stockbridge, most Shaysites resided in the western reaches of the communities, and opposed people in the more market-oriented eastern sections.[17] Nathaniel Austin of Sheffield summed up the importance of neighborhood ties for the organization of the Regulators. This Shaysite lived "in a part of the town of Sheffield where a universal disaffection to the measures of government prevailed" and joined in court disruptions due to pressure from his neighbors.[18]

Newspapers and tavern life furthered the organization of the Regulators. In 1789, noted geographer Jedediah Morse, "not less than 30,000 [newspapers were] printed every week in New England, and circulated in almost every town and village in the country." Most people could read them, according to Morse, who reported that "any person of mature age, who cannot both read and write, is rarely to be found." Widely circulated and read, newspapers provided an important mode of communication within rural New England during the uprising. They gave the dates of court sessions and printed accounts of the attacks upon debtor courts that took place in late 1786. Although usually carrying editorials favorable to government, newspapers still provided the Shaysites with necessary information and sometimes acted as a forum for dissenting opinions.[19]

Taverns filled an even more essential role than newspapers in the organization of armed activity. During the colonial and revolutionary eras, many farmers learned in taverns about events outside their communities. Innkeepers tacked up newspapers, and travelers gossiped about other parts of the state and country. In addition, inns served as the sites of town meetings and militia drills and as recruitment centers for patriot forces during the Revolution. Some rural tavern owners, bridging the gap between commercial and more traditional cultures, sided with their militant clientele and opened their doors to Shaysite activists. Massachusetts Regulators met at inns such as Clark's Tavern in Hubbardston and Merrick's Inn in Princeton for discussions of strategy. The practice evidently became widespread: tavern owners "have generally been very seditious, their houses have been the common rendezvous for the councils and the comfort of these people," complained Hampshire County militia leader William Shepard in 1787.[20] Many New England inns were not only Shaysite meetingplaces but recruitment centers for Regulator forces. Innkeeper Aaron Smith of Shrewsbury allowed a Shaysite company to organize on his premises in late 1786.[21] The owners of Conkey's Tavern in Pelham, the Upton Tavern in Fitchburg, the Old Goldsbury Inn in Warwick, and Fuller's Tavern in Ludlow, similarly permitted militants to recruit and to drill around their establishments.[22]

Many Shaysites had experience in camp and on the battlefield as militiamen or soldiers of the Continental line. As captains in the Revolutionary War, Daniel Shays, Luke Day, Agrippa Wells, Adam Wheeler, Luke Drury, Reuben Dickinson, Oliver Parker, and Seth Murray had drilled and recruited for the patriot forces. Former majors John Wiley and Jonathan Holman had done the same.[23] Many Regulators had served in the rank and file of the American forces. James Cole of Rehoboth, for example, had joined the twenty-second Massachusetts Regiment and had served for three months, starting on May 1, 1775. The same year, he had responded to an alarm in Rhode Island and had fought the British for sixteen days.

In May 1777, Private Cole had again battled the British in Rhode Island. In three months, he accepted a corporal's commission in the Continental army and remained in uniform until August 1780.[24] Other Regulators had similar experiences. Of 327 Shaysites from Amherst, Brookfield, Rehoboth, and Colrain, over 31 percent had taken part in the war. While only a few had enlisted in the Continental army, the veterans had been exposed to military training and had been bound together during warfare—facts that would become important during the postwar uprising.[25]

Having adequate means of coordination, the Shaysites demonstrated a decided system in their attacks. Like the American revolutionary crowds described by such historians as Pauline Maier, Edward Countryman, Dirk Hoerder, and Stephen Patterson, as well as the eighteenth-century English and French crowds analyzed by George Rudé, the Regulators carefully picked specific targets and seldom troubled inhabitants in surrounding areas.[26] When New Hampshire militants from the farming towns of Hampstead, Hawke, Sandown, Bedford, Goffstown, and Raymond attacked the statehouse in Exeter, they probably centered upon the assembly because it was the government institution nearest their homes.[27] On September 20, 1786, they quietly surrounded the building with the joint legislature still in it, posted "centinels at the doors and windows, with bayonets fixed to their muskets, and forbade any person from going in or coming out." Throughout the incident, the yeomen confined their operation to the grounds of the statehouse.[28]

During 1786, farmers in other New England crowds exhibited the same single-mindedness. Unlike New Hampshire yeomen, they lived at a distance from the capital and repeatedly attacked debtor courts held in inland towns. In each instance, however, the Regulators conducted their assaults in an organized way. During the September 25 incident at Springfield, Massachusetts, the Shaysites paraded toward the Court of Common Pleas "in good order" and harassed few people along the way. In Springfield, noticed one observer, the behavior of the crowd resembled "the regular movements of an army" as Regulators limited their activity to the courthouse itself.[29] On October 3, Shaysites in Bristol County showed similar internal coordination. According to militia leader David Cobb, "insurgents came unto the village green with military parade" and made their demands.[30] Another disturbance in Springfield on December 26 epitomized Shaysite organization. An hour before the attack, the Hampshire County sheriff had no idea of the approaching onslaught. "The expedition of theirs was conducted with as much secrecy and precaution as if it were an enterprise of the greatest magnitude and importance," reported retailer Samuel Lyman a day after the event.[31]

In the fall of 1786, the Regulators mounted organized attacks against debtor courts with a specific goal in mind. The Courts of Common Pleas gave creditors a means to collect specie obligations in the rural areas. In Massachusetts, through the courts, usually situated in inland market towns such as Springfield, Stockbridge, Northampton, Worcester, Concord, and Great Barrington, militants had been collared by retailers demanding payment of debts in hard money. In early 1784, Daniel Shays of Pelham, the nominal leader and namesake of the rebellion soon to come, was hauled into court by John Johnson for a twelve-pound debt. A few months later, a retailer from Brookfield prosecuted Shays for three pounds.[32] Merchant John Russell similarly took Regulator Abraham Gale to court for a small debt, and Silas Fowler was pressed for hard money by merchants William Phillips and Samuel Mather.[33] In Amherst, Shaysites John Billings and John Field received summonses from the Hampshire court for debts owed to retailers.[34]

Many other Regulators experienced the humiliation of court prosecution. In Hampshire County from 1784 to 1786, over 800 future Shaysites trudged to debtor court. During the same period, nearly 700 Regulator names appear in the Worcester debtor court files, while 64 Bristol County debtors taken to court eventually became Shaysites. Of the known Regulators in the three counties, about 66 percent had been dragged to court for unpaid debts.[35] For a few Shaysites such as Luke Day of Springfield and Thomas Lee of Rutland, Vermont, indebtedness led to imprisonment.[36]

Hauled to court and jailed by retailers, some future Shay-sites lashed out against their prosecutors. John Chapman of Uxbridge, Massachusetts, wanted to "put a stop to those iniquitous ways of obtaining wealth, by which a set of *plunderers* have for years been rioting on the spoils of the industrious." [37] For another Massachusetts yeoman, the solution seemed just as clear. "I am a man that gets his living by hard labor, not by a pension or monopolizing," he wrote in October 1786, "and I think that husbandry is as honest a calling as any in the world, the last temptation for fraud and lying—and I believe this country would flourish faster if there were less white shirts and more black frocks." Let "us oblige the merchants to shut up their shops and get their living by following the plough," he concluded.[38] One Hampshire County yeoman summarized the sentiments of many farmers who felt cornered by merchant-creditors. He had "labored hard all" his days and "fared hard," and had "been obliged to do more than my part in the war." Yet, he had been "loaded with class-rates, lawsuits, and had been pulled and hauled by sheriffs, constables and collectors and had [his] cattle sold for less than they were worth.... Great men," he feared, were "going to get all we have" and reduce independent farmers to peonage.[39]

To loosen the hold of retailers, some farmers recommended the closing of the courts. Yeomen in Bristol County had complained, through town petitions and county conventions, about a "too rigorous execution of the law." They had "petitioned the great and general court for some relief" but "could obtain none," and now they pledged to "oppose and prevent the sitting of the Inferior Court of Common Pleas, for the County of Bristol, or any other court that shall attempt to sit for the purpose of taking property by distress." [40] In late 1786, many yeomen may have been reluctant to follow a possibly violent course, but nevertheless, having found peaceful protest inadequate, they prepared for armed action. As Josiah Walker of Sturbridge, Massachusetts, told a friend, he "wished the insurgents had not taken up arms so soon, but said he did not know whether any other method than by arms would do." [41]

There was a precedent for such action. Yeomen had resorted to armed attacks against the Massachusetts courts during the

Revolution. On August 30, 1774, a crowd had assembled at Springfield and forced the judges to renounce their commissions. The Hampshire County court remained closed until 1780.[42] Also in August, several hundred farmers gathered at Great Barrington and "broke up the court, then sitting at that place." A month later at Worcester, a crowd "of about 5,000 collected and prevented the Court of Common Pleas from sitting (about 1,000 of them had fire-arms) and all drawn in two files, compelled judges, sheriffs, and gentlemen of the bar, to pass with them cap in hand, and read their disavowal of holding court." [43] Farmers in Taunton and Concord gave judges similar treatment. As wealthy Tory Henry Van Schaack later noted, "the first efficacious measure for obtaining a redress of grievances in 1774 was the breaking up of the courts of law by an unlawful assembly." [44]

During the 1780s, yeomen continued to close courts for reformist ends. The Shaysites, some of them veterans of the 1782 Ely disturbances, likewise attacked courts to achieve a temporary suspension of debt collection, hoping the closings would neutralize the demands of creditors until legislators enacted the more permanent measures of paper money and tender laws. In Hampshire County on August 29, 1786, the Regulators ordered the judges of the debtor court "to forbear doing any business at this court until the minds of the people can be obtained and the resolves of the convention of this county can have an opportunity of having their grievances redressed by the General Court." [45] Bristol County Shaysites such as Deliverance Bennett similarly demanded "that no executions or taxes should be levied for the space of twelve months" until "a redress of the present grievances can be legally obtained." [46] Worcester County Shaysites wanted judges to "adjourn until after a new choice of representatives." [47] Striking at a different target, New Hampshire militants made tempered demands. Regulators such as yeoman Joseph French of Hampstead determined "to do ourselves that justice which the laws of God and man dictate to us" and demanded "your honors to grant us the requests of our former petition [for paper money] and not drive us to a state of desperation." [48] On November 7, 1786, Shaysite Adam Wheeler encapsulated the reformist bent of most Regulators. "I had no intention to destroy the public government," he wrote in a letter addressed to the public, "but to have the courts suspended to prevent such abuses as have taken place by the sitting of those courts, distressed to see valuable members of society dragged from their families to prison." As with other Worcester Shaysites, Wheeler "did not intend to destroy law, but only to reform all those laws which were oppressive." [49]

The traditional nature of Shaysite reform can be seen in the Shaysite badge: a sprig of evergreen. The pine tree or evergreen had been a traditional symbol of liberty and independence on Massachusetts flags and coins. It first appeared on the seal of the Plymouth Colony in 1624 and later was seen on the pine-tree flag used at Bunker Hill, the New England jack, and the colors of the black Bucks of America during the Revolution.[50] In September 1777, on George Washington's march to Brandywine, the men also "wore a sprig of green in their caps." [51] Confronted by another threat to their independence in 1786, some Massachusetts farmers again put a sprig of green in their hats. The Shaysites soon began to be referred to as the "Green Bushers" and the "Bush Club" among some government supporters.[52]

In late 1786, then, events had not reached an irreconcilable stage. Dissatisfied yeomen, fearing the effects of tax collection and debt prosecutions, joined with family and neighbors in closing debtor courts to force legislators to consider their reformist proposals. "The stopping of the Judicial courts," observed George Richards Minot in 1788, "had been blended, in the minds of some people, with the redress of grievances" and had been "considered only as a mode of awakening the attention of the legislature" to rural demands.[53]

5
The Ideology and Politics
of Suppression

MERCHANTS AND PROFESSIONALS looked with horror upon the disruption of the legal process. In their eyes, the forced closings of the courts undermined the contractual basis of law, thus making property insecure and eventually leading to a general economic leveling. The blurring of socioeconomic divisions would in turn signal the complete destruction of a commercial society, ushering in anarchy and finally a tyrannical despotism by the lower classes. From their market perspective, the commercial and professional elite equated reformist objectives, militarily pursued, with radical attacks upon ordered society.

Fearing an end to their way of life, mercantile leaders took an uncompromising view of the Shaysite incursions. "Every man ought to show his colors and take his side: No neutral characters should be allowed, nor anyone suffered to vibrate between the two," asserted Massachusetts governor James Bowdoin.[1] This rigid attitude led to swift and repressive measures designed to combat the Regulators. In late 1786 and early 1787, New England leaders mounted armed attacks against desperate farmers who sought traditional justice in a variety of ways.

The Ideology of Reaction

The mercantile elite generally looked with dismay upon the court closings and worried about the consequences. The attacks upon debtor courts, temporarily releasing farmers from specie obligations, seemed to weaken the basis of the law. According to Hampshire County militia leader William Shepard, such attacks threatened the very existence of "fixed, permanent, and known laws." [2] Designed to enforce the law, the state itself seemed subverted by court disruptions. "If the courts of justice are not permitted to sit, or sitting are interrupted in their proceedings," Governor Bowdoin counseled the Massachusetts General Court in early September 1786, "the great end of government, the security of life, liberty, and property, must be frustrated, and government so far laid prostrate." General Benjamin Lincoln, merchant-speculator of Hingham, warned of a similar fate for government. Blocking "the avenues of private justice" in inland New England by attacks upon debtor courts, the Regulators were forming combinations "which have a tendency to stop the foundations of our constitution; to render totally futile the most implicit and absolute principles of government." [3]

In their attempts to undermine commercial relations, the Shaysites appeared insane to some merchants. Springfield retailer Samuel Lyman characterized them as "a party of madmen." Samuel Tyler, a store owner in Attleboro, likewise wrote to a friend about "the fury and madness of the people" in arms. By opposing the "virtuous sons of reason" who spoke out in favor of government, added Henry Knox, the Regulators fomented "a formidable rebellion against reason, the principle of all government." [4]

Predicting the subversion of government by mad Shaysites, merchants feared for their property. "We shall have no security of property" with continued assaults upon the Courts of Common Pleas, cautioned one Hampshire County retailer in late September 1786. "What honest man can live without government—what industrious man can live while his property is at the mercy of knaves and thieves?" [5] After repeated onslaughts had been made upon debtor courts, some Cambridge merchants similarly foresaw all "property afloat.... Private property will fall with them and lie wholly at the mercy of the most idle, vicious and disorderly set of men in the community." [6]

Expecting an end to private property, some government leaders accused the Regulators of seeking a general redistribution
of wealth—a leveling revolution. To Henry Knox, the Shaysites held "'that the property of the United States had been
protected from the confiscation of Britain by the joint exertions
of all, and therefore ought to be the common property of all
and he that attempts opposition to this creed ought to be swept
from the face of the earth.' In a word," Knox concluded in a
letter to George Washington, "they are determined to annihi-
late all debts public and private and have agrarian laws." By
December 4, Benjamin Lincoln held the same opinion. The
Regulators, he believed, sought an "agrarian law" of landed
equality.[7]

Such assessments of Shaysite motives, however, had little
basis in fact. The Regulators, themselves private property hold-
ers, never envisioned a society without private landownership
or backed schemes for a general redistribution of wealth. From
an agrarian viewpoint, the charges of Knox and Lincoln
seemed utterly absurd. But, challenged by farmers over the
payment of specie debts, some merchants and professionals
feared a partial loss of property. They sometimes exaggerated
their possible losses and equated rural reform with a type of
social revolution more probable in a society divided into proper-
tied and propertyless classes.

Fearing a redistribution of property and the subsequent de-
mise of commercial society, some government leaders and merchants warned of approaching chaos. "If suffered to prevail,"
a distraught Governor John Sullivan of New Hampshire
wrote in November, the Regulators would "plunge the community into anarchy." [8] Boston merchant Josiah Flagg likewise
cringed at "the impending danger which at present threatens
us with anarchy and confusion." "We are in this commonwealth on the very border of complete anarchy," echoed minister and land speculator Manasseh Cutler from Boston in
early October. Rufus King, a Massachusetts delegate to the
Confederation Congress, summarized mercantile fears: in late
October, he had "a good reason to despair of the Commonwealth and to give up all to wild confusion and despair." [9]

For all these men, the impending anarchy was pictured as

a descent into a Hobbesian state of nature. "The insurrections are a war levied upon society, and reduce us to the feeble and helpless state of nature where *might will always overcome right,*" wrote an observer in the *Hampshire Gazette*.[10] After a successful uprising, agreed Dedham lawyer Fisher Ames, "you will behold men who have ever been civilized, returning to barbarism, and threatening to become fiercer than the savage children of nature." The Shaysites would reduce New England to "a state of nature," a "rank among the savages taken somewhere below the Oneida Indians." [11]

According to merchants and professionals, an anarchic state of nature brought about by a successful uprising would give way to some form of tyranny. Believing competition to be the rule, they thought that a strong individual would eventually demonstrate superior power and rise above all others. "Wearied by anarchy, and wasted by intestine war," Fisher Ames argued, the masses "must fall an easy prey" to such coercion.[12] The resulting tyranny, based upon physical compulsion rather than reason, seemed an almost inevitable consequence of anarchy. "A state of general confusion," the "horrors of anarchy, and the effects of unrestrained violence and revenge" would probably "be followed by domestic despotism or foreign domination," warned Governor Bowdoin.[13]

Of Bowdoin's unpalatable alternatives, mercantile leaders thought domestic tyranny would appear first. "The experience of all ages and the historical page teach us that a popular tyranny" such as that sought by the Shaysites "never fails to be followed by the arbitrary government of a single person," forewarned Abigail Adams in late 1786. General William Shepard outlined the same sequence of events a week later. Crowds of angry farmers would "overturn the very foundations of our government and constitution, and on their ruins exert the unprincipled and lawless domination of one man." [14] As with the prewar British and patriot elite described by Bernard Bailyn, the postwar New England leadership feared some type of conspiracy leading to a loss of their power.[15]

In practical terms, the commercial elite imagined that the leaders of the Regulation plotted their own rise to power. William Cushing, a Massachusetts judge of the Supreme Judicial

Court, foresaw "evil minded persons, leaders of the insurgents," waging war "against the Commonwealth, to bring the whole government and all the good people of this state, if not continent, under absolute command and subjugation to one or two ignorant, unprincipled, bankrupt, desperate individuals." [16] Shaysite leaders, similarly reported an observer in New Hampshire, prepared to "elevate themselves on the distresses of their fellow citizens" by establishing a dictatorship.[17] According to such government supporters as Boston merchant Thomas Welch, "a number of bold and designing men" fomented the uprising for personal advancement. Some government leaders gave a more detailed prediction, warning that Daniel Shays would grasp rule. As William Shepard saw it, Shays hoped to "erect a military government for the coercion of the state, and by setting up his standard" in Massachusetts expected "to be supported by great numbers from all the states, and be able to declare himself dictator of the whole union." [18] William Williams, wealthy Berkshire County creditor, also charged Shays with designs to "conquer" Massachusetts and eventually to become "the tyrant of America." [19]

The mercantile elite, however, predicted a short-lived dictatorship for Daniel Shays. Revengeful British officials, they contended, provided the moving force behind the Shaysites, manipulating the Regulators in an effort to recapture their former colonies. As early as September 8, 1786, retailer Thomas Clarke of Roxbury hurriedly informed Governor Bowdoin of a Shaysite *"petition to the Parliament of Great Britain."* Four days later, Shrewsbury judge and ex-general Artemus Ward cautioned the governor about similar British-linked activity. He saw several persons riding "from county to county to stimulate the unwary to acts of disorder and violence, to poison the minds of others with unreasonable jealousies of their rulers, suggesting they are oppressed by them unnecessarily." The seditious horsemen seemed the obvious tools of "British emissaries." [20] The arrival of the new Canadian governor, Sir Guy Carleton, Lord Dorchester, in late October heightened fears of British involvement in the New England troubles. Government leaders believed that Dorchester, the British commander who withdrew the last English troops from the United States in 1783, carried British help to the Shaysites. By November 1786, wrote Samuel Osgood, an official in the Confederation Treasury Department, they seemed convinced of British plans to reinstitute "a monarchical government in this country" with "some of George's sons on the throne." [21]

Regulators vehemently denied any connection between themselves and the English. "As to the British emissaries and their combinations that you mention," replied Massachusetts yeoman Nehemiah Hinds in November 1786 to the charges of government supporters, "we will join heart in hand in the most complete discrimination between them and the virtuous." [22] "The idea which is eternally rung in the ears of the public, that the British are at the bottom of the present discontent in the country is a bug-bear, a mere invention of the court," opined Shaysite George Brock. [23]

Despite the fabricated nature of reports about English intervention in favor of the Regulators, the supposed bond between Great Britain and New England farmers created a real fear among anti-Shaysites. "Our eternal foes are still at work," one commentator had remarked about the British in the *Massachusetts Centinel* in April 1785. "They are making use of every method in their power, to interrupt our tranquility and sow the seeds of discord and dissension." [24] Less than a year later, Massachusetts political leader Nathan Dane expressed similar fears. "Great Britain would not have many scruples of conscience about disturbing our peace. That haughty nation feels sore and wounded and might be induced to buy peace in Europe at a dear rate in order that she might get back an inch of our territory," he told Boston merchant Samuel Phillips. [25] In this tense atmosphere, mercantile leaders too easily ascribed the Shaysite troubles to British influence.

All told, the commercial elite saw nothing but disaster from the court closings that took place in the fall and winter of 1786, expecting the overthrow of government, a subsequent anarchic state of nature, and ultimately the rule of a British tyrant. As the elite saw it, the Regulators left them with a sobering choice. "Cassius" in the *Worcester Magazine* outlined the alternatives: "Now is the time when men act before they reflect; every measure is taken to prejudice the unthinking part

of the community; the passions are inflamed, the solid principles of reason and truth scarcely examined," he wrote about
the court disturbances. "This is the crisis for us to choose,
whether we will be governed by the divine principles of reason, or by the caprice of a despot." [26] To many merchants and
professionals in late 1786, the options seemed alarmingly clear.

The Militias, Legislation, and a Government Army

Government leaders actually faced a number of alternatives
during the stressful last months of 1786. They could have
accepted proposals for paper money and tender laws, solving
the immediate problem by a few legislative moves. They could
have postponed the crisis by promising to consider rural suggestions after new elections. But rather than escape or post-
pone a confrontation, they chose aggressive measures to stop
court disruptions in the backcountry. "The state governments
were continually forced to submit to various kinds of popular
pressures, often expressed outside the regular legal channels,"
Gordon Wood has pointed out. "In this atmosphere Shays's
Rebellion represented something of an anomaly, largely because the farmers of western Massachusetts, unlike other
groups in the 1780s, found no release for their pent-up grievances in legislative action but instead were forcefully resisted
by the authorities." [27]

At first sight, the adverse reaction of government leaders
to the Regulation seems ironic. During the 1770s, they had
spearheaded an uprising against "oppressive British tyrants";
yet, only a few years later, they armed themselves against their
own constituents. In May of 1787, a Loyalist, one "Orina,"
captured the irony in a letter to four judges of the Massachusetts Supreme Court: "You did formally commit many irreg-
ularities, in opposing the king and the ministry of the nation
and wrongfully beguiled the people of this state and continent,
with the desultory notion that they should not be commanded
by any man whatsoever," he chided. "[How can you] justify
yourselves in punishing any or more of your brethren for
stopping, or endeavoring to stop any courts in this state?" [28]

But irony existed on the surface only. Leaders of the American Revolution had fought for political and economic self-

determination, seldom espousing egalitarian social principles. As James Kirby Martin has emphasized, the coming of the Revolution primarily represented a "struggle within the ruling class" and "a structural crisis in power and political placement among leaders in the colonies." Lesser colonial officers became involved in armed conflict against imperial officers to gain greater control over American affairs.[29] Struggling for power within the "ruling class," some patriot leaders such as Samuel Adams may have used urban crowds for their own ends, but they abhorred any spontaneous crowd activity that had leveling effects. As Pauline Maier has written, they "quickly learned that unrestrained popular violence was counter-productive. They organized resistance in part to contain disorder."[30] In July 1776, for example, a Hampshire County committee of correspondence headed by Deerfield retailer David Field discountenanced all unauthorized "mobs, riots, and tumultuous proceedings, and ye seizing and detaining ye persons and property of an individual."[31] Although seeking to overthrow the king, prominent Hampshire Whigs nevertheless emphasized orderly domestic behavior. In this sense, the reaction of the New England elite to Shaysite attacks showed continuity rather than change. During the 1780s, the revolutionary leadership maintained a prewar disdain and fear of extralegal, popular protest and met the Shaysites with military force.

Connecticut officials rapidly put down traces of impending armed protest. On October 29, 1786, a group of yeomen "bound themselves to be in readiness at a moment's warning, to embody" and stop the proceedings of the New Haven debtor court. But before the farmers could carry their plan into action, state leaders "got hint of the affair" and quickly arrested the heads of the movement. By abruptly halting "the whole conspiracy" at New Haven, they squelched the first signs of uprising in Connecticut and undoubtedly dissuaded discontented yeomen from future forceful action.[32]

In Vermont during the autumn of 1786, the authorities likewise put a speedy end to popular protest. In late October, county sheriff Benjamin Wait and state attorney Stephen Jacobs convinced seventy members of the Windsor County militia to defend the court. The militiamen, probably includ-

ing the few commercial farmers in the area, overpowered the
thirty yeomen who surrounded the courthouse and drove them
back to their homes.[33] During the Rutland County court disruption in November, militia heads Isaac Clark, Stephen Pearl,
and John Spafford armed their companies to confront the
Regulators. After both sides had discharged their guns, the
superior numbers of militia scattered the militants. Moreover,
the Vermont legislature passed a series of measures aimed at
the Regulators. A Riot Act passed on March 8, 1787, prohibited
more than twelve armed persons from assembling in public.
Offenders could be shot on sight by county sheriffs or captured
and assigned to the service of any Vermont citizen for an
indefinite period of time, thereby reducing convicted rioters
to a state of slavery. A Treason Act, approved on the same day,
strengthened the Riot Act by extending the death penalty
to anyone active in an insurrection against the Vermont government. Along with a quick militia response to agrarian
violence, the repressive legislation discouraged court disturbances and probably accounted for the small scale of armed
protest in the independent territory.[34]

The firm actions of New Hampshire leaders similarly limited crowd activity. When 200 yeomen encircled legislators in
the statehouse on September 20, 1786, Governor John Sullivan
promised immediate consideration of the paper money issue
if they would disperse. The Regulators, elated at Sullivan's
concession, agreed to the terms and retreated to the hills a few
miles from Exeter, vowing to return the next morning. Only
a few hours after they had left the capital, however, Sullivan
summoned the Rockingham County militia and three companies of lighthorsemen. Over 2,000 militiamen from the port
towns of Exeter, Portsmouth, and Londonderry, headed by
Joseph Cilley, a lawyer and vice-president of the New Hampshire Cincinnati, and including "gentlemen of the first rank
and education" such as lawyer William Plumer and political
leader Nicholas Gilman, responded to the call within hours
and marched against the yeomen. About thirty government
horsemen "came on the rear of the insurgents" and "took
possession of a bridge which cut off their retreat," while the
other state troops moved toward the surprised farmers. A few

yeomen fired at the approaching militiamen, but most, out-numbered, fled to the surrounding woods.[35]

To secure the government victory, Governor Sullivan made examples of thirty-nine militants, forcing them "with their heads uncovered and their hats under their arms, [to] march twice through the columns [of government soldiers], that in that humiliating condition they might behold a few of the many who were ready to defend government." He then imprisoned five of the farmers and tried them for treason in a military court martial.[36] A few days later, the governor outlawed all conventions, charging them with "a tendency to overturn and destroy constitutional authority and government."[37]

The legislature intensified these anti-Shaysite measures. On September 23, 1786, the New Hampshire Assembly gave the governor the power to "call forth a sufficient number of the militia, to quell any riot, insurrection, or attempt on the courts of justice."[38] Two weeks later, Sullivan toured the state "to establish and confirm government, and revive military discipline."[39] The governor's personal inspection of the militia, coupled with the swift dispersal of the farmers at Exeter, had its desired effect. Throughout the rest of the Shaysite troubles, only the farmers in Grafton County, who burned the court-house to the ground in December 1786, took action against established authority.[40]

Events in Massachusetts took a different turn. When Hampshire County yeomen had taken the first armed action of Shays' Rebellion on August 29, 1786, they had caught the Massachusetts establishment off guard. According to George Richards Minot, the first historian of the Rebellion, "the attack in the county of Hampshire was so sudden and violent, that from this cause perhaps, no recurrence was made to the militia."[41] The judges of the debtor court retreated to a nearby inn and adjourned the court session. Unlike officials in other states, Massachusetts leaders initially took no forceful action.

After recovering from the immediate shock of the attack, the authorities in Boston encountered the problem of insurgency within the rural militias. After the Northampton incident, Governor James Bowdoin and his council had formulated a policy for handling future assaults upon the courts, and as farmers surrounded the Worcester County court on September 5, Bowdoin and his advisors activated their plan, instructing Jonathan Warner to summon the Worcester militia in order to disperse the crowd. To the amazement of Bowdoin and Warner, the troops refused the call to action. "Notwithstanding the most pressing orders," explained Warner, "there did appear universally that reluctance in the people to turn out for the support of government." Some militiamen gave their officers a "flat denial." Others replied by "evasion or delay which amounted to the same thing." [42]

The unfavorable reaction of the Worcester militia, unlike the responses of militiamen in Connecticut, New Hampshire, and Vermont, can be explained in various ways. The number of militants in Worcester may have dissuaded many otherwise loyal militiamen from fighting. As Sheriff William Greenleaf reported, the 300 "Regulators (as they term themselves) took possession of the Court House, their numbers increased much faster and quicker than those for the support of authority, that induced a great number of the militia to join them as they appeared most formidable." [43] But just as important as numbers, the agrarian orientation of the militia made their hostility to the Regulators unlikely. In New Hampshire and Connecticut, where planned or actual insurgency arose near the merchant-dominated coast, coastal militiamen agreed to defend the government. Many Worcester state troops, however, farmed for a living; they backed agrarian reforms and resisted the attempt to use violence against their friends and neighbors. As Artemus Ward explained, the militia in Worcester "were too generally in favor of the people's measures" to fight for government.[44]

The militia in other parts of Massachusetts followed the example of the Worcester militia. In Berkshire, Hampshire, Bristol, and Middlesex counties, they generally deserted the government ranks. In Berkshire on September 13, for example, "the militia under the order of General Paterson marched into Great Barrington, [where] much the greatest part ... joined those in opposition to government at the Court House." [45]

The militia backing government usually came from commercially oriented areas. On September 25 in Springfield, the state troops who turned out "were not less than 200 of the most respectable and opulent gentlemen of this County," as well as a company of Continental officers. They included volunteers from the inland market towns of Springfield, Northampton, and Hadley.[46] A month later, over 2,000 recruits assembled in less than six hours at Cambridge to protect the court session there. In this largest display of support for government, the troops came mostly from Boston and its immediate vicinity and included the Massachusetts mercantile elite.[47]

Since the loyal militia could not check the Regulators in rural areas, some Massachusetts merchants and professionals demanded an alternative coercive policy to quiet disgruntled yeomen. On September 28, 1786, Governor Bowdoin instructed the General Court to "take the most vigorous measures, effectively to vindicate the insulted dignity of government" and to "enforce obedience to laws." Boston wholesaler and speculator James Swan likewise lobbied for some show of "force—and that effectively applied"; he felt firm measures would quickly end the disturbances. Some "eastern gentlemen" agreed with Swan's remedy, contending that "the discontents will never be settled but by the sword."[48] By October 1786, some forceful action seemed necessary to quell resistance in the countryside. As Roxbury retailer Samuel Dexter wrote the governor on October 3, he knew "too well the temper of these degenerate sons of worthy ancestors to suppose they can be reclaimed by soft and lenient methods. Giving way in any degree will be dangerous. All *reasoning* too would be lost upon them except the *ultima ratio regum*." Only drastic measures would restore "tranquility, good order, and due submission to the laws."[49]

A few mercantile leaders began leaning toward monarchy as a means of reestablishing the old order. As Southampton retailer Jonathan Judd, Jr., watched the crowd at Northampton on August 29, 1786, he felt that a "monarchy is better than the tyranny of this mob."[50] Connecticut lawyer and lexicographer Noah Webster exhibited the same propensity for monarchy: "I was once as strong a republican as any man in America," he informed the readers of the *Connecticut Courant* in November. "*Now,* a republican is the last kind of government I should choose. I would infinitely prefer a limited monarchy, for I would sooner be the subject of the caprice of one man than the ignorance of the multitude."[51] Similarly favoring a monarchical government amid the Shaysite troubles, Confederation president Nathaniel Gorham took action. Sometime in November 1786, he sent a letter to Prince Henry of Prussia, brother of Frederick the Great, asking "the Prince if he could be induced to accept regal powers on the failure of our free institutions." Prince Henry returned a curt refusal: "Americans had shown so much determination against their old king, that they would not readily submit to a new one."[52]

Most eastern leaders agreed with Prince Henry's assessment of the Gorham plan. Although seeking some means to suppress the Regulators, they had just fought a war for political liberation from a supposedly tyrannical king and did not support a reintroduction of monarchy. Rather than a king, some of the mercantile elite wanted troops of the Confederation to protect Massachusetts government. In early October 1786, Governor Bowdoin and his council secretly approached Secretary at War Henry Knox for federal troops. Knox, continually pressing for a national military force in the postwar era, brought the proposal to the Confederation Congress. Under his skillful guidance, the request easily gained legislative approval by the end of October. The Congress declared "that the aid of the federal government is necessary to stop the progress of the insurgents" or the Shaysites would "subvert the government, and not only reduce that commonwealth to a state of anarchy and confusion, but probably involve the United States in the calamities of a civil war." Fearing such a national disaster, Confederation legislators ordered a $530,000 requisition for a special force of 1,340 soldiers to put down the Massachusetts militants.[53] The troops, called for under the subterfuge of Indian troubles to avoid a possible popular outcry, would come primarily from New England and serve for three years.[54] Horrified by domestic upheaval and prodded by Henry Knox, the Congress of the Confederation thus provided for the establishment of a national army.

While some Confederation leaders were devising plans for an armed force, Massachusetts passed a spate of suppressive legislation in its fall session. The General Court first rejected agrarian reforms, bypassing proposals for paper money, a sweeping tender law, the reform and abolition of the Courts of Common Pleas, a reduction of the governor's salary, and a removal of the capital from Boston. They even laid aside a bill "safeguarding the persons of debtors from arrest for private contracts." [55] Blaming the postwar depression upon rural "habits of luxury," they prescribed "industry, sobriety, economy, and fidelity in contracts" to achieve economic prosperity. [56]

The General Court also enacted a number of measures directed against the Shaysites. On October 24, 1786, officials passed a new Militia Act that made "any officer or soldier who shall begin, excite, cause, or join in any mutiny or sedition" liable to "such punishment as by a court martial shall be inflicted." [57] Four days later, legislators put a Riot Act on the books, following a course that had been taken by British officials in response to American popular protest. Ironically engineered by ex-revolutionary Samuel Adams along with merchants Tristram Dalton and William Phillips, the law prohibited twelve or more armed persons from congregating in public and empowered county sheriffs to kill intransigent rioters. If found guilty of crimes under the act, the convicted rioters would "forfeit all their lands, tenements, goods, and chattels, to the commonwealth," and would "be whipped thirty-nine stripes on the naked back, at the public whipping post, and suffer imprisonment for a term not exceeding twelve months, nor less than six months." [58] On November 10, 1786, the assembly suspended the writ of habeas corpus. Following the precedent set during the Ely incident of 1782, the new legislation enabled the governor and the General Court to apprehend and imprison for an indefinite period without bail "any person or persons whatsoever, whom the Governor and Council shall deem the safety of the Commonwealth requires should be restrained of their personal liberty," despite "any law, usage, or custom to the contrary." It authorized the arrest and incarceration "*in any part of the Commonwealth any person* whom they shall *suspect* is unfriendly to government." [59]

On November 16, General Court members added a final
measure to the list of anti-Shaysite laws. Anticipating the
Sedition Act of 1798, they approved a bill "preventing the
making and spreading of false reports to the prejudice of
government." [60]

Massachusetts officials felt that legislation at best provided
only a temporary solution to their problems. They recognized
that the militants, although they might be quieted by armed
intervention, must eventually submit voluntarily to government rule for lasting peace. To break up Shaysite ranks, legislators passed an Act of Indemnity that pardoned all Regulators
who took an oath of allegiance to government. Although
maligned creditors could still sue repentant militants "for in-
juries done or committed to their property or persons," government leaders hoped the pardon offered a way for subjugated
yeomen to renounce their actions. In Bowdoin's words, the
General Court had held forth "punishments on the one hand
and pardon on the other," hoping to end armed protest in
Massachusetts.[61]

It became clear, however, throughout the last months of
1786, that the twin policies of government—federal troops and
legislation—had failed dismally. The Regulators, all but young
William Bemis of Spencer, rejected offers of indemnity and
continued to close courts during November and December, un-
hampered by government. Their success stemmed partly from
the inadequacies of the Confederation. Even though they
promised an army, congressmen possessed virtually no control
over national monetary policy. As Congressman Nathan Dane
wrote in January 1786, "the respective states hold the purse
strings of the Union." [62] Hardly cooperating with the central
government, every state except Virginia rejected the $530,000
requisition and effectively undermined the federal troop plan.

In Massachusetts, recruiting efforts foundered due to lack
of funds. By November 12, 1786, Commander Henry Jackson
had "not yet begun to recruit, *no money* is yet furnished." A
desperate Jackson scoured Boston for funds the next month
but met with frustration. "The subscription goes on very dull
and dreary, not more than £500 is yet subscribed. Deacon
Phillips, Mason, and a number of our rich men have not yet

subscribed," he glumly reported to Henry Knox on December 11, 1786.[63] Having "little confidence in government," observed Boston lawyer Christopher Gore, few "men of property" in the Massachusetts capital were willing to risk scarce specie on a project initiated by the weak Confederation.[64] In consequence, Jackson, although he had recruited about "ninety of the most ragged rascals you ever beheld," still needed cash to commence operations in January 1787.[65]

Recruitment in other states followed the Massachusetts pattern. In late 1786, Connecticut commander David Humphreys frantically sought men for his regiment, promising "Honor and Fortune!—to the enterprising and speculative." But Congress never got the necessary specie, and by January 1787 Connecticut recruitment officials had enlisted only 100 men.[66] Monetary problems likewise ground recruiting to a halt in Virginia and Maryland. In Rhode Island and New Hampshire, officials never even began enlisting men because of fiscal difficulties. All told, the Confederation's weak financial position doomed the federal troop plan to abject failure.[67]

As the economic impotence of the national government became clear, the mercantile elite in Massachusetts took matters into their own hands. Governor Bowdoin, a wholesaler himself, proposed on January 4, 1787, a special army of 4,400 troops to cope with agrarian discontent. Led by Benjamin Lincoln, a former revolutionary war general and a commander of the Suffolk militia, the force, composed of volunteers from Suffolk, Essex, Middlesex, Worcester, and Hampshire counties, would march toward Worcester on January 20 to defend the debtor court. Each government soldier would carry a bayonet, a cartridge box, and thirty rounds of ammunition. They would be given beef, bread, a half-pint of rum per day, and two pounds for a month's service.[68] Bowdoin hoped that this army would repel and apprehend "all and every such person and persons as shall in a hostile manner, attempt or enterprise the destruction, detriment or annoyance" of the Worcester court. Thereafter, the soldiers would march westward, restoring "system and order" to the countryside by convincing "the misguided of the abilities of government." [69]

Wealthy coastal merchants quickly made Bowdoin's suggested force a reality. To procure the needed funds, Benjamin Lincoln "went immediately to a club of the first characters in Boston, who met that night, and laid before them a full state of matters." He "suggested to them the importance of their becoming loaners of a part of their property if they wished to secure the remainder." Lincoln, a merchant-speculator and himself a personal friend of many wholesalers in the Massachusetts capital, was very persuasive. Within three days, such wealthy Bostonians as merchants Samuel Breck, Thomas Russell, Caleb Davis, and Joseph Barrell pledged about £4,000. Three days later, the sum had grown to "upwards of £6,000." By the end of January, 129 of the leading coastal merchants and professionals had loaned enough money for operations to begin. According to Henry Jackson, Lincoln had garnered "the whole of the monied men to support him." [70]

Some prominent merchant-speculators even joined the government army. Lincoln, commander of the troops, engaged in trade and speculated heavily in Maine lands for a livelihood.[71] The veteran officer Rufus Putnam, head of one regiment, had organized land speculators into the Ohio Company in early 1786 and simultaneously had speculated in Maine lands.[72] By the time of the Shaysite troubles, regimental leader David Cobb, son of Bristol County merchant Thomas Cobb, had become a large store owner and a judge of the Bristol debtor court.[73] During 1786, Yale-educated lawyer John Paterson, commander of government troops in Berkshire County, had speculated in Ohio lands and had paid over $3,600 for 20,000 acres in Maine. Paterson also invested in the New York Chanango land purchase with fellow government troop leaders and retailers William Walker, Moses Ashley, and John Egleston.[74] Essex County regimental officer Jonathan Titcomb of Newburyport made money in privateering before and during the war and turned to legitimate trade after the Revolution. His immediate subordinates—Jonathan Jackson and Moses Brown—similarly ranked among Newburyport's most prominent postwar merchants.[75]

The Society of the Cincinnati, an organization of the veteran officers of the American Revolution, provided a link between prominent merchants in the Lincoln expedition. In 1786, Lincoln headed the Massachusetts chapter of the Cincinnati. Under his leadership in October, the society drafted a letter to the General Court "expressive of [their] abhorrence of the late tumults and disorders and [their] determination to support the present government." Every member of the committee that wrote the petition—Lincoln, Henry Knox, William Eustis, John Brooks, William Hull, Henry Jackson, and Joseph Crocker—became either commanders in the expedition or prominent in the attempt to raise federal troops against the Shaysites. Along with these former officers, Cincinnati members John Paterson, Rufus Putnam, William Shepard, Benjamin Tupper, Moses Ashley, and David Cobb commanded troops against the rebels—an especially ironic fact considering the wartime protests of the officers over their pay.[76]

Membership in the Freemasons further showed the social solidarity among the state troop leaders. As officers in the Revolution, Lincoln, Paterson, Tupper, Hull, and Putnam had joined Washington Lodge No. 10. They displayed a continuing interest in the Freemasons after the war, enrolling in the Grand Lodge of Massachusetts.[77] Along with fellow merchants and professionals, these Masons headed the expedition against the Shaysites.

Other merchants and professionals, unwilling to fight themselves, encouraged their sons and forced their servants to join the government army. Boston lawyer James Warren and his wife, historian and playwright Mercy Otis Warren, prodded their son Harry to enlist in the expedition. Boston Judge William Cushing and Salem merchant William Pynchon urged their sons to do the same.[78] The sons of coastal merchants John Winthrop, Stephen Higginson, and George Cabot likewise bound themselves to Lincoln's army. Harrison Gray Otis, the son of Boston wholesaler Samuel A. Otis, even organized fellow Harvard students into a company of Independent Cadets for action against the Shaysites. And besides their sons, coastal merchants and professionals sent their servants. As Harvard student John Quincy Adams wrote from Boston on January 18, 1787, "the men have been selected who are to go from this town against the insurgents. They have taken almost all the servants in town." [79]

Other government soldiers in the rank and file generally came from coastal ports and inland market towns. Many people along the seaboard who had blamed farmers for wartime food shortages supported government measures during the postwar insurrection. "My sweep eastward has equaled my expectations," Noah Webster wrote New York publishers Hudson and Goodwin on September 10, 1786. "The people in Essex are warmly opposed to the present tumultuary proceedings in this state." [80] In the fall of 1786, the same anti-Shaysite sentiment swept Boston. According to lawyer James Sullivan, the capital practiced "its usual prudence. Every countryman who comes in, and offers to apologize for his own son or brother deluded is railed at and called a rebel." The "powers of government are so united in this metropolis that it is dangerous even to be silent. A man is accused of rebellion if he does not loudly approve every measure as prudent, necessary, wise, and constitutional." [81]

Enlistments in Lincoln's army reflected the coastal support of government. Suffolk County, the center of the mercantile interest, easily fulfilled its quota of 713 men, and Essex County, with its market town of Newburyport, furnished its allotted 500 soldiers for the Second Division. The remaining government soldiers came largely from inland market towns. Worcester County provided Lincoln with 600 men, only half its quota. The Worcester troops, organized by retailer Ebenezer Crafts and lawyer John Sprague, represented "the men of the best estates and the greatest property" living in market towns such as Worcester and Brookfield. From Middlesex County came 800 recruits, most of whom resided in towns east of Concord, which had economic ties with Boston and its environs. Hampshire County, the most agrarian area summoned for troop enlistments, provided the biggest disappointment to government supporters. Allotted 1,200 men, the county supplied only 400, who came mostly from market towns such as Hadley, Springfield, and Northampton. The rest of the farmers in inland Massachusetts either sided with the Shaysites or, as yeomen in Hopkinton observed, had their "own brothers and near relations among the insurgents and hence arises a reluctancy to engaging in the service of the Commonwealth." [82]

Some coastal blacks offered their services to government. In late 1786, Prince Hall, the head of the Boston African Lodge of Masons, wrote Governor Bowdoin that his fellow black Masons disapproved of "any plot or conspiracies against the state where we dwell." Possibly seeking government support for his plan to resettle in Africa, Hall pledged "to help and support, as far as our weak and feeble abilities may become necessary in this time of trouble and confusion, as you in your wisdom shall direct us." The governor, perhaps fearing such a large contingent of armed blacks in the Lincoln expedition, never called upon the 700 black Masons to join the state army.[83]

The Lincoln expedition also gained support from the clergy, and some ministers offered prayers for the government force. "A day of prayer at Mr. Thatch's church, Boston, for the army," Samuel P. Savage jotted in his diary on January 23, 1787. Other clergymen such as Thomas Allen of Pittsfield, Eleazer Storrs of Sandisfield, and Egremont's Alexander Steele promised divine rewards for helping the government.[84] Some ministers—for example, Manasseh Cutler—even recruited for Lincoln's army.[85] A few clergymen—Father James Whittiker, head of the pacifist Shaker sect in western Massachusetts, for one—counseled neutrality. "The spirit of party is the spirit of the world, and whoever indulges it, and unites with one evil spirit against another, is off from Christian ground," he advised his followers.[86] Baptist minister John Bigelow of Petersham similarly took a middle ground during the Shaysite disturbances. "There is in general a good agreement between me and the body of the people about worship," he told anti-Shaysite Baptist leader Isaac Backus in 1787. "I have said but little about the family quarrel that has been in this commonwealth the year past; but what I have said has been to condemn both sides." The cases of Whittiker and Bigelow, however, proved to be exceptions rather than the rule. As Barnabas Bidwell of Tyringham observed, "the gentlemen of learning and the liberal professions, especially the clergy, are universally for government." [87]

With the blessing of the ministry, five divisions of government troops marched toward Worcester on January 19, 1787, to protect the debtor court. But the aims of the government soldiers extended far beyond the immediate vicinity of the courthouse. In the words of John Avery, secretary of Massachusetts, the soldiers had armed to "totally defeat" the Shaysites by creating "a different way of thinking" among them.[88] The state troops held out a bleak prospect to the farmers and would push reformist yeomen to a more radical stance.

6
Rebellion, Social Banditry, and the End of Armed Insurgency

THE OFFENSIVE OF THE Massachusetts government served further to radicalize many farmers. After the passage of anti-Shaysite legislation and the formation of the Lincoln expedition, they came to recognize the fundamentally different outlooks that existed between themselves and their government and decided to oppose government rather than to rely upon the General Court to effect change. By January 1787 many yeomen had abandoned reformist protest and consciously undertook rebellion—the "opposition to lawful authority," in the words of eighteenth-century lexicographer William Perry.[1] The battle over the federal arsenal at Springfield on January 25 and its aftermath represented this third, most radical, stage of the New England uprising.

The Shaysites turned to a kind of social banditry after their defeat at Springfield. According to George Richards Minot, they "changed the mode of carrying on the contest" and determined "to harass the inhabitants in small parties by surprise."[2] For five months, hunted by better organized and equipped government soldiers, the rebels undertook raids against prominent military leaders, inland shopkeepers, and lawyers. As Eric Hobsbawm has observed in his study of social bandits in Europe, Massachusetts insurgents lashed out against the political and social elite with "a vague dream of some curb upon them, a righting of individual wrongs."[3] These incursions formed the fourth stage of the New England troubles.

By June 1787 raids upon the inland commercial elite gradually came to a halt. The anti-Shaysite policies of most New
England governments, a new Massachusetts government army,
and the possibility of migration to unoccupied western lands
contributed to the decline of insurgent armed action. As the
Tillys have observed about other rebel movements, conflict
ceased "not because few people were aggrieved or because the
state eschewed violence, but because collective violence grew
too costly." [4] Faced with government troops, some farmers
preferred migration to continued battle.

The Radicalization of Reformers

The anti-Shaysite legislation of the Massachusetts General
Court spurred many farmers to direct action. Some yeomen
found the militia law "very irritating"; [5] others exploded over
the Riot Act. Insurgent Aaron Broad, for example, met Robert
Forbes and their "conversation turned upon the Riot Act."
Broad read the words of the act to his friend and said, "I am
determined to fight and spill my blood and leave my bones
at the courthouse till Resurrection." [6] "Instead of giving quiet"
to discontented farmers, the act met with extreme opposition
and "added to their catalogue of grievances." [7] The suspension
of the writ of habeas corpus was another reason for resentment.
Daniel Shays and Luke Day felt a "horror" over its suspension,
and the revocation of the ancient English liberty likewise
seemed "dangerous if not absolutely destructive to a Republican government" to other rebels. Yeoman Daniel Gray, in an
address to "the people," opposed a suspension "by which those
persons who have stepped forth to assert and maintain the
rights of the people, are liable to be taken and conveyed even
to the most distant part of the Commonwealth." [8]

Raids taking place under the suspension of habeas corpus
caused much of this uproar. On the night of November 28,
1786, 300 lighthorsemen rode from Cambridge toward the
homes of three prominent insurgents in Middlesex County.
The government-backed company, commanded by Boston
lawyer Benjamin Hichborn and fellow Harvard graduate John

Warren, "consisted of lawyers, physicians, and merchants, [who] were joined by a number of Gentlemen from the county as they passed through it." [9] Reaching Groton at daybreak on November 30, they attacked the houses of Oliver Parker, Benjamin Page, and Job Shattuck. Shattuck resisted the armed band, but horseman John Rand slashed the rebel across the knee with a broadsword. The other two insurgents submitted to superior force. By December 1, the three rebels stared blankly at the walls of the Boston jail, far from their homes in Groton. In Worcester County on December 2, a group of coastal merchants and professionals armed themselves and rode into Shrewsbury in search of insurgents. They greatly "abused and threatened in his own house with pistols" Thomas Farmer, a prorebel tavernkeeper, and then "slightly wounded in the hand" yeoman John Hapsgood "for opposing their entrance" into his house. Returning to the capital, the lighthorsemen ordered other farmers on the Boston Post Road "to pull down fences and do drudgery for them, or they would instantly split their brains out." [10]

Inland farmers reacted immediately to the government raids. In Holden, Isaac Chenery railed against the intruders. They "have been cutting and hacking our people," he told his friend John Gill. When Gill "asked him who they have been cutting and hacking and what he meant, he said the Light-horse have been cutting and hacking at Shrewsbury and Groton. Shattuck of Groton and Hapsgood of Shrewsbury and these things are not to be suffered." A similar chorus of rage arose throughout the rest of the Massachusetts backcountry. According to yeomen in Ashburnham, the names of Shattuck, Page, Parker, and Hapsgood "inflamed the minds of the people against the officers of government" to an extreme degree.[11]

Such an intense response stemmed partly from insurgent fears of future government attacks. Farmer Henry Gale of Princeton, for example, feared that "the light horse would take him and abuse him as they did Captain Shattuck." Identifying with the imprisoned Groton insurgents, Gale believed that every rebel would "be taken" if they "did not get all together" and make the government feel their presence. Government raids thus led to both the desire and the necessity for greater solidarity and moved the rebels closer to a radical stance.[12]

Rumors surrounding the two raids further agitated rebels against the authorities. Some stories reported that Shattuck had been killed or that he had died of wounds in the Boston jail. Other accounts had it "that the eyes and breasts of women and children have been wounded, if not destroyed; the houses of the innocent broken open; their limbs mangled by the light horsemen."[13] Such rumors, true or false, structured an ambiguous, stressful situation within western and central Massachusetts. As with rumors circulating throughout the French countryside during the Great Fear of 1789, reports of government brutality provided yeomen with one more reason for radical action against the state.[14]

Agrarian anger and fear over the suspension of the writ of habeas corpus, coupled with resentment of other legislative measures, pushed some farmers toward rebellion by late 1786. "The seeds of war are now sown," Shrewsbury yeomen Thomas Grover and Elisha Pownell wrote to the towns of western Massachusetts on December 2. "Two of our men are now bleeding that were wounded by the lighthorse that came from Boston and Roxbury." No longer trusting government, the two farmers requested town selectmen "to let this letter be read, and for you and every man to supply men and provisions and relieve us with a reinforcement. We are determined to carry our point. Our case is yours." Silvanus Billings also condemned the "bloodshed and prisoners made by tyrants who are afighting for promotion to advance their own interest which will destroy the good people of this land." Fearing for the safety of "our lives and families which will be taken from us if we don't defend them," he directed fellow yeomen to "fly to our assistance and as soon as possible in this just and righteous cause as there must be." As did Grover and Pownell, Billings became convinced of the inadequacy of reform in the wake of the Groton and Shrewsbury incidents.[15]

Most Shaysites, however, had not been sufficiently radicalized to respond to Billings' call. Even though they complained about government legislation and, like farmer Francis Wilson of Holden, "did not want any of Bowdoin's pardons,"[16] they still looked upon the government as unfeeling and uncooperative rather than oppressive and hoped for a compromise between rural and mercantile interests through neutral arbitration by the state. As Boston lawyers James Fillebrown and James Winthrop told Governor James Bowdoin on December 13 after a tour of the inland areas, many Shaysites expected to disband after the General Court effected a "release of the Groton prisoners" and "a suspension of the Courts of Common Pleas till after the election."[17]

The actions of Massachusetts farmers during the last month of 1786 demonstrated their persisting reformism. Rather than leveling sweeping attacks upon authority, they continued the pressure tactic of court disruption to achieve temporary relief. The Shaysites in Worcester, attacking the debtor court on December 5, were worried about "the present expensive mode of collecting debts, which, by reason of the great scarcity of cash, will of necessity fill our gaols with debtors." They also added the new legislation to a list of grievances, singling out the "suspension of the writ of habeas corpus" and the "unlimited powers granted to Justices of the Peace and Sheriffs, deputy Sheriffs, and constables by the Riot Act." But apparently faith in the goodwill of legislators to act upon rural suggestions for reform still flickered, for the Worcester yeomen did not demand a fundamental alteration in government.[18]

On December 26, militants in Springfield enunciated the same temperate aims. Having stopped the Hampshire County debtor court, they ordered the judges "not to open said courts, at this time, nor do any kind of business whatsoever. But all kinds of business remain as tho' no such court had been appointed." The Shaysites evidently thought the temporary closing would force the General Court to pass paper money and tender laws.[19] As Daniel Shays informed fellow yeomen after the Springfield court had adjourned, "he was in hopes that he should not find it necessary to call them out anymore on the like occasion."[20]

The Lincoln expedition dispelled such reformist expectations. According to Daniel Shays, John Powers, Joel Billings, and John Bardwell, the government army sought to destroy "those who have stepped forth to ward off the evils that threaten the people with immediate ruin." In Sutton, another "body of men that call themselves Regulators" reacted in the same way. According to an observer, they felt "that if military force should be raised, for the purpose of apprehending and taking up the said body of men, under the present situation of government, that they will embody and defend themselves at the risk of their lives." [21]

Besides endangering their lives, insurgents believed that the state army would wrench them from the soil, parcel out their farms among wealthy speculators, and reduce them to wage laborers or, as Shaysite Joseph Whipple of New Braintree feared, force them to "come under Lordships." [22] As a result, some rebels, ironically adopting a slogan made popular by the seaboard patriot elite during the Revolution, cried out against possible enslavement. "Transactions of public affairs have a direct tendency to involve the common people in a state of slavery," warned a group of Amherst insurgents on January 12, 1787. James Adams of New Braintree likewise alerted fellow farmers to the determination of government soldiers "to bring us into slavery." [23]

For the first time in the New England disturbances, Shaysites placed the blame for their difficulties directly upon government. Lincoln's army had been approved by the General Court and had been financed by Governor Bowdoin and other Commonwealth officials. The close connection between the state and the commercial interest had become clearer, and Shaysites such as John Bardwell, charging Massachusetts leaders with misusing power, characterized government rule as "the cruel hand of tyranny." [24]

As they began to perceive the government as tyrannical, some rebels became more conscious of their own group identity. Opposing a ruthless, commercially oriented government, they became more and more aware of the need for agrarian solidarity to protect their common way of life. Although it evolved haphazardly among farmers and country artisans, a consensus of rural unity developed by late January 1787. Along with Norman Clark, many insurgents felt that "almost every individual who derives his living from the labor of his hands or the income of a farm" backed the uprising in some way. Rebels such as Luke Day began to equate the Shaysite ranks with "the body of the people." [25]

As a majority of the population, the Shaysites further argued, yeomen deserved major political power. Echoing the ideology of the Revolution in early 1787, Amherst rebel John Billings felt that "we are a republic. Government rests upon the shoulders of the people. The staff of government is in the hands of the people." As the rightful guardians of political power, added rebel sympathizer William Whiting, the rural majority possessed a right of revolution against tyrannical government: "Whenever any encroachments are made either upon the liberties or properties of the people, if redress cannot be had without, it is virtue in them to disturb government." [26]

Fearing enslavement by government troops, some Shaysites repudiated the existing government. In early 1787, Isaac Chenery unabashedly told a Captain Webb of his intent to overthrow the Massachusetts government. Webb "asked him whether he would live in a state of nature, whether he would knock down government." Chenery "answered yes. I had rather be under the devil than such a government as this." On January 20, 1787, Shays, Bardwell, Powers, and Billings similarly asked the countryside to "immediately assemble in arms to support and maintain not only the rights, but the lives and liberties of the people." They wanted to smash "tyrannical government in Massachusetts." The future might be uncertain, but the rebels felt that the time for compromise had passed. As Daniel Shays told a friend on January 17, he "knew no more what government to set up, than he knew of *the dimensions of eternity.*" He even "was sorry he ever engaged in the *scrape,* but he had his hand to the plough and could not now look back." [27] Hunted by state troops and fearing the loss of land and family, Shays and his compatriots saw little choice other than a direct attack upon government.

Pondering the Shaysite threats, the seaboard elite began to sense the ambiguity of the revolutionary legacy. "Opinions which perhaps were excessively dissimulated previous to and during the late revolution seem to produce effects materially different from which they were intended," wrote Henry Knox in February 1787. "For instance, the maxim that all power is derived from the people and that all government is influenced [by them is] perverted by a certain proportion of the people.... The object and ultimate end of republican government being thus delusively established in their minds they have no hesitation of embracing any means for the accomplishment of their purposes." The insurgents, agreed lawyer Fisher Ames, "turned against their teachers the doctrines, which were inculcated in order to effect the late revolution." [28]

Some British observers found the situation full of irony. "Strange that the ungrateful multitude should turn upon the illustrious patriots, who led them to seek such happiness," loyalist Jonathan Mallet sarcastically wrote from London in early 1787. An English commentator in the *Bath Chronicle* captured the same irony: "America exhibits a curious scene at this time, rebellion growing out of rebellion; particularly in that seedling-bed and hot-bed of discontent, sedition, riot and rebellion Massachusetts Bay." [29]

Ironic or not, the goals of the Shaysites had shifted from reform to rebellion. In January 1787 some yeomen renounced the Massachusetts government and planned to overthrow it.

Confrontation at Springfield

During late 1786 and early 1787, farmers systematically planned for an assault upon government. Already linked by family ties, the Shaysites divided western and central Massachusetts into four regimental areas in early December. Rather than constructing a rigid hierarchical order with supreme power invested in a single commander, they formed "committees of the people" to assume leadership in each county. Hampshire County farmers, for example, instituted a Committee of Seventeen. The head of each committee, sometimes local militia leaders such as Daniel Shays or Luke Drury, had the responsibility for writing "to the several towns in their respective regiments in the name and behalf of this committee, requesting them to meet and organize." Designated yeomen carried letters to towns in inland Massachusetts, exhorting small landholders to support the Shaysite cause and to hold "themselves in readiness to march at a moment's warning" like the minutemen of 1775. Once formed, each regiment considered its plan of action on a majority basis.[30] As Richard M. Brown has observed generally about rural rebellions in revolutionary America, "the protagonists of the backcountry rebellion rose from the people but, unlike John Adams of the patriot movement, for example, did not rise above them."[31]

Daniel Shays, a revolutionary war veteran from Pelham, functioned within this collaborative organizational structure. In a revealing conversation with his former revolutionary commander Rufus Putnam about his role in the uprising, Shays shouted: "I at their head! I am not." Putnam questioned the farmer about his supposedly pivotal role in planning the Hampshire County court closing. Shays replied that he "never had any hand in the matter; it was done by a committee." While the name of Daniel Shays undeniably provided yeomen with a rallying cry and a symbol of unity like the mythical "Captain Swing" of nineteenth-century England, Shays himself acted simply as one influential member of the Hampshire County "committee of the people."[32]

Once organized into regiments, Massachusetts farmers began to plan the overthrow of the state government. This scheme involved a take-over of the federal arsenal in Springfield. Built in 1778, this arsenal of the Confederation government housed 7,000 muskets with bayonets, 1,300 barrels of powder, and a large quantity of shot and shell. All told, the building held 450 tons of military stores. Although it probably offered an alluring target for yeomen wielding old guns and wooden clubs, the arsenal did not come under attack in late 1786. Insurgent inaction puzzled Hampshire militia commander William Shepard. "I am surprised they have not seized the arsenal long before this time and erected their standard at Springfield," he wrote in December to Henry Knox.[33] Shepard's bewilderment, however, stemmed from his misunderstanding of rebel goals. In late 1786, the Shaysites still professed reformist ends and consciously confined their activity to the immobilization of the debtor courts, a traditional target of agrarian protest. Since an attack upon the arsenal involved a fundamental challenge to government, they left the federal storehouse untouched despite two incursions into Springfield during the last months of 1786.

By January 1787, however, radicalized farmers readied for an attack on the magazine. They planned to surround the building and capture its stores while Benjamin Lincoln and his army waited for trouble in Worcester. After garnering arms from the magazine, explained Shays, rebels planned to "march directly to Boston, plunder it, and then ... *to destroy the nest of devils, who by their influence, make the Court enact what they please,* burn it and lay the town of Boston in ashes." By such extreme measures, farmers such as Shays believed "it was in their power to overthrow the present constitution" and free themselves from a merchant-dominated government.[34]

To achieve their designs, yeomen slowly filtered into the Springfield area and surrounded the arsenal. On January 21, more than 300 Berkshire yeomen, artisans, and farm laborers walked over sixty miles in snow and cold to take possession of the Chicopee bridge immediately north of the arsenal. About 1,000 men marched from their Hampshire County homes to nearby West Springfield and, according to eyewitness Thomas Dwight, "placed guards at the old ferry on the west of the Connecticut River and at one Samuel Leonard's, innkeeper, about two miles from the river beyond Agawam bridge" on the Boston Post Road.[35] Along with a few men from Bristol County and Vermont, over 1,000 farmers and day laborers from Worcester and Middlesex counties traveled to Palmer, east of the arsenal, the same day. The strategic positions of the three agrarian companies effectively severed communications between the 1,000 Hampshire County militiamen defending the federal storehouse and the rest of Massachusetts. The loyal militia, probably recruited from market towns such as Springfield, Northampton, Hadley, and Deerfield, stood isolated from the 4,400-man government army in Worcester. "There are numerous bodies of insurgents in different places all around me, cutting off communications with the country," wrote Major General William Shepard to Hartford wholesaler Jeremiah

Wadsworth. "I am environed on every side, excepting that which leads to Connecticut." [36]

Encircling Shepard and his men, the Shaysites first harassed shopkeepers around Springfield and Northampton—obvious targets for farmers dragged to court by retailers for unpaid debts. On January 23, they captured prominent store owner Warham Parks of Westfield. The same day they made prisoners of retailer Robert Breck and "several other gentlemen with their ladies," all from the market center of Northampton. They then marched into West Springfield and commandeered "about 4,000 bushels of grain and several barrels of beef and pork" from store owner Justin Ely. Besides the need for food, revenge for Ely's many prosecutions of inland farmers may have provided a motive for the attack.[37]

After dealing with local retailers, the Shaysites leveled their muskets at the federal arsenal. According to their plan, Berkshire rebels would assault the arsenal from the north, Worcester and Middlesex farmers from the northeast, and Hampshire yeomen from the west. The three-pronged onslaught, the insurgents hoped, would overwhelm Shepard and his militiamen. By January 24, the farmers were prepared for a clash. They "would lodge in Springfield the next night or in *Hell*," promised yeoman John Wheeler. "*Hell* was not full enough—some more men must be killed." Other farmers expressed the same resolve, vowing "to take the ground and arms which General Shepard now occupies." [38]

But a miscarried message doomed rebel plans. On January 25, the Hampshire farmers sent an ultimatum to Shepard. Luke Day, writing for "the body of the people assembled in arms," demanded "that the troops in Springfield lay down their arms" and "return to their homes under parole." Shepard had twenty-four hours to comply; if he did not, Day pledged "to give nor take no quarter." Simultaneously, Day sent a note to fellow Shaysites, informing them of the postponement of operations from January 25 to January 26.[39]

Intercepted by Shepard's men, Day's letter never reached the Shaysites in Chicopee and Palmer, who proceeded with their original plans.[40] At four o'clock in the afternoon of Jan-

uary 25, a small agrarian army of 1,500 determined farmers
approached the arsenal. They "came on impetuously but in
good order with their pieces shouldered," forced by four feet
of snow into two open columns of twelve-man platoons. The
columns advanced within 250 yards of the arsenal and then
halted. William Lyman and Samuel Buffington, Northampton
retailers and aides to General Shepard, galloped up to the
insurgent ranks and threatened the Shaysites with the arsenal
cannon. "If they proceeded to advance or put their troops in
motion," they warned, the farmers "would inevitably be fired
on" and would have to fight men they "had once been accustomed to obey" during the Revolution. "That is all we
want, by God," cried Adam Wheeler. As Lyman and Buffington rode back to the magazine, Daniel Shays "laughed at the
information" and told his men that they would take "the Hill
on which the arsenal and Public Buildings stand." A battle
"was all he wanted." "March, God Damn you, march!," he
shouted. The time for compromise had passed.[41]

As the Shaysites neared the arsenal, "three field pieces and
a howitz[er] were placed so as to rake them" at "the two wide
roads at the entrance of the plain." According to Thomas
Dwight, a retailer from Springfield, Shepard fired two of his
cannon at the approaching Shaysites "at such an elevation as
not to injure them, humanely wishing to frighten them to lay
down their arms. This had no other effect than to lower the
heads of two or three of their platoon in front." In desperation,
the militiamen then aimed two cannon directly at the rebels
and fired fourteen or fifteen rounds of grapeshot into their
ranks. When the smoke cleared, the blood of four dead and
twenty wounded farmers stained the snow-covered ground
around the arsenal as the bulk of the farmers retreated from
Springfield to nearby towns. As Shaysite Eli Parsons told
government soldier Elnathan Haskell a few days after the
Springfield defeat, Day's miscarried message "occasioned their
failure—they must have carried it, if their measures had been
properly concerted."[42]

Despite the setback at Springfield, insurgents tried to re-
group their regiments and continue the fight. On January 26,

Worcester and Middlesex farmers united with Berkshire rebels around Amherst; Hampshire Shaysites linked up with the group a day later. About 100 Shaysites from Berkshire County, hearing of the Springfield battle and wishing to join the insurgent ranks, met with opposition: a government party headed by lawyer Theodore Sedgwick, a leader of the conservative western Massachusetts faction within the General Court, confronted the rebels and killed two of them before they made their way to Springfield.[43]

This rural army did not abandon plans to overthrow the government. According to Worcester retailers Jonathan Sprague and Joseph Allen, the insurgents "discovered no marks of submission either by surrendering their arms or taking the oath of allegiance."[44] They still felt it better "to die by the bayonet than by the halter" and prepared for another confrontation, circulating accounts of the Springfield attack "calculated to inflame the minds of the people against government" and encouraging fellow yeomen to meet them at Petersham in order to make a last stand against the state army. Some Shaysites entertained hopes for success. Daniel Shays, for example, "knew General Lincoln was coming against him, but as he would bring with him nobody but shopkeepers, lawyers, and doctors, he could easily defeat him."[45]

As the Shaysites marched from Amherst to Petersham, they raided the stores of a number of Hampshire County retailers. On January 27, groups from Amherst, Greenwich, and New Salem captured four area storekeepers at South Hadley—Sunderland retailers Cotton Graves, Noadiah Leonard, and Martin Cooley as well as Deerfield store owner Ebenezer Barnard—two Shaysites losing their lives in the incident. On January 29, rebels attacked Chesterfield retailer Joshua Healy, dragging him to a Shaysite camp where he was held for twelve days.[46] Two days later, they planned the same treatment for prominent Springfield tradesman Jonathan Dwight. About sixty "Shays men beset Colonel Dwight's house with design to take the Colonel and a horseman whom they heard were there." Not finding Dwight, the party "carried off a young man whom the Colonel had left to take care of his family." The raiders then marched from Springfield to Amherst, where they attacked the homes of the town's store owners and confiscated some of their property.[47]

Another agrarian attack upon country retailers ended in a minor battle. On February 2, Worcester store owners John Stanton and Samuel Flagg traveled to Leicester "in order to secure a debt they had against one Southgate." Southgate's father answered their knocks and said he would call his son. As the store owners waited, forty Shaysites surrounded the house. Returning from the rural army "in order to get provisions and with orders to take up any government men they might find," the farmers captured the retailers and took them to a makeshift headquarters at Hamilton's Inn in New Braintree. Government horsemen soon heard of the incident. As the 120 government soldiers closed in for the rescue, a few yeomen formed a picket guard "to go to hail the party sent by government" while another 30 Shaysites, like the Minutemen of Lexington and Concord, "placed themselves behind some fences and some in one place and some in another." On sight of oncoming horsemen, the picket guard jumped up, "fired upon the government party," and then retreated. As the government troops galloped toward the withdrawing husbandmen, the other line of Shaysites opened fire upon the troops. After the shooting had stopped, Worcester County sheriff Jonathan Rice and state trooper David Young lay wounded on the ground "in violent spasms." The troops found no rebels. The farmers had disappeared "with all possible speed into the woods" and made their way toward Petersham, expecting a large-scale confrontation with the full body of Lincoln's army in the near future.[48]

General Benjamin Lincoln also looked forward to battle at Petersham. Hearing of the Springfield battle at Worcester, he had immediately marched west. His army of 3,000—1,400 men short due to the unfulfilled allotments of the inland counties—had doggedly pursued the insurgents, moving from Springfield to Amherst to Hadley and finally ending in Pelham. On February 2, Lincoln concocted a scheme to quell the uprising. Planning to march from Pelham to Petersham the next night, he hoped to surprise and disperse the Shaysites.

Lincoln executed his plan with precision. During the night

of February 3, the government troops began a thirty-mile trek to Petersham. Halfway through the march, the weather abruptly changed. "The wind rose to a great height and blew snow with excessive violence," wrote government soldier Thomas Thompson. "The old paths were all filled up immediately. The wind and snow seemed to come in whirls and eddies and penetrated the all of my clothes and filled my eyes, ears, neck, and everything else which, added to the severe cold, made the march distressing as words can describe it." Even though "the greater part of the way was half leg high" in snow and more than half the men suffered frostbite, the government troops trudged forward and reached the Shaysite camp during the early hours of February 4. The appearance of government soldiers shocked the rebels. As one government trooper observed, "the movement was so unexpected and sudden, that they were immediately thrown into disorder.... [They] had not time to call in their out parties or even their guards." [49] Within thirty minutes, the rebels abandoned Petersham and scattered to the nearby countryside.

A number of factors may have accounted for the debacle. In the midst of a violent snowstorm, the Shaysites probably never expected another army to appear. Rebels may also have been taken unaware because Lincoln attacked on a Sunday. Besides time and weather, the size and artillery of Lincoln's army may have daunted the farmers. Lincoln commanded 3,000 men while the rural forces numbered less than 2,000. Lincoln also had an advantage in firepower, for his troops managed to haul a number of cannon to Petersham. According to George Richards Minot, Lincoln had "his flanks covered from any sudden impression, by a very deep snow, so crusted as nearly to bear a man"; he "knew therefore that he could not be annoyed, but in front, in a very narrow sled path which, having a part of his artillery advanced, he could command to a very great distance." [50] As a government soldier contended, "the great advantage Lincoln's army had always enjoyed was at this critical moment of infinite consequence—in having an artillery." [51]

Immediately after Lincoln's victory, the reassured leaders in the East moved to consolidate their position. Rufus King,

Newburyport merchant and later prominent Federalist diplomat and senator, hoped that "the most extensive and minute attention will now be paid to the eradicating of every seed of insurgency." [52] On February 4, the Massachusetts General Court, as if to justify the reality it had created, declared a state of "open, unnatural, unprovoked, and wicked rebellion." The act gave Governor Bowdoin "almost absolute powers" for "extirpating the spirit of rebellion; quieting the minds of the good people of the commonwealth and to establish the just authority and dignity" of government. Under its provisions, the governor could "exercise martial law, and in every respect treat the citizens in arms against the state and their adherents as open enemies." [53] Legislators simultaneously passed measures for raising an additional 2,600 government troops. Coastal merchants again loaned specie to supply the new regiments: Boston wholesaler William Phillips gave £2,235; fellow merchant Samuel Breck offered £365; and Salem merchant Elias Haskell Derby furnished another £100. In all, at least nine seacoast merchants loaned over £4,000 to outfit the contingent and show the continued commitment of the coastal elite to crush the Shaysites. [54]

Not completely confident in the lasting triumph of arms, representatives on February 16 also blocked the possibility of Shaysite-oriented legislation by passing a Disqualification Act. Shaysites could "not serve as jurors, be eligible to any town office or any other office" in the Commonwealth for three years. The act additionally disqualified "their votes for the same term of time, for any officer civil or military, within this Commonwealth." At the same time, recognizing the important cultural function of teachers and tavern owners, it barred rebels from "holding or exercising the employments of school-masters, innkeepers, or retailers of spiritous liquors, or either of them." [55]

This anti-Shaysite legislation, combined with Lincoln's triumph at Petersham, marked the end of the third stage of the Shaysite struggle. Most rebels now abandoned their plans for a massive assault on Boston. The fundamental nature of the confrontation, however, militated against a quick resolution. The last action had not been taken.

"To Harass the Inhabitants in Small Parties by Surprise"

According to government commander Jonathan Warner, "the bitter rebellious spirit of the insurgents" in Worcester County "continued unsubdued and stubborn" after the rout at Petersham. Few countrymen, he wrote on February 7, had "surrendered their arms, and numbers assert that when General Lincoln's army is discharged they shall be able to defend themselves." On the eighteenth, Major General William Shepard described to Governor Bowdoin a similar sentiment among Hampshire County yeomen: "Insolent menaces have been and still are in circulation. Inflammatory letters have been handed about to prevent the evil spirit of sedition and rebellion from evaporating." In Berkshire County, the rebels likewise seemed "as rancorous and seditious as ever," swearing that "they had rather die in the field than submit." On February 15, for example, from Vermont Eli Parsons exhorted "the People" to arms:

> Will you now tamely suffer your arms to be taken from you, your estates to be confiscated, and even swear to support a constitution and form of government, and likewise a code of laws, which common sense and your consciences declare to be iniquitous and cruel? And can you bear to see and hear of the yeomanry of this commonwealth being patched and cut to pieces by the cruel and merciless tools of tyrannical power, and not resent it *even unto relentless bloodshed?* . . . You, as citizens of a republican government [have an obligation] to support those rights and privileges that the God of nature hath entitled you to.

By "all the sacred ties of friendship, which natural affection inspires the human heart with," Parsons told the farmers "immediately to turn out, and assert your rights" and *"Burgoyne* Lincoln and his army."[56] Such continued opposition to government resulted in a number of raids upon the inland market elite that mark the fourth stage of Shays' Rebellion.

Seeking asylum, many Shaysites initially traveled to Vermont and New York. On February 7, Daniel Shays and the brothers Luke and Elijah Day reached Bennington, Vermont; the Shaysite stalwarts Eli Parsons, Joel Billings, Reuben Dick-

inson, and John Nash arrived a week later. By the end of
March, more than "2,000 souls" had trudged into the independent territory with "livestock, household furniture, and all
the moveable property" they possessed, despite government
orders to "arrest all persons concerned in the present rebellion,
who shall be moving out of this state with their property and
effects." [57] Other Shaysites also defied the state decree, crossing
the Massachusetts border into New York. In early February,
Royall Tyler, government trooper and future playwright, saw
"columns of refugee rebels" moving toward New Lebanon.
Masses of farmers from Berkshire County, agreed government
suppliers James Prince and Joseph Ruggles, fled to "the other
side of the line in New York." [58] By March, between 2,500
and 3,000 insurgents had escaped Lincoln's army by moving
to neighboring states.

Rural New England family ties facilitated the migration
from Massachusetts. Luke and Elijah Day, for example, found
shelter with their brother Giles Day in Marlborough, Vermont. For Shaysite John Fox, the home of his brother
Hubbard in New Canaan, New York, offered refuge. Some
rebels stayed with relatives in Pittsford, Vermont, and many
"were dispersed about in private families" in New York. [59]
Some Shaysites undoubtedly emigrated without familial contacts, but bonds of kinship expedited the migration of many.
Affording hunted farmers needed protection from the government army, these bonds created the possibility of continued
Shaysite resistance after the rout at Petersham.

Protected by their families, a few Shaysites began planning
fresh forays against the Massachusetts government. A party
of five yeomen reached Quebec on February 24, 1787, where
they met with Canadian governor Lord Dorchester and asked
for arms and ammunition. According to Massachusetts government spies, Dorchester promised aid to the rebels through
pro-British Indian chief Joseph Brant. [60] Two considerations
may have prompted Dorchester to support the Shaysites. Before leaving England in October 1786, Abigail Adams had
reported from London, the new Canadian governor "gave it as
his solid opinion, that he should live to see America sue to
Britain for protection and to be received again by it." [61] For

Dorchester, British aid to the rebels may have represented the first step toward reintegrating the United States into the British Empire. Besides furthering long-range goals, such assistance to the insurgents may have helped England indirectly in the struggle over the forts along the Canadian–United States border; continued troubles in New England, Dorchester probably believed, would divert American attention from the northern garrisons and give the British a free hand in the area.

Some rebels may have seriously reassessed their attitude toward the British and considered accepting the English weapons. "I arrived from Canada where I was well-treated by them which was my eternal enemies which at first appearance seemed strange. It might appear not stranger than my avowed friends to seek my life and plunder me in my absence," wrote Shaysite John Wiley in April 1787.[62]

Acting upon the promise of weapons, the Shaysites began a series of assaults upon merchants and lawyers, noted state military leaders, and government officials in western and central Massachusetts. During the night of February 26, at least 120 farmers and agricultural laborers in New Lebanon, New York, organized, "paraded, and marched three divisions" eastward. The insurgents included brothers Uriah, Amos, and Shubel Woodruff, Phillip Austin and his brother Nathaniel, as well as brothers Caleb and Henry Clark. Most of these Shaysites formerly lived in West Stockbridge, Sheffield, Egremont, and Tyringham, Massachusetts, with a few, such as Barnabas Minlee and William Pixley, coming from New York towns along the state line.[63] Together, the farmers tramped through the snow, reaching the Massachusetts border "well armed and well provided with ammunition" in the early hours of February 27. They promised "death" to prominent retailers and professionals in Berkshire County.[64]

To fulfill their vow, the rebels first entered Stockbridge, one of the largest market centers in Berkshire County during the late eighteenth century. Once in the town, they marched directly to the home of Elisha Williams, storekeeper, Yale graduate, and noted government supporter, and pounded on the shutters. "God Damn you open your door," they cried out. With "curses and threatenings," the band kicked down a heavy wooden door and rushed into the house. They searched the building "from bottom to top for arms, ammunition, etc." and then took a "pretty roughly handled" Elisha Williams prisoner. The insurgents then surrounded the home of physician Erastus Sargeant, a sergeant in Lincoln's army. The Shaysites "drove their bayonets through the windows," jumped into the building, and grabbed Sargeant, thrusting a bayonet toward his "wife's breast, with a demand of arms and ammunition." After "getting what arms and ammunition they could find," they dragged the doctor to their temporary headquarters at Bingham's Tavern.[65]

The same fate awaited other retailers and professionals in Stockbridge. The Shaysites burst into the home of Silas Pepoon, one of the most prominent store owners in Berkshire County, and captured him along with his son Daniel. Proceeding to the residence of Timothy Edwards, son of renowned minister Jonathan Edwards and owner of the first store in Berkshire County, the rebels seized him and his son Edward.[66]

The Shaysites next advanced on the law office of Yale-educated Theodore Sedgwick. As an aide to General John Paterson in the Lincoln expedition and leader of an attempt to capture the insurgents in January, Sedgwick was a natural target for the Shaysites. The rebels forcibly entered his law office, intending to kill him, but found only frightened law students. Sedgwick himself had traveled to Boston a few days earlier. Disappointed, the Shaysites pulled law students Ephraim Williams and Harry Hopkins from their beds and took them to Bingham's Tavern.

The raiders continued their attacks upon commercial leaders in Stockbridge, ransacking seventeen other houses and apprehending more than twenty other store owners and professionals. Among their prisoners were land speculator Moses Ashley; Jahleel Woodbridge, a judge of the Berkshire debtor court; county treasurer Henry Dwight; and retailer Jonathan Woodbridge. According to Benjamin Lincoln, the captives represented "the most influential characters" in the town.[67] Significantly, the Shaysites restricted their raids to the homes of about thirty merchants and professionals, leaving the rest of Stockbridge undisturbed.

After departing from Stockbridge, the rebels made their way to Great Barrington—another major market center in postwar Berkshire County. Taking the prisoners with them, they kidnapped nineteen retailers and professionals from that town, after which they broke into the county jail and released all debtors from their cells.[68]

News of insurgent exploits soon reached government troops stationed in nearby Pittsfield. Although most of Lincoln's army had been dismissed on February 22, eighty government soldiers still remained, waiting for replacements. The troops, headed by merchant and militia general John Ashley, rode off in sleighs to pursue the rebels. A few Berkshire men joined the troopers on the march, including Elnathan Curtis, owner of grist and sawmills in Stockbridge; Dr. Jonathan Ingersoll; and Thomas Ives, Yale-educated lawyer and confidant of Theodore Sedgwick. With the government soldiers, these men wanted to rescue their "friends and property." [69]

During the evening of February 27, government supporters found the Shaysites and their captives outside Sheffield. At sight of the approaching government troops, the rebels shoved their prisoners "by point of bayonet, into the front of the battle and kept them there for a breastwork"; a few minutes later, they began to attack "by scattering fire from a considerable distance." State troopers returned the fire, and the shooting continued at close range for over six minutes. After the firing stopped, more than thirty yeomen lay dead or wounded on the frozen ground. On the government side, three soldiers were killed and dozens wounded. The insurgent attack upon retailers and professionals in Stockbridge and Great Barrington had ended in the bloodiest battle of the Massachusetts troubles.[70]

Despite their losses at Sheffield, the Shaysites persisted in their assaults upon country traders. One target was Josiah Woodbridge, who operated a large potash works in South Hadley throughout the 1780s and had lent money and supplies to the government during the uprising. On March 2, rebels burned Woodbridge's glassmaking factory to the ground.[71] A week later, a few insurgents slipped into Nobletown, New York, and burned a store owned by two Massachusetts retailers. The Sheffield owners, "gentlemen who had exerted themselves in favor of government," lost "400 pounds of wheat, other kinds of grain, and a large assortment of English and West India goods." On March 26, Pittsfield lawyer and retailer Woodbridge Little saw his barn burn to the ground. "I would only infer that it does not appear that the evil spirit has entirely departed" or that the rebels had "such marks of penitence as could be wished," he wrote.[72]

The Shaysites struck again in Westfield on April 4, when they tried to burn the general store of Enoch Loomis. A few days later, some rebels lashed out against retailer and potash factory owner William Moore of Greenfield. During the night of April 9, they cautiously moved into Greenfield and placed some "combustibles" at the northwest corner of Moore's store. Flames, kindled by gusts of wind, consumed half the building before the trader and his friends extinguished the blaze, saving "a large adjoining pearl ash works with excellent accommodations." To an observer in the *Hampshire Gazette,* the incident afforded "one instance, among several others, of the fulfillment of the threatenings made by the disaffected to government." [73]

Besides attacking retailers, the Shaysites employed hit-and-run tactics to combat a more immediate problem: the Lincoln expedition. Government troops had marched to Berkshire County to quell discontent after their victory at Petersham. Although Lincoln had dismissed the force in late February, over 2,000 replacements followed within two weeks. Relentlessly pursued by these state troops, the insurgents launched a number of forays against noted military leaders.

The Shaysites first attempted to capture the expedition commander, Benjamin Lincoln. In early April, Lincoln journeyed to New Lebanon, Massachusetts. The arduous campaign of the preceding months had tired the 300-pound warrior, and he hoped that New Lebanon's hot springs would afford some comfort. As he was enjoying the waters, a group of rebels crossed the New York border and marched toward the unprotected general. Lincoln, however, got the news in time and quickly fled. About ten minutes later, over 120 yeomen armed with clubs and muskets descended upon the unoccupied hot springs.[74]

Other Shaysites terrorized Major General William Shepard who, in the minds of some, symbolized the defeat at Springfield and bore responsibility for the death of four rebels during the melee; he had become the "murderer of brethren." [75] In early April, one Shaysite sent him a threatening letter: "William Shepard I write you this to let you know we have determined to kill you. I write in haste for my anger being up to the very heavens and crying aloud for vengance." [76] Two weeks later, a band of nine Shaysites moved toward the major general's home in Westfield and burned his fences and woodlands "beyond recovery for many years." They then mutilated two of his horses "by cutting off their ears and digging out their eyes before they were killed." Shepard, away from home during the raid, escaped harm.[77]

Other prominent military leaders endured similar treatment from the Shaysites. In late February, reported Shepard, four farmers hiding in Vermont returned to Massachusetts "for the purpose of assassinating Captain Caleb Chapin" of Bernardston. Chapin evaded the party but was in constant fear of another attempt on his life for the rest of the year. On May 3, Shaysites terrorized government commander Josiah Osgood of Wendell, Massachusetts. "Prepare ye for death for your life is short and terrible," they wrote to him. "You have had your day and ours is acoming and then you and a great many more will be as bad off as those that is in the torments of hell." Ebenezer Mattoon, another officer of the state troop, likewise "suffered much in person and property" from the Shaysites. Raids directed at his Amherst home eventually forced Mattoon to move his "family to a neighboring town for shelter." [78]

The Shaysites also attacked a few political leaders in western Massachusetts. Throughout the uprising, a group of representatives from the inland regions, many of them retailers or lawyers, had repeatedly sided with the dominant mercantile interest, voting for anti-Shaysite legislation. Becket representative Nathaniel Kingsley was one of these, and on May 8 about

twenty armed Shaysites crossed the New York border and
marched directly to Kingsley's home. Not finding him, they
"took all the arms in the house, about twenty," and "went off
whither could not be found." A few insurgents launched a
similar foray against John Starkweather, the Lanesboro representative. On June 13, a party of farmers in New York slipped
over the state line, broke into Starkweather's house, and manhandled him.[79] Like the raids against merchants and military
leaders, the attacks on members of the House demonstrated
the continuing militance of the Shaysites.

The End of Armed Insurgency

In June 1787, Shaysite raids, for a number of reasons, ground
to a halt. For one, a new group of Massachusetts legislators
continued the anti-Shaysite policies of their predecessors. In
the statewide election of April 1787, only 77 of the 203 House
members gained reelection, and about half of all incumbent
senators were ousted from their seats.[80] To make the change-
over almost complete, Governor James Bowdoin fell from
office. Bowdoin, hated by inland farmers for measures passed
during his administration and blamed by many merchants and
professionals for the western uprising, lost to an ever-popular
John Hancock by a three-to-one margin in a heavy voter
turnout. These new legislators, contended one Shaysite, would
"please we poor folks" and recall "them tarnal great men that
Bowdoin sent up here last winter. I believe Governor Hancock
will put his negative to anything that ain't answerable to the
good cause." Rebels had another reason to be in good spirits:
Shaysites in Shrewsbury, Boylston, Barre, New Braintree, Sutton, and Sterling won offices in elections on the town level
despite the disqualification act.[81]

But despite the hopes of many yeomen, new lawmakers on
the state level enacted measures more favorable to the mercantile interest. The Massachusetts General Court first elected
anti-Shaysite Samuel Adams to the Senate presidency and
Boston lawyer James Warren as the Speaker of the House.
Acting under coastal leadership, the General Court refused to
seat three Shaysites—Samuel Willard, Luke Drury, and Josiah
Whitney—elected to the House and then rejected a paper

money proposal by an overwhelming 103-to-47 vote. Legislators also lent their support to inland retailers directly affected by the uprising, awarding shopkeepers such as Aaron Brown of Groton complete monetary reimbursements for property destroyed by the Shaysites. Finally, they created a special court of oyer and terminer to try the rebels. Held during April and May 1787, the hearings led to death sentences for thirteen rebels who were eventually pardoned and to the hangings of Berkshire insurgents John Bly and Charles Rose. Other Shaysites escaped prosecution by taking an oath of allegiance to government.[82]

Although accepted by many farmers due to his informal, democratic style, the new governor, John Hancock, pushed additional anti-insurgent measures in the General Court. The governor, himself a prosperous Boston merchant who told a friend in 1766 that extra-legal crowds were "what I abhor and detest as much as any man breathing," proposed to "adopt every vigorous and efficacious method, necessary to suppress the present traitorous opposition to the laws." To implement an antirebel policy, Hancock requested and received from the General Court a £3,000 requisition for 800 new government soldiers. In June, the troops marched from Boston toward Berkshire County with instructions to "kill, slay, and destroy if necessary, and conquer by all fitting ways, enterprises, and means whatsoever, all and every one of the rebels." Following the example of New Hampshire governor John Sullivan, Hancock joined the government force in August and made a military tour of western Massachusetts. As Mercy Otis Warren later observed, Hancock did not "contravene the wise measures of his predecessor. He was equally vigilant to quiet the perturbed spirits of the people, and to restore general tranquility." [83]

The insurgents felt added pressures from other New England states. Rhode Island once again proved the exception, when in March its legislature considered a bill that would have barred Massachusetts rebels from the state. The proposal was soundly rejected after Shaysite Samuel Willard of Massachusetts, "one of the principal springs of insurgency," was allowed to raise his voice in the debate.[84] Throughout the rest of 1787, Rhode Island gave no help to Bowdoin or Hancock and even provided shelter to a few rebels although its close proximity to Boston made it a poor place of refuge.

Unlike proinsurgent Rhode Island, the other New England states sided with the Massachusetts government and barred organized Shaysite activity within their borders. Early in 1787, New Hampshire Governor John Sullivan offered his whole-hearted support. "You may rest assured, sir," he informed Governor Bowdoin, "that no measure shall be wanting, in this state, to prevent the rebels from receiving countenance or protection." The next month, Sullivan commissioned armed agents to stop Shaysite recruitment of New Hampshire farmers.[85]

Connecticut gave Massachusetts similar help. In February, Governor Samuel Huntington vowed to capture "any of the insurgents who attempt to screen themselves from justice by seeking an asylum in this state."[86] Three months later, he provided more forceful support when Berkshire Shaysites John Hurlburt and Jonah Barnes, along with country artisan William Mitchell and one Captain Tanner from New York, began to recruit farmers in Litchfield County "to assist Shays in the completion of his army." Representative Hezekiah Swift of Salisbury, expounding on "the righteousness of the cause" and the "necessity and justice of the insurgents having recourse to arms," likewise convinced some farmers to enlist in the rural force. By May 15, over 100 yeomen in the town of Sharon had joined the Shaysites while others in Salisbury, Kent, and Norfolk volunteered their help.[87] Learning of the rebel recruitment efforts, Governor Huntington issued a proclamation "to quiet the disorders that appear to be prevalent among the people and for the establishment of government and good order in the most effectual manner." He also appointed four leading officials to "consider intelligence" about possible trouble in western Connecticut and "prevent any insurrections of the people."[88] On May 18, the governor sent a special mission composed of Hartford merchants Samuel Canfield, Uriah Tracy, Heman Swift, and Swift's deputy to Litchfield County. The four-man team reached Sharon a day later, captured the leading recruiters for the Shaysite army, and carried them to jail amidst "bitter excretions of some women who called themselves Shays women." Farmer Ithamar Saunders tried to liberate the imprisoned rebels, but authorities defeated the move with armed force. By June 22, the decisive actions of Samuel Huntington had effectively checked the spread of Shaysism in Connecticut.[89]

New York Governor George Clinton also adopted coercive measures to support the Massachusetts government. Initially, Clinton had taken no action, allowing some insurgents to take refuge in New York. In late February, however, the governor abruptly changed his mind. The confrontation at Sheffield, only forty miles from Albany and near the landed estates of Dutchess County, seemed to threaten New York with insurrection and may have rekindled memories of the 1766 New York tenant uprising. To Clinton, the incident appeared so alarming that he immediately called into action three militia companies from Dutchess County and the Columbia County brigade. The governor then personally traveled with the militia to the Massachusetts border, expecting that the show of force would "prevent the insurgents from spreading their evil councils" in his state. By late March, the military parade had largely achieved its desired effect. According to New York merchant's agent Colin McGregor, "the Governor and others who went to examine the situation of matters, lately returned, having left everything in peace and quietness."[90]

After initial hesitation, Vermont also neutralized the Shaysites within its borders. During most of the Shays' uprising, both Ethan Allen and Governor Thomas Chittenden had refused to cooperate with Massachusetts officials. Allen, probably the most influential man in Vermont, thought "that those who held the reins of government in Massachusetts were a pack of damned rascals and that there was no virtue among them." Scoffing at the plea of the Massachusetts government for help, he "did not think it was worth anybody's while to try to prevent them that had fled into this state for shelter from cutting down our maple trees."[91] Thomas Chittenden assumed a similar stance. On February 18, after the Vermont House had pledged its full support to the Massachusetts government, the governor vetoed the decision and later bottled up a new measure in committee. The governor felt "that whenever people

were oppressed they will mob" and "did not conceive the nature" of the insurgent "offense to be such that it was the duty
of this state to be aiding in hauling them away to the halter." [92]

In May 1787, however, Chittenden and Allen abandoned
their prorebel policy. Possibly fearing trouble in their own
bailiwick, and prodded by conservative Vermont legislators,
they now permitted aid to the Massachusetts authorities. On
May 7, Vermont officials dispersed over 100 insurgents "in
convention" at Shaftsbury "for continuing opposition to government." A month later, a number of "respectable gentlemen"
captured Shaysites Gideon Dunham and George Baker at
Onion River, delivering "them to the proper authorities" in
Massachusetts. By late August, Ethan Allen boasted of Vermont's assistance to Massachusetts. "I dare say, that the government of this state has been very friendly to yours," he told
Royall Tyler. "Such persons as have been criminals, and have
acted against law and society in general, and have come from
your state to this, we send back to you." [93]

The policy of the British also hampered continued Shaysite
resistance to the Massachusetts government. In mid-1787, the
ministry apparently changed its attitude toward the rebels.
Believing that the New England tumults had already retarded
"any operations the Americans may mediate against the Indians" near the northern forts, Foreign Minister Lord Sidney
saw little reason to aid the Shaysites and advised his Canadian subordinate Lord Dorchester that "active assistance would
at this present moment be a measure extremely imprudent."
The Canadian governor heeded the orders of his superior.
Thus, the British reneged on promises of armed support. [94]

One other factor played an important part in bringing the
troubles to a close: migration and resettlement on unoccupied
lands. Harried by hostile governments, some rebels took advantage of the vast expanses of American territory and moved
to areas where subsistence farming could be resumed and
their way of life preserved. In late 1787, for example, Shaysite William Hencher left his farm in Brookfield, Massachusetts, and resettled in Newtown, New York. Reuben Dickinson of Amherst, engaged in both the Ely and Shaysite
troubles, likewise uprooted his family and started farming on

free land in Thetford, Vermont. Abraham Gale and Norman Clark from Princeton took up residence in the pioneer town of Clarkesville, New Hampshire, while a group of such prominent insurgents as Daniel Shays, Adam Wheeler, and Henry Gale banded together and resettled at Eadie Brook near Beattie Mountain outside Sandgate, Vermont.[95] Other Shaysites migrated to the unsettled Ohio territory. "The malcontents are moving there in large numbers, and the banks of the Ohio will soon be covered with plantations," observed French minister Louis Guillaume Otto on October 23, 1787.[96] As with other vacant areas, the Ohio valley offered shelter to the rebels and provided a means to end the Shaysite troubles without a final confrontation.

Most Shaysites, however, stayed in Massachusetts amidst an economic upswing. In 1788, reported Boston lawyer William Tudor "the exports of our state exceed the imports last year by £230,000 and upwards. The town of Boston alone that year exported £1,213." [97] The Massachusetts government also eased the credit situation, passing a one-year tender act in June 1787. But as Samuel Eliot Morison has observed, the favorable balance of trade "did more to salve the wounds of Shays' Rebellion than all the measures passed by the General Court." [98]

Yet, the Shaysites did not forget the burdens that had been placed upon them. Abandoning armed protest, they continued to fight their case in opposing the adoption of the new federal Constitution.

7
Shays' Rebellion and the Constitution

THE UPRISING OF New England farmers in 1786 and 1787 has a historic significance much deeper than that of a regional chronicle. For it is clear that Shays' Rebellion played an integral part in the genesis and formation of the United States Constitution adopted at Philadelphia in September 1787. The crisis atmosphere engendered by agrarian discontent strengthened the resolve of the nationalists and shocked some reluctant localists into an acceptance of a stronger national government, thereby uniting divergent political elements of commercial society in the country at large.

Besides affecting the formation of the Constitution, the Shaysite troubles influenced the ratification debates in New England, and especially in Massachusetts. The ratification contest generally pitted backcountry Antifederalists against merchants, professionals, and urban artisans. Following the pattern of Shaysite resistance to government, Massachusetts antifederalism represented an attempt to save a subsistence-oriented way of life from the penetrating edge of a commercial society. As Van Beck Hall has argued, "the debate over the Constitution, instead of raising the curtain on new divisions that would exist in a new political era, actually climaxed the political struggles of the earlier period." In both the formation of the Constitution at Philadelphia and the ratification debates in Massachusetts, then, Shays' Rebellion assumed an important role.[1]

During the 1780s, most state leaders had been oriented toward a commercial society. New England legislators usually gained their livelihoods through merchant or professional enterprises. In the middle states, lawyers such as James Wilson of Pennsylvania and New Jersey's William Paterson along with such wholesalers as Philadelphia merchants George Clymer and Thomas Mifflin exercised leadership. A few merchants in and around Charleston, South Carolina, lawyers such as North Carolina's William Davie and John Rutledge of South Carolina, and such plantation owners as Pierce Butler, Charles Pinckney, and Richard Dobbs Spaight of the Carolinas held the reins in the southern states. Together, merchants, professionals, and planters dominated the political life of the United States.

Despite common ties to a commercial society, American leaders disagreed over the political system. For most leaders of the Confederation and many coastal wholesalers, a strong national government seemed imperative. Some prominent Confederation officials, headed by Secretary at War Henry Knox and congressional leader James Madison of Virginia, consistently pushed for a more powerful national government. In March 1785, Knox advocated a new government established "upon more national principles," probably sensing the impotence of the weak Confederation from his position of national power. According to Rhode Island representative and Baptist minister James Manning, almost "every member of Congress" similarly pointed "to a crisis within the Federal government" and demanded a more centralized political system.[2]

Some New England merchants joined Confederation officials in endorsing a stronger national government. Feeling the damaging consequences of a depressed postwar economy, they blamed losses upon an inefficient Confederation and cried out for a more powerful central government. In late 1785, New Hampshire wholesaler John Sparhawk demanded a strengthened "union of the United States by delegating ample powers to Congress."[3] Many Boston merchants echoed Sparhawk's plea. According to Massachusetts political leader Nathan Dane, "the restrictions laid by the British on our trade" along with the subsequent credit crisis in New England created a "disposition especially among mercantile men, to lodge a power somewhere in the Union." In 1785, pressure laid upon the Massachusetts legislature by coastal merchants produced a resolution "to propose to the several states a convention of delegates for the express purpose of a *general revision of the Confederation.*" As Confederation delegate Rufus King observed on June 11, 1786, "the merchants through all the states are of one mind, and in favor of a national system." [4]

In September 1786, both Confederation officials and merchants pressed for an implementation of the nationalist plan at a general economic convention in Annapolis. Led by Alexander Hamilton, they focused upon the "delicate and critical" economic situation of the United States and cautioned fellow leaders about possible financial collapse and resulting anarchy unless the states quickly instituted measures for a more vigorous national government. [5] "If we do not control events we shall be miserably controlled by them," warned Massachusetts lawyer Theodore Sedgwick. [6]

Despite the obvious economic problems facing the United States in late 1786, many state officials rejected the nationalist arguments. Having gained influence and prestige through positions in the state governments and recognizing the possible dangers that a stronger national government posed to their state-based power, they ignored the nationalist-inspired Annapolis meeting. Connecticut, Maryland, South Carolina, and Georgia snubbed it, while Massachusetts, New Hampshire, Rhode Island, and North Carolina waited until the last moment. In consequence, the delegates from the latter states arrived after the convention had adjourned. Because only Virginia, Delaware, Pennsylvania, New Jersey, and New York were represented, the delegates at Annapolis decided not "to proceed on the business of their mission, under the circumstances of so partial and defective a representation." They then recommended another convention to be held at Philadelphia in May 1787 and disbanded on September 14, 1786. Although some historians have contended that the delegates went home prematurely to secretly further the nationalist cause, nationalist Rufus King privately expressed disappointment over the failure at Annapolis:

Foreign nations had been notified of this convention, the friends to a good government through these states looked at it with anxiety and hope; the history of it will not be more agreeable to the former, than it must be seriously harmful to the latter.[7]

In the time between the abortive Annapolis meeting and the proposed Philadelphia convention, nationalist resolve intensified, and some localists accepted the necessity for a stronger national government. The resulting union of American leaders originated at least in part from the domestic upheavals taking place in 1786 and 1787. To the nationalists, Shays' Rebellion reflected the overall inadequacy of a political system dominated by semisovereign states. Prolonged domestic conflict in Massachusetts, one of the most respected and influential states in the Confederation, disclosed the vulnerability of individual states in the loose-knit union. For nationalist-minded leaders such as George Washington, no "stronger evidence" could be given "of the want of energy in our governments than these disorders." At the same time, the Massachusetts insurrection brought into full relief the impotence of the federal government. Even though "Congress have been much alarmed at the prospect of the insurgents," wrote Confederation delegate John Stevens of New Jersey, it possessed few means to arm troops against the rebels. Confronted with such debility, nationalists such as Foreign Secretary John Jay felt that "the inefficiency of the Federal government becomes more and more manifest."[8]

The New England rebellion also convinced some state-oriented leaders of the need for a more powerful national government. For many localists, Shaysite activity came as a shock. "The commotions in Massachusetts daily become more alarming," exclaimed planter William Blount of North Carolina in late 1786. "The disturbances in Massachusetts Bay have been considerable, and absolutely threaten the most serious consequences," agreed Virginia planter William Grayson that November. "How it will end, God only knows; the present prospects are, no doubt, extremely alarming."[9]

Much of the localist fear of the disturbances stemmed from the perceived goals of the Shaysites and the supposed effects that a successful insurrection might have upon commercial relations. Along with New England merchants and professionals, officials in the middle and southern states feared that the insurgents sought a general redistribution of property. Frightened Pennsylvania merchant and legislator Charles Pettit thought that the Shaysites envisioned "a total abolition of all debts both public and private and even a general distribution of property." Events in Massachusetts likewise convinced South Carolina slaveholder Edward Rutledge that the rebels would "stop little short of a distribution of property—I speak of a general distribution." Such an event, cautioned Rutledge, would destroy commercial exchange and lead to economic anarchy.[10]

Pockets of backcountry resistance to debt and tax collection in the middle and southern states caused added concern among American leaders. In Maryland on June 8, 1786, "a tumultuary assemblage of the people" rushed into the Charles County courthouse and closed the court. Like the Massachusetts rebels, the insurgents demanded a suspension of debt suits and an adjournment of the court until the Maryland Assembly issued paper money. Just after the Charles County court incident, yeomen in Harford and Calvert counties organized public boycotts against government sales of debtor property. In Cecil County, farmers circulated unsigned handbills that threatened state officers with violence in the event of government seizure of property for unpaid taxes.[11] By early 1787, widespread agrarian protests had created fear among state leaders. Alexander Hamilton, engaged in some Maryland debt suits, felt that the disturbances portended a general movement against "every well wisher to the Constitution, laws, and peace of their country."[12] Governor William Smallwood likewise condemned "riotous and tumultuous" proceedings and dreaded further "violence and outrages" against the Maryland government.[13]

Officials in South Carolina confronted similar protests. During May of 1785, sheriffs and deputies were "threatened in the execution of their duty; and at length the people in the district of Camden grew outrageous." They "planted out centinels to intercept the sheriffs, and put the laws at defiance." In one incident, Colonel Hezekiah Mayham "being served by the sheriff with a writ obliged him to eat it on the spot." [14] The next month, farmers assaulted the Camden courthouse in a demonstration against debt collections, successfully blocked the consideration of debt suits, and sent the judges scurrying home.[15] Yeomen also struck out against debt collections in other South Carolina districts, preventing debtor courts "by tumultuous and riotous proceedings from determining actions for debt." Although partially calming farmers with the Pine Barrens Act and a £100,000 emission of paper money, South Carolina officials nonetheless feared future attacks upon debtor courts. If the legislature allowed "creditors to sue debtors," warned Judge Aedanus Burke, "the people would not suffer it." Not even "5,000 troops, the best in America or Europe, could enforce obedience to the Common Pleas." About the same time, Governor William Moultrie informed the assembly that "confusion and anarchy" still threatened the state.[16]

New Jersey officials also faced outbreaks of rural violence. As early as January 1785, wrote minister Joseph Lewis, "a spirit of rebellion caught hold of the greatest part of the community" around Morristown. Farmers refused to pay taxes and blocked attempts by sheriffs to auction debtor property. In one case, yeomen in Mendham armed themselves with clubs and forcibly stopped the sale of "some property at vendue" that a constable had "distrained for taxes." [17] A year later, brothers John, Ralph, Jacob, and Abraham Schenck planned an attack upon the Hunterdon County debtor court. Driven by "the madness of poverty" and angered by debt prosecutions, they surrounded the building and "began to nail up the courthouse." [18] In July 1786 Jersey farmers assaulted the Elizabethtown debtor court, planted a stake in the ground, and impaled an effigy of Governor William Livingston on the pole.[19]

Yeomen in Virginia similarly protested against debt collections. In March and April 1787, they complained of their heavy load of debts and taxes, seeking relief through peaceful protest. Some husbandmen formed associations and boycotted property sold at auction. Others flooded the legislature with petitions for paper money and tender laws, hoping the measures would alleviate the credit crisis in Virginia. Rebuked by the state assembly, some yeomen, wrote John Dawson to James

Madison, began "following the example of the insurgents in Massachusetts and preventing the courts proceeding to business." On the eve of the May court session, the King William County courthouse "with all the records of the county, was burnt down." [20] In late August, over 300 yeomen stormed the Greenbrier County court, successfully stopping its proceedings. And in Amelia County, "disorderly people of desperate circumstances" obstructed the county debtor court session.[21] Throughout the state in 1787, Madison reported, Virginia officials watched the "prisons and courthouses and clerk's offices willfully burnt." [22] Backcountry resistance to debt collections caused concern among some Virginia leaders. "The friends to American honor and happiness," wrote Richard Henry Lee from Philadelphia in September, "here all join in lamenting the riots and mobbish proceedings in Virginia." Planter Archibald Stuart, closer to the outbreaks of violence than Lee, "trembled with the apprehensions of a rebellion." [23]

The same fear of domestic insurrection seized Pennsylvania leaders. On November 29, 1786, 200 yeomen, "about twenty armed with guns, and the rest with clubs, marched into York, and by force attempted to rescue some goods and chattels that had been executed for taxes." On January 25, 1787, the same husbandmen staged another attack, assembling "at the house of Justice Sherman, where a public sale of some cattle seized for taxes was to have been held, and effecting a rescue of them."[24] Although they satisfied many farmers with an issue of paper money, Pennsylvania leaders feared trouble. To Pennsylvania official Michael Hahn, the York incidents appeared "epidemic, the infection of which has spread itself from the eastward and therefore ought to be cautiously as well as spiritedly treated." The "wild fire" of the Massachusetts rebellion, agreed Lutheran minister Henry Melchior Muhlenberg, "may cause a conflagration in the rest of the independent states because combustible materials, both physical and moral, are heaped up here." [25] While state leaders in Rhode Island, North Carolina, New York, and Georgia avoided trouble by issuing paper money, other state elites, including those in Pennsylvania, felt the anger of discontented farmers.

Fearing continued domestic turmoil, many state leaders oriented to the Confederation began to accept the idea of a stronger national government. Massachusetts, the state most plagued by domestic unrest, saw the need in late 1786. According to Henry Knox, the uprising "wrought prodigious changes in the minds of men in that state respecting the powers of government—everybody says they must be strengthened and that unless this shall be effected, there is no security for liberty and property." [26] Shays' Rebellion taught Connecticut Lieutenant Governor Oliver Wolcott, formerly a staunch localist, the same lesson. The Massachusetts uprising pointed to "such radical defects in our general system as will, unless soon remedied, produce unhappy convulsions." The "authority or rather the influence of Congress and the system connected with it, I consider at about an end," Wolcott wrote to his son on February 18, 1787.[27] To Pierce Butler, a South Carolina planter and lawyer, a strengthened national government also seemed to be "the only thing at this critical moment that can rescue the states from civil discord." [28]

By contributing to a change in the outlook of some localists, rural outbursts in New England and throughout the country may have made a general convention in Philadelphia possible. Backcountry violence did not *cause* the May 1787 meeting—in fact, the assembly had been planned before the most extreme Shaysite activity had occurred—but domestic unrest helped to ensure in certain quarters a favorable reaction toward the meeting. Developing at a critical juncture in time, the rebellion convinced the elites of sovereign states that the proposed gathering at Philadelphia must take place.

George Washington believed that the Shaysite disturbances so shocked localists "that most of the legislatures have appointed and the rest will appoint delegates to meet at Philadelphia." The revolutionary war hero attributed his own presence at the Constitutional Convention in May to the Massachusetts troubles. Fellow Virginian Edward Carrington likewise considered the "tendency to anarchy" in Massachusetts a major reason that the convention was well attended. From his perspective, it jarred into action state leaders "who had consigned themselves to an eve of rest." James Madison saw a similar connection between Shays' Rebellion and the formation of the Philadelphia convention. To the Virginian, the insurrection seemed "distressing beyond measure to the zealous friends of the Revolution." It furnished "new proofs of the necessity of such a vigor in the general government as will be able to restore health to any diseased part of the Federal body." "To bring about such an amendment of the Federal Constitution," wrote Madison, state leaders pinned their hopes on the convention "to be held in May next in Philadelphia." [29] The actions of state assemblies confirmed Madison's observation. Of the twelve states represented at the gathering—the pro-agrarian Rhode Island refused to send delegates—eight appointed delegates from October 16, 1786, to February 28, 1787, during the most threatening stages of Shays' Rebellion.[30]

As well as helping to guarantee good attendance, fears over agrarian uprising affected decisions made at the federal convention. North and South, delegates sought to block paper money and tender laws, two measures tied to backcountry discontent and insurrection. Connecticut lawyer Oliver Ellsworth "thought this a favorable moment to shut and bar the door against paper money" and tender laws. "The mischiefs of the various experiments which had been made, were now fresh in the public mind and had excited the disgust of all the respectable part of America." [31] To guard against the two measures, convention members proposed that no state shall "coin money, emit bills of credit, making anything but gold and silver coin a tender in payment of debts." [32] By this decision, observed Benjamin Rush, the delegates gave America the "advantage of a future exemption from paper money and tender laws." [33]

State leaders also framed provisions to guard against future domestic unrest. According to some prominent Americans, the Shaysite turmoil had hurt the prospects of merchants engaged in international trade. "Shutting up the courts of *justice*," contended a group of Boston wholesalers and lawyers, "loudly proclaims to our foreign creditors their *total insecurity*." British merchants, they warned, eventually would withdraw all credit and would completely cut commercial ties with their American counterparts due to fears of property loss at the hands of the rebels.[34] Perceiving a similar link between the Shaysite troubles and commercial stagnation in 1786, George Washington felt "the commotions among the Eastern people have sunk our national character much below par," bringing American "credit to the brink of a precipice."[35] Washington may have accurately described the situation. As early as November 1786, a London journal instructed "all our traders not to have any trans-Atlantic dealings, except for ready money" due to the "flames of civil war" bursting forth in New England.[36]

Making a connection between domestic turmoil and commercial decline, most state leaders agreed upon the urgent need for some coercive measures to suppress future insurgency. "A certain portion of military force is absolutely necessary in large communities. Massachusetts is now feeling the necessity," Alexander Hamilton told the Philadelphia convention on June 18, 1787.[37] Virginia planter George Mason expressed the same sentiments a month later. "If the General Government should have no right to suppress rebellions against particular states, it will be in a bad situation indeed," he told fellow delegates. "As rebellions against itself originate in and against individual states, it must remain a passive spectator of its own subversion."[38]

To suppress future rural rebellions and slave insurrections, state officials recommended two types of military force. Some delegates at Philadelphia pushed for national control of the militia. George Mason "introduced the subject of regulating the militia. He thought such power necessary to be given to the General Government." Since "the states neglect their militia now," agreed James Madison, "the discipline of the militia is evidently a *National* concern, and ought to be provided for in the *National* Constitution." He warned that "without such a power to suppress insurrections, our liberties might be destroyed by domestic faction."[39] Other delegates suggested a national army to put down uprisings. In times of widespread domestic upheaval, Pinckney of South Carolina had "but a scanty faith in the militia. There must also be a real military

force. This alone can effectively answer the purpose. The
United States have been making an experiment without it,
and we see the consequences in their rapid approaches to
anarchy." [40] "The apprehension of the national force will have
a salutary effect in preventing insurrections," added merchant-
speculator John Langdon of New Hampshire.[41]

State leaders in Philadelphia provided for both types of
military force in the proposed Constitution. They conferred
upon the proposed Congress powers "for calling forth the
militia to execute the laws of the Union, suppress insurrections
and repel invasions; to provide for organizing, arming, and
disciplining the militia, and for governing such part of them
as may be employed in service of the United States." Although
they did not create a standing army, the nationalists additionally provided Congress with the ability "to raise and support armies" for a maximum of two years.[42]

After giving military powers to the proposed national government, the delegates assured the states of protection against
domestic discord. According to the provisions of the so-called
guarantee clause, the national government would give each
state protection "on application of the legislature, or of the
Executive (when the legislature cannot be convened) against
domestic violence." [43] "The object," noted Pennsylvania lawyer
James Wilson who himself had been the target of a Philadelphia crowd in 1779, "is merely to secure the states against
dangerous commotions, insurrections, and rebellions." [44] Shays'
Rebellion may have motivated Wilson's support of the clause.
"I believe it is generally not known on what a perilous tenure
we held our freedom and independence" during the Massachusetts troubles, he explained. "The flames of internal insurrection were ready to burst out in every quarter . . . and from
one end to the other of the continent, we walked in ashes
concealing fire beneath our feet." [45] Instructed by experience
gleaned during the Shaysite uprising, delegates at Philadelphia
such as James Wilson passed the guarantee clause. In addition,
they agreed upon a suspension of the writ of habeas corpus
"in cases of rebellion" and, to discourage rebels from hiding
in bordering states as the Shaysites had done after February
1787, the delegates proposed that:

A person charged in any state with treason, felony, or other crime, who shall flee from justice, and be found in another state, shall on demand of the executive authority of the state from which he fled, be delivered up.

Although not dominating the Philadelphia debates, concern with domestic unrest proved important to many decisions made at the convention.[46]

Framed at least partly in response to mercantile fear of rural insurrection, the proposed Constitution gained support from the commercial interest and met stiff opposition from the yeomanry in Massachusetts. According to Henry Knox, "the new Constitution is received with great joy by all the commercial part of the community. The people of Boston are in raptures with it as it is." Besides the "commercial part of the state," added Knox, "all the men of considerable property, the clergy, the lawyers, including the judges of the court, and all the officers of the late army" advocated the "most vigorous government."[47] Among the ranks of the Massachusetts nationalists stood former governor James Bowdoin, Governor John Hancock, "three judges of the supreme court—fifteen members of the Senate, twenty from among the most respectable clergy—ten or twelve of the first characters of the bar—Judges of Probate, High Sheriffs of Counties, and many other respectable people, merchants, etc.," including wholesalers William Phillips, Caleb Davis, John Coffin Jones, Thomas Russell, and Tristram Dalton.[48]

In contrast, Massachusetts Antifederalism gained its impetus from the rural areas. "The *whole opposition,* in this commonwealth, is *that cursed spirit of insurgency* that prevailed last year," contended Henry Jackson who sat in the gallery of the Massachusetts state house during the debates. Jackson's friend Henry Knox likewise ascribed resistance to the Constitution "to the late insurgents, and all those who abetted their designs." Although somewhat overrating the influence of Shaysism and downplaying the importance of Maine farmers and the pacifist whalers of Nantucket in the Antifederalist cause, Knox and Jackson nevertheless captured the Shaysite orientation of the opponents to the Constitution. Direction of the Antifederalists fell to twenty-nine former insurgents, among them Phanuel Bishop of Rehoboth and a few farmers from Maine.[49]

Of the few merchants and professionals opposing the Constitution, most offered only lukewarm resistance to the proposed government. Antifederalist merchant Elbridge Gerry of Marblehead, for example, accepted the basic tenets of the Constitution. On October 18, 1787, he told legislative leaders Samuel Adams and James Warren that he believed the federal plan had "great merit and by proper amendments, may be adapted to the 'exigencies of government,'" pledging "to support that which is finally adopted." Two years later, the Marblehead merchant admitted to his overall approval of the Constitution. "I was never for rejecting the Constitution, but for suspending the ratification until it could be amended," he explained to his friend John Wendall.[50] Lawyer James Sullivan similarly accepted the general premises of the new government, objecting merely to specific provisions. "I have this day seen the report of the Convention and cannot express the heartfelt satisfaction I have from it," he wrote on September 23, 1787. "I am more than pleased, having only one doubt, which is, whether the object of the judicial power is well defined." By mildly criticizing the Constitution, merchants and lawyers such as Gerry and Sullivan stood out conspicuously among the mercantile elite, but they provided little leadership to the rural-based Antifederalist movement.[51]

The objections to the proposed Constitution revealed the rural orientation of most Massachusetts Antifederalists. To Antifederalists such as "Cornelius," the new government laid the foundation "for throwing the whole power of the federal government into the hands of those who are in the mercantile interest; and for the landed, which is the greatest interest of this country, to lie unrepresented, forlorn, and without hope."[52] Some Antifederalists believed that the mercantile elite would seize power through the proposed national military force. With national military power, argued farmer Amos Singletary of Sutton, "lawyers and men of learning, and monied men" expected to "get all the power and all the money into their own hands, and then they will swallow up all us little folks, like the great Leviathan," degrading independent farmers to tenants or wage laborers. Fearing such a fate for Massachusetts farmers, Phanuel Bishop warned delegates at the ratification convention that "the liberties of the yeomanry are at an end." Antifederalists such as farmer Samuel Nasson consequently urged fellow representatives to "show to the world that you will not submit to tyranny" by defeating the Constitution.[53]

The showdown between the commercial and the agrarian interests came on February 6, 1788. As convention president John Hancock took the roll call, a vast majority of seaboard delegates joined hands with representatives from inland market towns such as Worcester, Stockbridge, and Springfield in approving the document. Of the towns with Shaysite sympathies, ninety voted against the Constitution, and a mere seven supported the plan. The rest of the opposition centered in other Maine and western Massachusetts farming communities.[54] After the ballots had been tabulated, Hancock announced the results. The Constitution had passed by a slim margin of 187 to 168.

The victory of the nationalists arose from a variety of factors. Holding the ratification assembly in Boston undoubtedly gave the mercantile group an undue influence over convention proceedings and made possible the superior organization of the commercial interest. The coastal site of the convention also imposed a significant financial burden upon some inland towns for transportation costs, prohibiting about fifty Antifederalist towns from sending delegates.[55] The pronationalist outlook of most newspapers in Massachusetts furthered the nationalist cause while the addition of amendments during the final days of the session probably coaxed a few yeomen into the nationalist ranks. A last-minute endorsement of the Constitution by a supposedly bedridden Governor Hancock similarly helped the nationalists. According to Boston merchant Caleb Gibbs, if Hancock had not "appeared in convention, it was more than probable that *important* question would have been lost."[56] Moreover, five states had already ratified the document by the time of the Massachusetts contest, lending legitimacy to nationalist arguments. Coupled with the fears generated by Shays' Rebellion, these factors united the mercantile interest against the Shaysites and their sympathizers who opposed the Constitution.

Shays' Rebellion, then, marked an important point in the social development of the United States, as evidenced by the reaction of the dominant commercial elite to it on the regional and national levels. As George Washington wrote to George Richards Minot after the publication of Minot's *History of the Insurrections in Massachusetts* in 1788, "the series of events which followed from the conclusion of the War, forms a link of no ordinary magnitude, in the chain of the American Annals. That portion of domestic History, which you have selected for your narrative deserved particularly to be discussed." [57]

Notes

Preface

1. Diary of George Richards Minot, June 9, 1787, Theodore Sedgwick Papers, Massachusetts Historical Society, Boston.
2. George Richards Minot, *The History of the Insurrections in Massachusetts In the Year 1786 and the Rebellion Consequent Thereon* (Boston, 1788), pp. 60, 189.
3. Ibid., pp. 3–4; Minot to George Washington, August 7, 1788, in the "Character of Judge Minot," *Massachusetts Historical Collections* 8 (1801): 99. For this same argument, see Robert Feer, "George Richards Minot's History of the Insurrections: History, Propaganda, and Autobiography," *New England Quarterly* 35, no. 2 (June 1962): 218–26.
4. Ramsey to John Eliot, November 26, 1788, quoted in Feer, "Minot's History," p. 203.
5. Josiah Holland, *The History of Western Massachusetts*, 2 vols. (Springfield, 1855), 1:297, 299.
6. John Fiske, *The Critical Period of American History, 1783–1789* (Boston, 1888), pp. 178, 179, 181.
7. Andrew McLaughlin, *The Confederation and the Constitution, 1783–1789* (1905; rpt., New York: Collier, 1962), p. 111. For the same interpretation, see Josephine Canning, "The Shays' Rebellion," *American Historical Register* 2 (July 1895): 1266; and Frederick Holland, "Rutland County Insurrection, 1786," *New England Historical and Genealogical Society Register* 26 (1872): 131.
8. Jonathan Smith, "The Depression of 1785 and Daniel Shays' Rebellion" (1905), *William and Mary Quarterly* 5, no. 1 (January 1948): 77–78.
9. Joseph P. Warren, "The Confederation and Shays Rebellion," *American Historical Review* 11 (October 1905): 42; also see his "Shays Rebellion" (Ph.D. thesis, Harvard University, 1900).
10. Albert Farnsworth, "Shays's Rebellion in Worcester County, Mas-

sachusetts" (Ph.D. thesis, Clark University, 1927), p. 1; idem, "Shays's Rebellion," *Massachusetts Law Quarterly* 12, no. 5 (February 1927): 40, 42. For Beard's interpretation of Shays' Rebellion, see Charles Beard, *The Rise of American Civilization,* 2 vols. (New York: Macmillan, 1927), 1:307.

11. Robert East, "The Massachusetts Conservatives in the Critical Period," in *The Era of the American Revolution,* ed. Richard B. Morris (New York: Harper & Row, 1939), p. 349.

12. Millard Hansen, "The Significance of Shays' Rebellion," *South Atlantic Quarterly* 39, no. 3 (July 1940): 305. For the same view, see Bernard Donovan, "The Massachusetts Insurrection of 1786" (Ph.D. thesis, Boston College, 1938); and Franklin Mullaly, "The Massachusetts Insurrection of 1786–1787" (M.A. thesis, Smith College, 1947).

13. Richard B. Morris, "Insurrection in Massachusetts," in *America in Crisis,* ed. Daniel Aaron (New York: Knopf, 1952), p. 22.

14. Sidney Kaplan, "Veteran Officers and Politics in Massachusetts, 1783–1787," *William and Mary Quarterly* 9, no. 1 (January 1952): 48.

15. Robert Taylor, *Western Massachusetts in the Revolution* (Providence: Brown University Press, 1954), p. 167.

16. Marion Starkey, *A Little Rebellion* (New York: Knopf, 1955), p. 5.

17. Louis Hartz, *The Liberal Tradition in America* (New York: Harcourt, Brace, 1955), pp. 74, 78; interestingly, Hartz gives an incorrect date for the Rebellion (p. 75).

18. Robert Feer, "Shays' Rebellion" (Ph.D. thesis, Harvard University, 1958), p. 509.

19. Pauline Maier, "Popular Uprisings and Civil Authority in Eighteenth Century America," in *Interpreting Colonial America,* ed. James Kirby Martin (New York: Free Press, 1973), pp. 332, 334, 337. Maier originally published this article in *William and Mary Quarterly* 27, no. 1 (January 1970): 3–35.

20. Alden Vaughan, "The 'Horrid and Unnatural Rebellion' of Daniel Shays," *American Heritage* 27, no. 4 (June 1966): 53.

21. Van Beck Hall, *Politics without Parties: Massachusetts, 1780–1791* (Pittsburgh: University of Pittsburgh Press, 1972), p. 210.

22. Alfred Young, Afterword to *The American Revolution,* ed. Alfred Young (De Kalb, Ill.: Northern Illinois University Press, 1976), p. 459.

23. Jackson Turner Main, *The Social Structure of Revolutionary America* (Princeton, N.J.: Princeton University Press, 1965); Edward Countryman, "'Out of Bounds with the Law': Northern Land Rioters in the Eighteenth Century," in Young, *American Revolution,* pp. 37–70; Barbara Karsky, "Agrarian Radicalism in the Late Revolutionary Period," in *New Wine in Old Skins,* ed. Erich Angermann, Marie-Luise Frings, and Hermann Wellenreuther (Stutt-

gart: Klett, 1976), pp. 97–114; E. P. Thompson, *The Making of the English Working Class* (New York: Knopf, 1963); and Eric Hobsbawm, *Primitive Rebels: Studies in Archaic Forms of Social Movements in the Nineteenth and Twentieth Centuries* (New York: Norton, 1959).

Chapter 1

1. Jackson Turner Main, *The Social Structure of Revolutionary America* (Princeton, N.J.: Princeton University Press, 1965), p. 18. For the urban-rural continuum, see Edward Cook, Jr., *The Fathers of the Towns: Leadership and Community Structure in Eighteenth Century New England* (Baltimore: Johns Hopkins Press, 1976), chap. 7; and Van Beck Hall, *Politics without Parties: Massachusetts 1780–1791* (Pittsburgh: University of Pittsburgh Press, 1972), p. 36.
2. *Massachusetts Centinel,* June 24, 1786. For statistics on the agrarian population, see Main, *Social Structure,* pp. 41–43.
3. Rodney Loehr, "Self-Sufficiency on the Farm," *Agricultural History* 26, no. 2 (April 1952): 41.
4. *Massachusetts Centinel,* June 24, 1786; *American Husbandry* (1775; rpt., New York: Kennikat, 1939), p. 50.
5. Gregory Stiverson, "Early American Farming: A Comment," *Agricultural History* 50, no. 1 (January 1976): 38. For a similar view, see Boguslaw Galeski, "Sociological Problems with the Occupation of Farmers," *Annals of Rural Sociology* 26, no. 1 (January 1968): 19. For the premarket orientation of most farmers, see Robert Mutch, "Yeoman and Merchant in Pre-Industrial America: Eighteenth-Century Massachusetts as a Case Study," *Societas* 7, no. 3 (Autumn 1977): 279–302.
6. The aggregate data for Whately can be found in Susan Baxendale, "Whately in Shays' Rebellion" (graduate paper, May 1969, University of Massachusetts Library, Amherst). According to Richard Sutch and Roger Ransom, *One Kind of Freedom* (New York: Oxford University Press, 1978), adults needed twenty pounds of flour, and each child ten pounds per year to subsist. James Lemon, *The Best Poor Man's Country: A Geographical Study of Early Southeastern Pennsylvania* (Baltimore: Johns Hopkins Press, 1972), p. 155, gives the meat requirements; he also computes the amount of hay and corn needed by a farmer (p. 153). According to Lemon, a farmer needed one bushel of grain per acre for next year's planting. After it was milled, the grain of the farmer yielded only 71 percent of edible flour. Oliver Evans, *The Young Mill-Wright and Miller's Guide* (1795; rpt., Philadelphia, 1850), p. 275.
7. According to Matthew Patten, one adult could cultivate one acre of land per day, although this obviously would have varied with

the individual. Entry for May 25, 1785, in Matthew Patten, *The Diary of Matthew Patten of Bedford, New Hampshire, 1754–1788* (Concord, N.H., 1903), p. 505. At twenty-nine, the Whately yeoman probably could have cleared most of his land. Percy Bidwell and John Falconer, *History of Agriculture in the Northern United States, 1620–1860* (Washington, D.C.: Government Printing Office, 1925), pp. 80–82. Baxendale, "Whately in Shays' Rebellion."

8. The crop yields have been computed on the basis of the entry for October 19, 1789, in George Washington, *The Diaries of George Washington,* ed. John Fitzpatrick, 4 vols. (New York, 1925), 1:27; and Edward Jenkins, "Connecticut Agriculture," in *History of Connecticut,* ed. Norris Osborn, 4 vols. (New York, 1925), 2:326. Both sources, as well as many others, agree that Indian corn commonly yielded about thirty bushels per acre, wheat about twenty bushels.

9. Surplus beef is computed from Lemon, *Best Poor Man's Country,* p. 155. It is assumed that the miller will take 4 percent of the grain. For the miller's share in New England, see Harry Weiss and Robert Sim, *The Early Grist and Flouring Mills of New Jersey* (Trenton: New Jersey Historical Society, 1956), p. 24. See Theodora Orcutt Account Book, in J. H. Temple, *History of the Town of Whately, Massachusetts* (Boston, 1872), pp. 71–72, for women's spinning.

10. For prices, see Carroll Wright, "Historical Review of Wages and Prices, 1752–1860," *Annual Report of the Massachusetts Bureau of Statistics* 16 (1885): 209; and William Weeden, *Economic and Social History of New England,* 2 vols. (Boston, 1891), 2:903. Indian corn sold for 4s. a bushel in 1786 and beef sold for 3d. a pound in 1785. Wright, "Historical Review," p. 209. Needed articles cost from £12 to £50 a year, depending upon family size. Main, *Social Structure,* p. 117. Examples of the cost of required articles: salt, £1 5s. per bushel; shoes, 7s. per pair (Wright, "Historical Review," p. 209); nails, 5d. per pound (Patten, *Diary,* p. 508); rum, 2s. 2d. per gallon (Patten, *Diary,* p. 497); and medicine, variable though usually very expensive (Levi Shepard Account Book, Forbes Library, Northampton, Mass.; and "Diary of Mrs. Martha Moore Ballard," in Charles Nash, *The History of Augusta* [Augusta, 1904], pp. 238, 243, 256).

11. Brookfield Tax Lists, 1784, Massachusetts State House, Boston.

12. Amherst Tax Lists, 1779, Massachusetts State House, Boston.

13. Samuel Deane, *The New England Farmer* (Worcester, 1790), p. 138. Deane, an agricultural reformer, looked with disdain upon the traditional attitudes of the farmers. He wanted a "more spirited and rational husbandry."

14. For the comparison of Indian corn with other crops, see James Swan, *National Arithmetick* (Boston, 1786); Lemon, *The Best Poor*

Man's Country, p. 182; and Elton Hall, "Sailcloth and Sailmaking in Connecticut before 1860," *Chronicle of Early American Industries* 31, no. 4 (December 1978): 63. *American Husbandry,* p. 39.

15. For crop diversification, see Deane, *New England Farmer.*

16. Ibid., p. 66. Also see Brooke Hindle, *The Pursuit of Science in Revolutionary America, 1735-1789* (Chapel Hill: University of North Carolina Press, 1956), pp. 194-95, 366-67, for yeomen's refusal to use new agricultural techniques.

17. Jedediah Morse, *The American Geography* (Elizabethtown, N.J., 1789), p. 182. Also see *American Husbandry,* p. 40; Lemon, *Best Poor Man's Country,* pp. 150, 169; and *Independent Chronicle,* April 27, 1786.

18. For the basis of these computations, see above, nn. 8 through 12. In British sterling, the farmer's surplus amounted to £25 16d. in an *ideal* year.

19. A. V. Chayanov, *The Theory of Peasant Economy* (1924; rpt., Homewood, Ill.: Irwin, 1966), p. 78.

20. Marquis de Chastellux, *Travels in North America,* 2 vols. (Chapel Hill: University of North Carolina Press, 1963), 1:79. This common view can be found in Robert Brown, *Middle-Class Democracy and the Revolution in Massachusetts, 1691-1780* (New York: Cornell University Press, 1955); and *American Husbandry,* p. 52.

21. Some examples of tenantry can be found in John Worthington Account Book, December 20, 1786, Springfield Public Library, Springfield, Mass.; Joseph Hadfield, *An Englishman in America, 1785: Being the Diary of Joseph Hadfield,* ed. Douglas Robertson (Toronto: Hunter-Rose, 1933), p. 219; Timothy Dwight, *Travels in New England and New York,* 4 vols. (New Haven, 1821), 3:11-12; and Sidney Kaplan, "Harvard College and Shays' Rebellion," *Boston Public Library Quarterly* 7, no. 2 (April 1955): 110-11.

22. Quoted in Jackson Turner Main, *Political Parties before the Constitution* (New York: Norton, 1974), p. 96 n. Also see Lee Newcomer, *The Embattled Farmers: The Massachusetts Countryside in the American Revolution* (New York: King's Crown Press, 1953), p. 14; and Michael Merrill, "Cash Is Good to Eat: Self-Sufficiency and Exchange in the Rural Economy of the U.S.," *Radical History Review* 3, no. 4 (Fall 1979): 65.

23. Eric Wolf, *Peasants* (Englewood Cliffs, N.J.: Prentice-Hall, 1966), p. 2.

24. Joel Halpern and John Brode, "Peasant Society: Economic Changes and Revolutionary Transformations," in *Biennial Review of Anthropology, 1967,* ed. Bernard Siegel and Alan Beals (Stanford, Calif.: Stanford University Press, 1967), p. 58; for the same position, see the note about F. S. Tefft and R. O. Sinclair, p. 92.

25. Deane, *New England Farmer,* pp. 88, 330, 136.

26. For this general position, see James Henretta, "Families and Farms: *Mentalité* in Pre-Industrial America," *William and Mary Quarterly* 35, no. 1 (January 1978): 3–33.

27. Patten, *Diary,* August 7, 1784, p. 489; October 14, 1786, p. 513; June 20, 1785, p. 507; June 22, 1785, p. 507.

28. Ibid., May 26, 1785, p. 505; June 26, 1786, p. 523; July 13, 1785, p. 508; September 10, 1784, p. 490.

29. Chastellux, *Travels,* 1:80.

30. For cornhusking and barn raising, see Patten, *Diary,* October 28, 1785, p. 513; June 22, 1784, p. 486; and Jared Van Wagenen, Jr., *The Golden Age of Homespun* (Ithaca: Cornell University Press, 1953), p. 38.

31. Patten, *Diary,* February 25, 1784, p. 479; December 31, 1784, p. 497.

32. Henretta, "Families and Farms," p. 15.

33. Ferdinand Tönnies, *Community and Association: Gemeinschaft and Gesellschaft* (1896; rpt., London: Oxford University Press, 1955), pp. 67–68. For one of the finest theoretical discussions of barter in an agrarian economy, see Aristotle, *Politics* (New York: Modern Library, 1943), p. 67.

34. Main, *Social Structure,* pp. 41–43; and Lemon, *Best Poor Man's Country,* p. 179.

35. Diary of Abner Sanger, 1774–82, June 11, 1775, and August 4, 1775, Manuscript Division, Library of Congress, Washington, D.C. Sanger's diary is one of the few diaries of a day laborer in the revolutionary era still in existence.

36. Ibid., October 1, 1774; October 5, 1774; May 15, 1775.

37. Ibid., December 1, 1774; March 13, 1775; March 22, 1775; July 1, 1775; July 3, 1775.

38. Carl Bridenbaugh, *The Colonial Craftsman* (Chicago: University of Chicago Press, 1950), p. 147. Also see Main, *Social Structure,* p. 11. The nonspecialized nature of country artisans' work in England can be found in Adam Smith, *An Inquiry into the Nature and Causes of the Wealth of Nations* (1776), ed. Edwin Cannan (1776; rpt., New York: Modern Library, 1937), p. 17.

39. William Nutting, "Diary of 1787," January 13, 1787, *Groton Historical Series* 1 (1887): 15.

40. James Parker, "The Diary of James Parker," July 1, 1786, *New England Historical and Genealogical Society Register* 69 (1915): 301.

41. Main, *Social Structure,* p. 134.

42. Arthur Cole, "The Tempo of Mercantile Life in Colonial America," *Business History Review* 23, no. 3 (Spring 1959): 292–93.

43. Main, *Social Structure,* p. 135. Coastal merchants generally made 60 percent profit on most goods. James Hedges, *The Browns of Providence Plantation: Colonial Years* (Cambridge: Harvard University Press, 1952), p. 187. Norman Gras, *The Massachusetts First Na-*

tional Bank of Boston (Cambridge: Harvard University Press, 1937), p. 530.

44. Robert East, *Business Enterprise in the American Revolutionary Era* (New York: AMS, 1938), p. 313; Queries: Connecticut, June-July 1784, in Thomas Jefferson, *The Papers of Thomas Jefferson,* ed. Julian Boyd, 18 vols. (Princeton, N.J.: Princeton University Press, 1950–), 7:336.

45. For subscription list, see the Winthrop Sargent Papers, Massachusetts Historical Society, Boston. East, *Business Enterprise,* pp. 271, 279–81; and Main, *Social Structure,* p. 139, contain evidence of other land deals at the time.

46. Van Beck Hall, *Politics without Parties,* p. 44 n.

47. Warren to John Adams, January 28, 1785, *Warren-Adams Letters,* 2 vols. (Boston: Massachusetts Historical Society, 1925), 2:249.

48. Hancock to Osborne, February 24, 1755, quoted in W. T. Baxter, *The House of Hancock: Business in Boston, 1724–1775* (Cambridge: Harvard University Press, 1945), p. 190.

49. John Schaar, "Legitimacy in the Modern State," in *Power and Community: Dissenting Essays in Political Science,* ed. Philip Green and Sanford Levinson (New York: Pantheon, 1969), p. 299.

50. Samuel Collins to Stephen Collins, March 29, 1788, Box 37, Stephen Collins and Son Papers, Library of Congress, Washington, D.C. Also see Jonathan Webb to Samuel B. Webb, January 1787, vol. 7, Samuel B. Webb Papers, Sterling Library, Yale University, New Haven.

51. Main, *Social Structure,* p. 137.

52. Hall, *Politics without Parties,* pp. 35–36. Retailers generally received a two-year extension of credit from the wholesalers; see Baxter, *The House of Hancock,* p. 192.

53. William Nelson, *The Americanization of Common Law: The Impact of Legal Change in Massachusetts Society, 1760–1830* (Cambridge: Harvard University Press, 1975), p. 118.

54. C. B. MacPherson, *The Political Theory of Possessive Individualism* (London: Oxford University Press, 1962), p. 3.

55. Hall, *Politics without Parties,* p. 45.

56. For the transformation of society in Massachusetts, see Bernard Bailyn, *New England Merchants in the Seventeenth Century* (Cambridge: Harvard University Press, 1955). Daniel Scott, *From Office to Profession: The New England Ministry, 1750–1850,* (Philadelphia: University of Pennsylvania Press, 1978), specifically deals with the transformation of the clergy.

57. Joseph Lewis, "Diary or Memorandum Book," *Proceedings of the New Jersey Historical Society* 60, no. 1 (January 1942): 62.

58. Hall, *Politics without Parties,* pp. 50–51.

59. *American Husbandry,* p. 46.

60. Main, *Political Parties,* p. 85.

61. Queries: Massachusetts, July 1784, in Jefferson, *Papers,* 7:342. The same can be found for Philadelphia in Eric Foner, *Tom Paine and Revolutionary America* (New York: Oxford University Press, 1976), p. 21. Of the artisans examined by Joseph Ott, "Rhode Island Housewrights, Shipwrights, and Related Craftsmen," *Rhode Island History* 31, nos. 2 and 3 (Spring 1972): 65–80, at least 41 percent worked directly in shipbuilding trades. According to a January 24, 1764, petition by "merchants, planters, and traders" to the king, most "mechanics" depended upon "the merchant for employment." *Records of the Colony of Rhode Island,* 7 vols. (Providence, 1856–62), 6:381.

62. Queries: Connecticut, June-July 1784, in Jefferson, *Papers,* 7:332.

63. Lawrence Romaine, "Gideon French of Boston, Tallow-Chandler, 1784–1789," *Old-Time New England* 5, no. 2 (Fall 1959): 53.

64. Samuel Collins to Stephen Collins, February 23, 1787; Ezra Collins to Stephen Collins, May 2, 1787, Box 34, Collins Papers. One barrel of shoes contained from 100 to 105 pairs; see the above citations, and William Vans, Jr., to Stephen Collins, December 8, 1786, Box 33. Also see Benno Forman, "Salem and Craftsmen circa 1762: A Contemporary Document," *Essex Institute Historical Collections* 107, no. 1 (January 1971): 68.

65. John Hall, "The Journal of James Weston, Cordwainer, of Reading, Massachusetts, 1788–1793," *Essex Institute Historical Collections* 92, no. 2 (April 1956): 191.

66. Joseph Ott, "Rhode Island Furniture Exports, 1783–1800, Including Information on Chaises, Buildings, Other Woodenware, and Trade Practices," *Rhode Island History* 31, no. 1 (February 1977): 3–14.

67. Bridenbaugh, *Colonial Craftsman,* p. 165. Also see Main, *Political Parties,* p. 374; and Foner, *Tom Paine,* pp. 35–36.

68. Mary Baker, "Anglo-Massachusetts Trade Union Roots, 1730–1790," *Labor History* 14, no. 3 (Summer 1973): 390.

69. Bernard Farber, *Guardians of Virtue: Salem in 1800* (New York: Basic, 1972), p. 199.

70. Jonathan Tucker, "The First Voyage from India to Salem, 1786–1787," *Essex Institute Historical Collections* 75, no. 1 (January 1939): 44–52. Seamen got £2 8s. on this voyage. For New Haven figures, see Queries: Connecticut, June-July 1784, in Jefferson, *Papers,* 7:333. Some seamen, especially in Boston and Providence, were black and thus had an added reason to distrust their superiors. Jesse Lemisch, "Jack Tar in the Streets: Merchant Seamen in the Politics of the American Revolution," *William and Mary Quarterly* 25, no. 3 (July 1968): 371–407. For the overall integration of "mechanics and laborers" in the "mercantile interest," see John Adams to James Warren, October 20, 1775, in Edmund Burnett, ed., *Letters of Members of the Continental Congress,* 8 vols. (Wash-

ington, D.C.: Government Printing Office, 1931–36), 1:240; and Hall, *Politics without Parties,* p. 23.
71. Stephen Higginson and Brook Watson Testimony, February 28, 1775, in Peter Force, *American Archives,* 4th ser. (Washington, D.C., 1837), 1: 1638–47.
72. Seth Jenkins Testimony, February 28, 1775, ibid., p. 1650.
73. Brook Watson Testimony, February 28, 1775, ibid., p. 1640; Hall, *Politics without Parties,* p. 32.
74. Mutch, "Yeoman and Merchant," pp. 287–91.
75. Henretta, "Families and Farms," p. 15.
76. E. P. Thompson, "The Moral Economy of the English Crowd in the 18th Century," *Past and Present,* no. 50 (February 1971), p. 136.
77. Robert Brenner, "Agrarian Class Structure and Economic Development in Pre-Industrial Europe," *Past and Present,* no. 70 (February 1976), pp. 30–75; idem, "The Origins of Capitalist Development: A Critique of Neo-Smithian Marxism," *New Left Review* 104, no. 1 (July-August 1977): 25–92. Similarly, Daniel Chriot and Charles Ragin, "The Market, Tradition, and Peasant Rebellion; The Case of Romania in 1907," *American Sociological Review* 40, no. 4 (August 1975), locate the roots of the 1907 Romanian peasant uprising in the reaction of "the strong residual peasant traditionalism" against "the rapid penetration of market forces," p. 430. For the same view, see Eric Hobsbawm, *Primitive Rebels: Studies in Archaic Forms of Social Movements in the Nineteenth and Twentieth Centuries* (New York: Norton, 1959), p. 67; Charles Tilly, *The Vendee* (Cambridge: Harvard University Press, 1967), pp. 114–19; Barrington Moore, *The Social Origins of Dictatorship and Democracy: Lord and Peasant in the Making of the Modern World* (Boston: Little, Brown, 1967), p. 474; and Eric Wolf, *Peasant Wars of the Twentieth Century* (New York: Harper-Row, 1969), pp. 277–78.
78. Stephen Riley, "Doctor William Whiting and Shays' Rebellion," *Proceedings of the American Antiquarian Society* 66, no. 1 (January 1956): 142–44.

Chapter 2

1. George Chalmers, *Opinions on Interesting Subjects of Public Law and Commercial Policy Arising from American Independence* (London, 1784), p. 44.
2. Otto to Count de Vergennes, May 17, 1785, in Paul Sifton, "Otto's Memoire to Vergennes, 1785," *William and Mary Quarterly,* 22, no. 4 (October 1965): 634.
3. H. J. Habakkuk, "Population, Commerce, and Economic Ideas,"

in *The New Cambridge Modern History,* 14 vols. (Cambridge: Harvard University Press, 1965), 8:33.

4. Data compiled from James Shepard, "Commodity Exports from the British North American Colonies to Overseas Areas, 1768–1772," *Explorations in Economic History* 8, no. 1 (Fall 1970): 12–41.

5. Habakkuk, "Population, Commerce, Economic Ideas," 8:34–35; Shepard, "Commodity Exports," pp. 12–41.

6. Aa Rasch, "American Trade in the Baltic, 1783–1807," *Scandinavian Historical Review* 13, no. 1 (1963): 34, 37.

7. See James Lydon, "Fish and Flour for Gold: Southern Europe and the Colonial American Balance of Payments," *Business History Review* 34, no. 2 (1965): 182, for the prewar trade. For postwar problems in the Mediterranean, see H. G. Barnby, *The Prisoners of Algiers: An Account of the Forgotten American-Algerian War, 1785–1797* (New York: Oxford University Press, 1966), pp. 70–75; and Jefferson to Francis Eppes, December 11, 1785, in Thomas Jefferson, *The Papers of Thomas Jefferson,* ed. Julian Boyd, 18 vols. (Princeton, N.J.: Princeton University Press, 1950–), 8:45.

8. Higginson to John Adams, August 8, 1785, in Stephen Higginson, "The Letters of Stephen Higginson," *Annual Report of the American Historical Association, 1896,* ed. J. Franklin Jameson, 2 vols. (Washington, D.C., 1897), 1:723.

9. Jefferson to Count de Vergennes, August 15, 1785, in Jefferson, *Papers,* 8:389. Also see John Stover, "French-American Trade during the Confederation," *North Carolina Historical Review* 35, no. 4 (October 1958): 406.

10. Marechal de Castries to M. de Sourdeval, October 23, 1783, in Henri See, "Commerce between France and the United States, 1783–1784," *American Historical Review* 31, no. 4 (July 1926): 733. For other obstacles to French-American trade, see Charles Ritcheson, *Aftermath of Revolution: British Policy toward the United States, 1783–1795* (New York: Norton, 1971), pp. 23–26.

11. For New England prewar business contacts in Britain, see Richard Sheridan, "The British Credit Crisis of 1772 and the American Colonies," *Journal of Economic History* 20, no. 2 (June 1960): 169–70.

12. For an analysis of the United States in the revolutionary era as a newly independent, "underdeveloped" nation, see Seymour Martin Lipset, *The First New Nation: The United States in Historical and Comparative Perspective* (New York: Basic, 1963).

13. U.S. Department of Commerce, Bureau of the Census, *Historical Statistics of the United States,* 2 vols. (1975), 2:1175, provides import data.

14. D. A. Farnie, "The Commercial Empire of the Atlantic, 1607–1783," *Economic History Review,* 2d ser., 15, no. 2 (1962): 215.

15. For 1745 and 1763, see Marc Egnal and Joseph Ernst, "An Eco-

nomic Interpretation of the American Revolution," *William and Mary Quarterly,* 29, no. 1 (January 1972): 3–32.

16. Bancroft to William Frazer, November 8, 1783, in George Bancroft, *History of the Formation of the Constitution,* 2 vols. (New York, 1883), 1:333.

17. William Weeden, *Economic and Social History of New England,* 2 vols. (Boston, 1891), 2:819.

18. Febiger to J. Sobotken, June 15, 1785, in "Extracts of a Merchant's Letters, 1784–1786," *Magazine of American History* 8, no. 4 (May 1882): 352; Stephen Higginson to John Adams, July 20, 1786, in Higginson, "Letters," 1:740. Also see *Independent Chronicle,* June 22, 1786, and *Hampshire Herald,* February 7, 1786.

19. Lord John Sheffield, *Observations on the Commerce of the American States with Europe and the West Indies* (London, 1783), p. 264; Sheffield to Silas Deane, September 22, 1783, in "The Deane Papers: Correspondence between Silas Deane and His Brother," *Collections of the Connecticut Historical Society* 23 (1930): 130. Also see Edmund Burnett, "Observations of London Merchants on American Trade," *American Historical Review* 18, no. 4 (July 1913): 769–80.

20. Chalmers, *Opinions,* p. 46.

21. King to Daniel Kilham, October 12, 1785, King-Kilham Papers, Butler Library, Columbia University, New York.

22. Replies to Queries: New Hampshire, June 1784, Jefferson, *Papers,* 7:344; W. T. Baxter, *The House of Hancock: Business in Boston, 1724–1775* (Cambridge: Harvard University Press, 1945), p. 272 n.; Benjamin Baldwin, "Debts Owed by Americans to British Creditors, 1763–1802" (Ph.D. thesis, Indiana University, 1932), p. 10.

23. Replies to Queries: Rhode Island, June 1784, in Jefferson, *Papers,* 7:338; Carl Bridenbaugh, ed., "Patrick McRobert's Tour through Part of the North Provinces of America," *Pennsylvania Magazine of History and Biography* 59 (1935): 150. According to George Brooks, Jr., *Yankee Traders, Old Coasters, and African Middlemen* (Brookline: Boston University Press, 1970), p. 16 n, Rhode Island merchants had eighteen ships engaged in the slave trade and made £40,000 annually from slave cargoes from the 1730s to the beginning of the American Revolution. A good example of a slave-trade voyage from Rhode Island to Africa can be found in James Hedges, *The Browns of Providence Plantation: Colonial Years* (Cambridge: Harvard University Press, 1952), pp. 76–81. Also see Peter Force, *American Archives,* 4th ser. (Washington, D.C., 1837), 1:1643. Gilman Ostrander, "The Making of the Triangular Trade Myth," *William and Mary Quarterly* 30, no. 4 (October 1973): 635–44, put this trade in proper perspective, although he may have overstated his case.

24. Baldwin, "Debts Owed by Americans," p. 10. According to Rhode

Island "merchants, planters, and traders" in 1764, "the ability to pay for such quantities of British goods [£120,000]" came from the West Indies trade. *Records of the Colony of Rhode Island,* 7 vols. (Providence, 1856–62): 6:379. Shepard, "Commodity Exports," pp. 12–41, has computed that New England merchants sold over 66 percent of their goods in the West Indies from 1768 to 1772.

25. Adams to Secretary Livingston, June 23, 1783, in John Adams, *The Works of John Adams,* ed. Charles Francis Adams, 10 vols. (Boston, 1853–56), 8:74.

26. *Boston Town Records, 1785* (Boston, 1903), pp. 77; James Manning to Caleb Evans, July 21, 1785, in Reuben Guild, *The Early History of Brown University* (Providence, 1897), pp. 404–5. Also see William Chase to Edward Forbes, June 25, 1785, Box 8, Nicholas Low Papers, Manuscript Division, Library of Congress, Washington, D.C., for added evidence on Rhode Island merchants.

27. *Massachusetts Centinel,* May 7, 1785. According to Samuel Eliot Morison, *The Maritime History of Massachusetts, 1783–1860* (Boston: Houghton Mifflin, 1921), p. 34, Boston launched 125 ships annually before the war and built only 15 to 20 annually after the Revolution.

28. "A Patriot," *Connecticut Courant,* January 9, 1792.

29. Margaret Martin, "Merchants and Trade of the Connecticut River Valley, 1750–1820," *Smith College Studies in History* 24, nos. 1–4 (October 1938–July 1939): 134–35. Also see Replies to Queries: Connecticut, June–July 1784, Jefferson, *Papers,* 7:335.

30. Stephen Hubbard Account Book, 1785–89, Jones Library, Amherst, Mass.; Levi Shepard Account Book, 1786–87, Ledger, Forbes Library, Northampton, Mass.

31. Replies to Queries: Connecticut, June–July 1784, in Jefferson, *Papers,* 7:334–35. See William Gregory, "Scotchman's Journey in New England in 1771," *New England Magazine,* ed. Mary Powell, 12, no. 3 (1895): 352, for a description of a New Haven retailer-wholesaler. Also see Martin, "Merchants and Trade," pp. 3, 23, 40, 42, for a general analysis of valley trade patterns. Over 95 percent of all ships leaving New Haven in 1764 and 1765, for example, sailed to the British islands. New Haven, Connecticut: A List of Frigates Outward, September 17, 1762, to June 24, 1801, Bureau of Customs, National Archives, Washington, D.C.

32. Barnabas Deane to Silas Deane, October 14, 1785, in "Deane Papers" (Conn.), p. 215. Peter Colt to Jeremiah Wadsworth, April 23, 1786, Jeremiah Wadsworth Papers, Connecticut Historical Society, Hartford; Sebor to Silas Deane, July 1, 1785, in "Deane Papers" (Conn.), p. 213.

33. Compiled from U.S. Department of State, *Historical Statistics,* 2:1175.

34. Higginson to John Adams, August 8, 1785, in Higginson, "Letters,"

1:719; Gay to Benjamin Holmes, October 7, 1785, Gay-Otis Collection, Butler Library, Columbia University, New York.

35. Replies to Queries: Massachusetts, July 1784, in Jefferson, *Papers,* 7:339.

36. Jackson and Bromfield to William Reeve, April 15, 1767, in Kenneth Porter, *The Jacksons and the Lees: Two Generations of Massachusetts Merchants, 1765–1844,* 2 vols. (Cambridge: Harvard University Press, 1937), 1:177, 165–66. Higginson to John Adams, December 30, 1785, in Higginson, "Letters," p. 732; Abigail Adams to John Quincy Adams, September 6, 1785, in Abigail Adams, *Letters of Mrs. Adams,* ed. Charles Francis Adams, 2 vols. (Boston, 1840), 2:114.

37. Deane to Samuel Webb, July 16, 1785, in "The Deane Papers," *Collections of the New York Historical Society,* 5 vols. (New York, 1890), 5:458; Deane to Jeremiah Wadsworth, December 14, 1784, no. 593, Emmett Collection, New York Public Library, New York. The number of English merchant bankruptcies can be found in the English *Manchester Mercury,* 1786 and 1787.

38. British merchants' withdrawal of credit before the war can be found in Sheridan, "The British Credit Crisis of 1772." According to English merchant John Lane, New England traders owed London credit houses over £1 million sterling in 1775. Force, *American Archives,* 4th ser., 1: 1648; *Morning Herald* (London), August 27, 1784; Merrill Jensen, *The New Nation: A History of the United States during the Confederation, 1781–1789* (New York: Knopf, 1950), p. 188.

39. Protheroe and Claxton to Christopher Champlin, January 23, 1786, in "Commerce of Rhode Island," *Collections of the Massachusetts Historical Society,* 7th ser. (1915), 10:272.

40. *Morning Herald* (London), August 27, 1784; Jonathan Jackson to Thompson and Gordon, December 30, 1784, in Porter, *Jacksons and Lees,* 2:370; Joseph Russell to Jeremy Belknap, May 2, 1785, in "The Belknap Papers," *Collections of the Massachusetts Historical Society,* 6th ser. (1891), 4:295.

41. Ethan Allen to Ira Allen, August 18, 1786, Ira Allen Papers, Wilbur Library, University of Vermont, Burlington; Higginson to John Adams, December 30, 1785, in Higginson, "Letters," 1:732; Spear to Marcy Spear, July 8, 1786, in Robert Haas, "The Forgotten Courtship of David and Marcy Spear," *Old-Time New England* 7, no. 3 (January 1962): 67.

42. Ethan and Ira Allen agreement, May 1, 1787, Ira Allen Papers.

43. Tax Evaluations: Boston, 1785, Massachusetts State Library, Boston. For the same situation among Newburyport merchants, see Benjamin Labaree, *Patriots and Partisans: The Merchants of Newburyport, 1764–1815* (Cambridge: Harvard University Press, 1962), p. 63.

44. John Waters, *The Otis Family in Provincial and Revolutionary*

Massachusetts (New York: Norton, 1968), p. 199; Samuel Otis to Joseph Otis, April 10, 1785, Box 4, Otis Papers, Butler Library, Columbia University, New York, show the familial help given to economically distressed Samuel A. Otis. Jean Joseph Marie Toscan to the French government, 1785, in Constance Sherman, "Through an Eighteenth Century Looking Glass," *New England Quarterly* 27, no. 4 (December 1954): 520. Samuel A. Otis to Henry Knox, March 5, 1788, Henry Knox Papers, Massachusetts Historical Society, Boston.

45. Richard Pares, *Yankees and Creoles: The Trade between North America and the West Indies before the Revolution* (Cambridge: Harvard University Press, 1956), p. 163, and n. 75. In 1768, Boston merchant John Hancock owed the British merchant house of Hayley and Hopkins £6,700; Nicholas Brown and Company of Providence owed the same trading house £8,018 in 1774. Hedges, *The Browns of Providence,* p. 183.

46. Tyler to Samuel Peters, April 20, 1786, in Kenneth Cameron, ed., *The Church of England in Pre-Revolutionary Connecticut* (Hartford: Transcendental Books, 1976), p. 232; Cleveland to Zebulon Butler, September 23, 1786, Zebulon Butler Papers, Wyoming Historical and Geological Society, Wilkes-Barre, Pa.; Swan to Jeremiah Wadsworth, April 5, 1786, Boston Public Library, Boston.

47. Compiled from the Hampshire County Court Records, Northampton, Mass.

48. Compiled from the Worcester County Court Records, Worcester, Mass. William Pynchon, *The Diary of William Pynchon of Salem,* ed. Fitch Oliver (Boston, 1890), p. 211.

49. Compiled from the Bristol County Court Records, Taunton, Mass.

50. Lee Newcomer, *The Embattled Farmers: The Massachusetts Countryside in the American Revolution* (New York: King's Crown Press, 1953), p. 135. Unfortunately, the actual court records for Berkshire County no longer exist to permit a statistical analysis.

51. *New Haven Gazette,* December 14, 1786.

52. E. P. Walton, ed., *The Records of the Governor and Council of Vermont,* 8 vols. (Montpelier, 1875), 3:360.

53. William Plumer Autobiography, 1836, 18:22, William Plumer Papers, Library of Congress, Washington, D.C.

54. Edwards to Jeremiah Powell, May 24, 1780, 202:203, Massachusetts Archives, Boston.

55. Compiled from Hampshire County Court Records, and from Bristol County Court Records.

56. Compiled from Hampshire County Court Records.

57. Hampshire County Court Records.

58. Compiled from Oliver Dickinson Account Book, 1783–93, Jones Library, Amherst, Mass.

59. Whitney Bates, "The State Finances of Massachusetts, 1780–1789"

(M.A. thesis, University of Wisconsin, 1948), pp. 158–64. Rufus
King to John Adams, October 3, 1786, Box 1, Rufus King Papers,
New York Historical Society, New York, provides the quote.

60. Van Beck Hall, *Politics without Parties: Massachusetts, 1780–1791*
(Pittsburgh: University of Pittsburgh Press, 1972), p. 29. Also see
Richard Herschcopf, "The New England Farmer and Politics, 1785–
1787" (M.A. thesis, University of Wisconsin, 1947), p. 18; Charles
Bullock, "A Historical Sketch of the Finances and Financial Policy
in Massachusetts from 1780 to 1905," *Publications of the American
Economic Association*, 3d ser., 8 (1907): 281; and Nathaniel Ames,
"Extracts from the Diary of Nathaniel Ames," *Dedham Historical
Register*, ed. Sarah Baker, 5 (1894): 32.

61. Conway Petition, *Massachusetts Gazette*, January 20, 1784; Palmer
Town Petition, 1786, House Doc. 2234, Massachusetts Archives,
Boston. Quoted in Charles Hudson, *The History of Marlborough,
Massachusetts* (Boston, 1862), pp. 189–90. Robert Feer, "Shays'
Rebellion," (Ph.D. thesis, Harvard University, 1958), p. 530. Dur-
ing the same period, only four towns in the coastal counties of
Essex and Suffolk complained about taxation.

62. Manning to Caleb Evans, September 13, 1784, in Guild, *Early History of Brown*, p. 389.

63. Town of Tinmouth, October 2, 1786, in *State Papers of Vermont:
General Petitions, 1778–1787*, ed. Edward Hoyt, 17 vols. (Montpelier, 1918–), 8:217. Also see "John Clark's Journal," *Proceedings
of the Vermont Historical Society* 10, no. 4 (December 1942): 188.

64. Tyler to Samuel Peters, April 20, 1786, in Cameron, *Church of
England*, p. 232.

65. Replies to Queries: Connecticut, June–July 1784, in Jefferson, *Papers*,
7:332. Mason Green, *Springfield 1636–1886* (Springfield, 1888), p.
311. According to Charles Bullock, "A Historical Sketch of Finances," p. 276, the vast majority of state taxes levied between 1780
and 1785—roughly £1,200,000 of £1,407,895—were actually collected. See Jere Daniell, *Experiment in Republicanism: New Hampshire Politics and the American Revolution, 1741–1794* (Cambridge:
Harvard University Press, 1970), p. 187, for New Hampshire taxation.

66. Town of Greenwich, Mass., January 16, 1786, Petitions Folder,
Shays' Rebellion Box, American Antiquarian Society, Worcester.

67. Stephen Riley, "Doctor William Whiting and Shays' Rebellion,"
Proceedings of the American Antiquarian Society 66, no. 1 (January 1956): 144.

68. Otto to Count de Vergennes, September 20, 1786, in Bancroft,
Formation of the Constitution, 2:396.

69. *Independent Chronicle*, August 10, 1786.

70. E. L. Quarantelli, "Nature and Conditions of Panic," *American
Journal of Sociology* 60, no. 2 (1954–55): 273. Conway Petition,

Massachusetts Gazette, January 20, 1784. Merchants and professionals no doubt understood the implications of land seizure. As Alexander Hamilton noted in 1788, "a power over a man's support is a power over his will." John Jay, Alexander Hamilton, and James Madison, *The Federalist Papers,* ed. Clinton Rossiter (New York: New American Library, 1961), p. 441.

71. *Acts and Laws of the State of Connecticut* (Hartford, 1786), p. 61. Charges included five shillings for the prisoner's food each week as well as fees for his commitment and discharge (p. 66). *Massachusetts Spy,* June 23, July 7, 28, 1785.

72. Charles Martyn, *The Life of Artemus Ward* (New York: Artemus Ward Press, 1921), p. 276.

73. Quoted in Robert Moody, "Samuel Ely: Forerunner of Daniel Shays," *New England Quarterly* 5, no. 1 (January 1932): 115.

74. Compiled from the Two-in-One Book: Hampshire County House of Correction, July 2, 1784–1830, Forbes Library, Northampton, Mass.

75. Worcester County Jail Records, vol. 1, Worcester Collection, American Antiquarian Society, Worcester.

76. Joseph Hawley to Caleb Strong, June 24, 1782, Bancroft Collection, New York Public Library, New York.

77. *Massachusetts Gazette,* October 20, 1786. Even Connecticut lawyer-politician Oliver Ellsworth understood the plight of the New England farmer: "When trade is embarrassed, the merchant is first to complain, but the farmer in event bears more than his share of the loss." *Connecticut Courant,* March 10, 1787.

Chapter 3

1. Eric Hobsbawm, *Primitive Rebels: Studies in Archaic Forms of Social Movements in the Nineteenth and Twentieth Centuries* (New York: Norton, 1959), pp. 10, 5.

2. Knox to Henry Jackson, December 17, 1786, Revolutionary Autographs, American Miscellaneous, J. Pierpont Morgan Library, New York.

3. Marvin Michael Kay, "The North Carolina Regulation, 1766–1776: A Class Conflict," in *The American Revolution,* ed. Alfred Young (De Kalb, Ill.: Northern Illinois University Press, 1976), pp. 71–123.

4. Compiled from Robert Feer, "Shays' Rebellion" (Ph.D. thesis, Harvard University, 1958), pp. 540–46.

5. Charles Whittemore, *A General of the Revolution: John Sullivan of New Hampshire* (New York: 1961), p. 199.

6. E. P. Walton, ed., *Records of the Governor and Council of Vermont,* 8 vols. (Montpelier, 1875), 3:362; Charles Sedgwick, *A General History of the Town of Sharon* (Amenia, N.Y., 1898), p. 80.

7. Quoted in Robert East, "The Massachusetts Conservatives in the Critical Period," in *The Era of the American Revolution,* ed. Richard B. Morris (New York: Harper-Row, 1938), p. 360.
8. Van Beck Hall, *Politics without Parties: Massachusetts, 1780–1791* (Pittsburgh: University of Pittsburgh Press, 1972), p. 184.
9. Robert Taylor, *Western Massachusetts in the Revolution* (Providence: Brown University Press, 1954), pp. 112, 121–22; Walton, *Records of the Governor,* 3:358.
10. Walton, *Records of the Governor,* 3:361–63.
11. John Kaminski, "Democracy Run Rampant: Rhode Island in the Confederation," in *The Human Dimensions of Nation Making: Essays on Colonial and Revolutionary America,* ed. James Kirby Martin (Madison: University of Wisconsin Press, 1976), pp. 255, 257.
12. *Massachusetts Gazette,* August 14, 1786; Richard Herschcopf, "The New England Farmer and Politics, 1785-1787" (M.A. thesis, University of Wisconsin, 1947), pp. 121–24.
13. George Richards Minot, *The History of the Insurrections in Massachusetts in the Year 1786 and the Rebellion Consequent Thereon* (Boston, 1788). For the fact that the town of Worcester refused to send a delegate to the convention, see *Worcester Magazine,* 4th week, August 1786; the quotation can be found in ibid., 1st week, September 1786.
14. Minot, *History of the Insurrections,* p. 34. Legislative Drafting Fund of Columbia University, *Constitutions of the United States,* 3 vols. (New York, 1962), 2:12; the New Hampshire Constitution gave the same right to its citizens in exactly the same words (2:11); J. R. Pole, "Shays' Rebellion: A Political Interpretation," in *The Reinterpretation of the American Revolution, 1763–1789,* ed. Jack Greene (New York: Harper-Row, 1968), p. 429.
15. For town petitions, see Feer, "Shays' Rebellion," pp. 540–46. For the cry of the Massachusetts conventions for paper money, see Worcester County Convention Petition, September 28, 1786, in Samuel Eliot Morison, ed., *Sources and Documents Illustrating the American Revolution* (London: Oxford University Press, 1923), p. 211; Stephen Mix Mitchell to William Johnson, September 14, 1786, vol. 2, William Samuel Johnson Papers, Connecticut Historical Society, Hartford; *Massachusetts Gazette,* September 5, 1786.
16. Kaminski, "Democracy Run Rampant," p. 246.
17. Sedgwick, *General History of Sharon,* p. 80.
18. *New Hampshire Gazette,* July 20, 1786.
19. Whitney Bates, "The State Finances of Massachusetts, 1780–1789" (M.A. thesis, University of Wisconsin, 1948), p. 166.
20. Quoted in Thomas Weston, *History of the Town of Middleboro, Massachusetts* (Boston, 1906), p. 578.
21. Petition, September 25, 1786, in Charles Hudson, *A History of Marlborough, Massachusetts* (Boston, 1867), p. 191.

22. Samuel Holden Parsons to William Johnson, October 2, 1786, in *The Life and Letters of Samuel Holden Parsons,* ed. Charles Hall (New York, 1905), p. 470.

23. Minot, *History of the Insurrections,* p. 34.

24. Town of Dracut, September 29, 1786, Petitions Folder, Shays' Rebellion Box, American Antiquarian Society, Worcester.

25. Minot, *History of the Insurrections,* pp. 34–37; Feer, "Shays' Rebellion," pp. 540–46.

26. Barbara Karsky, "American Radicalism in the Late Revolutionary Period," in *New Wine in Old Skins,* ed. Erich Angermann, Marie-Luise Frings, and Hermann Wellenreuther (Stuttgart: Klett, 1976), p. 93.

27. Minot, *History of the Insurrections,* pp. 34–37. For the towns, see Feer, "Shays' Rebellion," pp. 540–46.

28. Sedgwick to Aaron Burr, August 7, 1774, in Matthew Davis, *Memoirs of Aaron Burr,* 2 vols. (New York, 1838), 1:93.

29. Richard Cranch to John Adams, October 3, 1786; Charles Storer to John Adams, September 16, 1786, Adams Family Papers, Massachusetts Historical Society, Boston; Samuel Bates, ed., *Braintree Town Records* (Randolph, 1886), p. 568. Also see William Wetmore to Unknown, May 8, 1786, Addendum 1, Wetmore Collection, Sterling Library, Yale University, New Haven. Although a merchant, Austin got little support from the commercial interest and later retracted his position. Sidney Kaplan, "Honestus and the Annihilation of the Lawyers," *South Atlantic Quarterly* 48, no. 3 (July 1949): 401–20.

30. Robert Moody, "Samuel Ely: Forerunner of Shays," *New England Quarterly* 5, no. 1 (January 1932): 108–11.

31. Whittemore, *General of the Revolution,* pp. 184–85.

32. Hall, *Politics without Parties,* pp. 186–87.

33. George Billias, "The Massachusetts Land Bankers of 1740," *University of Maine Studies,* 2d ser., 61, no. 17 (April 1959); John MacInnes, "Rhode Island Bills of Public Credit 1710–1755" (Ph.D. thesis, Brown University, 1952), pp. 218–19, 237, 497.

34. Replies to Queries: Massachusetts, July 1784, in Thomas Jefferson, *The Papers of Thomas Jefferson,* ed. Julian Boyd, 18 vols. (Princeton: Princeton University Press, 1950–), 7:341.

35. October 12, 1786, in Fisher Ames, *The Works of Fisher Ames,* ed. Seth Ames, 2 vols. (Boston, 1854), 2:96. Also see Mary Cranch to Abigail Adams, February 9, 1787, Adams Family Papers.

36. Noah Webster, *A Collection of Essays and Fugitive Writings* (Boston, 1790), p. 41.

37. Jonathan Jackson, *Thoughts upon the Political Situation of the United States of America* (Worcester, 1788), p. 35.

38. C. B. MacPherson, *The Political Theory of Possessive Individualism* (London: Oxford University Press, 1962), p. 85.

39. Quoted in William Smith, "Springfield in the Insurrection of 1786," *Connecticut Valley Historical Review* 2 (1877): 80.

40. *New Hampshire Gazette,* June 3, 1785. Also see Webster, *Collection of Essays,* p. 130.

41. *Massachusetts Centinel,* December 2, 1786. Also see *Hampshire Herald,* September 26, 1786, and *Massachusetts Gazette,* April 3, 1786; Robert East, *Business Enterprise in the American Revolutionary Era* (New York: AMS, 1938), pp. 279–81. Dane to Captain Wales, January 31, 1786, Nathan Dane Papers, Library of Congress. Washington, D.C.; Hall, *Politics without Parties,* pp. 43, 44 n; Amory to Dowling and Sons, October 16, 1786, in William Weeden, *Economic and Social History of New England,* 2 vols. (Boston, 1891), 2:847 n.

42. Sewall to George Thatcher, October 16, 1786, in "The Thatcher Papers," *Historical Magazine,* 2d ser., 6, no. 5 (November 1869): 257–58.

43. *Worcester Magazine,* last week, August 1786.

44. Ibid., 4th week, August 1786.

45. Quoted in Jackson Turner Main, *Political Parties before the Constitution* (New York: Norton, 1974), p. 115 n.

46. *Boston Gazette,* April 11, 1749.

47. *Worcester Magazine,* 4th week, August 1786.

48. Webster to Pickering, August 10, 1786, Pickering Papers, Massachusetts Historical Society, Boston.

49. Pole, "Shays' Rebellion" p. 419.

50. William Manning, *The Key of Liberty,* ed. Samuel Eliot Morison (Billerica, Mass.: Manning Association, 1922), p. 52.

51. Pole, "Shays' Rebellion," p. 423. Jackson Turner Main, *Political Parties before the Constitution,* p. 93.

52. Legislative Drafting Fund, *Constitutions,* 2:12.

53. Samuel Eliot Morison, "The Struggle over the Adoption of the Constitution of Massachusetts, 1780," *Proceedings of the Massachusetts Historical Society* 50 (May 1917): 338, 354; idem, *The Maritime History of Massachusetts, 1783–1860* (Boston: Houghton Mifflin, 1921), pp. 28–29.

54. Legislative Drafting Fund, *Constitutions,* 2:10.

55. Secretary of State, *Connecticut State Register and Manual, 1976* (Hartford: Commonwealth of Connecticut, 1976), p. 55.

56. For the text of the Vermont Constitution, see John Williams, ed., *State Papers of Vermont: Laws of Vermont, 1785–1791,* 17 vols. (Montpelier, 1918–), 14:100–10.

57. Pole, "Shays' Rebellion," p. 419.

58. Allen Johnson et al., eds., *Dictionary of American Biography,* 22 vols. (New York: Scribners, 1946), 2:498–501; 9:418–19; 18:192–93.

59. Kaminski, "Democracy Run Rampant," p. 249.

60. Patrick Conley, "Rhode Island and Division, 1787–1790," *Rhode Island History* 31, no. 4 (Fall 1972): 99.
61. Samuel Hough, "Castiglioni's Visit to Rhode Island," *Rhode Island History* 26, no. 2 (April 1967): 64.
62. *United States Chronicle,* June 1, 1786.
63. *New Jersey Journal,* August 23, 1786.
64. Man in Boston to Providence, July 27, 1786, in *Providence Gazette,* August 5, 1786.
65. The Anarchiad, *New Haven Gazette,* December 28, 1786.
66. *United States Chronicle,* May 25, 1786.
67. Dana to Elbridge Gerry, September 2, 1787, Lloyd C. Stevens Collection, Morristown National Historic Park, Morristown, N.J.
68. *American Museum* 2, no. 4 (October 1787): 397. For the activity of New York merchants, see East, *Business Enterprise in the American Revolutionary Era,* p. 283.
69. Kaminski, "Democracy Run Rampant," pp. 254, 259–60.
70. Webster to Hudson and Goodwin, September 28, 1786, Noah Webster Papers, New York Public Library, New York.
71. John R. Bartlett, ed., *Records of the State of Rhode Island,* 10 vols. (Providence, 1856–65), 10:220; Irwin Polishook, *Rhode Island and the Union, 1774–1795* (Evanston: Northwestern University Press, 1969), pp. 133–42.
72. Jackson Turner Main, *The Antifederalists: Critics of the Constitution, 1781–1788* (New York: Norton, 1961), p. 59; Allan Nevins, *The American States during and after the Revolution* (New York: Macmillan, 1924), p. 535.
73. Hall, *Politics without Parties,* p. 203.
74. Strong to Nathan Dane, July 2, 1786, Addendum 1, Wetmore Collection, Sterling Library, Yale University, New Haven.
75. Humphreys to Washington, November 1, 1786, George Washington Papers, Library of Congress, Washington, D.C.
76. Albert Batchellor, ed., *Early State Papers of New Hampshire,* 42 vols. (Manchester, N.H., 1890–), 20:420.
77. Ibid., pp. 491, 587, 672, 676, 696.
78. Williams, *State Papers of Vermont,* 14:63.
79. Daniel Chipman, *The Life of Nathaniel Chipman* (Boston, 1846), pp. 66–68.

Chapter 4

1. Samuel Ellsworth, *There Shall Be Wars and Rumors of Wars before the Last Day Commeth: Solemn Predictions of Future Events Plainly Manifested by the Planets* (Bennington, Vt., 1787), pp. 4–5.
2. William Greenleaf to Gov. James Bowdoin, n.d., 190:235, Massachusetts Archives, Boston, notes that the Shaysites called themselves

Regulators; for the Shaysite aim of "moderating government," see ibid., Insurgent Report, September 26, 1786, 190:290. In *The Crowd in History: A Study of Popular Disturbances in France and England, 1730–1848* (New York: Harper-Row, 1964), p. 42, George Rudé quotes some 1766 English food rioters who "declared they were Regulators."

3. *New Hampshire Gazette,* August 10, 1786; *Independent Chronicle,* August 31, 1786.

4. Man in Providence to Baltimore, July 1, 1786, in *New Jersey Gazette,* August 28, 1786. Also see *New Hampshire Gazette,* August 3, 1786; and Luther Riggs, ed., *The Anarchiad: A New England Poem* (New Haven, 1861), pp. 95–96.

5. Ronald Banks, *Maine Becomes a State: The Movement to Separate Maine from Massachusetts, 1785–1820* (Middletown, Conn.: Wesleyan University Press, 1970), pp. 18–25.

6. James Lemon, *The Best Poor Man's Country: A Geographical Study of Early Southeastern Pennsylvania* (Baltimore: Johns Hopkins Press, 1972), p. 178.

7. The number of "fighting men" was obtained from Jedediah Morse, *The American Geography* (Elizabethtown, N.J., 1789), p. 172. The number of Shaysites has been compiled from the various newspaper accounts and the oaths of allegiance taken after the rebellion, vol. 190, Massachusetts Archives.

8. Webster to James Bowdoin, March 15, 1787, "Bowdoin-Temple Papers," *Collections of the Massachusetts Historical Society* 9 (1907): 181. The various figures have been compiled from the oaths of allegiance primarily found in vol. 190, Massachusetts Archives, Boston. The average acreages can be found in Barbara Karsky, "Agrarian Radicalism in the Late Revolutionary Period," in *Old Wine in New Skins,* ed. Erich Angermann, Marie-Luise Frings, and Hermann Wellenreuther (Stuttgart: Klett, 1976), p. 112. For the difficulty in defining the term *gentleman* for eighteenth-century America, see *Worcester Magazine,* 3d week, August 1786.

9. For aggregate data, see U.S. Department of Commerce, *Historical Statistics* (1957), p. 756. The participation of Green and Carter in the Shaysite troubles can be found in vol. 190, Massachusetts Archives, under their respective towns. For Sash, see Sidney Kaplan, "A Negro Veteran in Shays' Rebellion," *Journal of Negro History* 33, no. 2 (April 1948): 123–29. Few Indians were found in the Shaysite ranks. By 1785, the Stockbridge Indians of the westernmost part of the state had left Massachusetts. Electa Jones, *Stockbridge: Past and Present* (Springfield, 1854), p. 228.

10. *New England Historical and Genealogical Register* 30 (1876): 298. For a general analysis of women in the period, see Nancy Cott, "The Bonds of Womanhood: 'Women's Sphere'" in *New England, 1780–1835* (New Haven: Yale University Press, 1977).

11. Two women in Pelham to Sally, March 3, 1787, in *Massachusetts Gazette,* March 20, 1787.

12. Aggregate data can be found in Morse, *American Geography,* pp. 171–72; and Isaac Backus, *A Church History of New England,* 2 vols. (Providence, 1784), 2:420–22.

13. Isaac Backus, *An Address to the Inhabitants of New England* (Boston, 1787); *Manual of the Second Congregational Church* (Amherst, 1924), pp. 6–7; First Congregational Parish Tax List, January 8, 1787, Jones Library, Amherst, Mass. William McLoughlin's contention that "the Separate-Baptists in western Massachusetts were prominent among the supporters of Daniel Shays" may be overstated: "The Role of Religion in the Revolution," in *Essays on the American Revolution,* ed. Stephen Kurtz and James Hutson (Chapel Hill, N.C.: University of North Carolina Press, 1969), p. 206.

14. Hinds Petition, May 1787, 189:367, Massachusetts Archives. Aggregate data compiled from the oaths of allegiance mainly in vol. 190, Massachusetts Archives, and the various town genealogical data.

15. William Newton, *The History of Barnard, Vermont,* 2 vols. (Montpelier, n.d.), 2:43, 322, 91.

16. Charles Pease, *History of Conway* (Springfield, Mass., 1917), p. 60.

17. Sarah Sedgwick and Christina Marquand, *Stockbridge: 1738–1939* (Stockbridge, 1939), p. 150. Data for Springfield compiled from vol. 190, Massachusetts Archives.

18. Austin to James Bowdoin, n.d., 189:337, Massachusetts Archives.

19. Morse, *American Geography,* p. 145. Also see Kenneth Lockridge, *Literacy in Colonial New England: An Inquiry into the Social Context of Literacy in the Early Modern West* (New York: Norton, 1974). For the anti-Shaysite bias of New England newspapers, see Paul Marsella, "Propaganda Trends in the *Essex Journal* and *New Hampshire Packet,* 1787–1788," *Essex Institute Historical Collections* 114, no. 3 (July 1978): 164–75. In fact, the *Hampshire Gazette* of Northampton, Mass., was established partially as a reaction to the insurgents. Nevertheless, the *Hampshire Gazette* did carry letters by rebels. Almanacs fulfilled some of the same functions as newspapers, carrying dates of the court sessions and at least once some pictures about the rebellion.

20. John Holland, Jr., Testimony, May 5, 1787, 189:401, Massachusetts Archives. For a general analysis see Edward Field, *The Colonial Tavern* (Providence, 1897), pp. 4, 258. Taverns fulfilled the same role during periods of rural rioting in Europe. E. J. Hobsbawm and George Rudé, *Captain Swing* (New York: Pantheon, 1969), p. 60. Shepard to James Bowdoin, February 18, 1787, "Bowdoin-Temple Papers," p. 143.

21. Shrewsbury, Mass.: Records, p. 90, New York Historical Society, New York.

22. Mary Crawford, *Old New England Inns* (Boston, 1907), pp. 42–45; John Goldsbury, "Shays' Rebellion," typescript (Warwick, R.I., 1933), Jones Library, Amherst; Alfred Noon, *The History of Ludlow, Massachusetts* (Springfield, 1912), p. 70.

23. Sidney Kaplan, "Veteran Officers and Politics in Massachusetts, 1783–1787," *William and Mary Quarterly* 9, no. 1 (January 1952): 51, gives other insurgent captains.

24. Secretary of the Commonwealth, *Massachusetts Soldiers and Sailors of the Revolutionary War*, 17 vols. (Boston, 1896–1908), 3:766.

25. Based on a comparison of ibid. and the oaths of allegiance in vol. 190, Massachusetts Archives.

26. Rudé, *The Crowd in History*, p. 254; Pauline Maier, *From Resistance to Revolution* (New York: Vintage, 1972), p. 13; Dirk Hoerder, *Crowd Action in Revolutionary Massachusetts, 1765–1780* (New York: Academic Press, 1977); Stephen Patterson, *Political Parties in Revolutionary Massachusetts* (Madison: University of Wisconsin Press, 1973), p. 99; Arthur Schlesinger, "Political Mobs and the American Revolution, 1765–1776," *Proceedings of the American Philosophical Society* 99, no. 4 (1955): 244–50; Edward Countryman, " 'Out of Bounds of the Law': Northern Land Rioters in the Eighteenth Century," in *The American Revolution,* ed. Alfred Young (De Kalb, Ill.: Northern Illinois University Press, 1976), p. 42; and Theodore Crackel and Martin Andresen, "Fort William and Mary: A Case Study in Crowd Behavior," *Historical New Hampshire* 29, no. 4 (Winter 1974): 213. This point of view disagrees with Robert Feer, "Shays' Rebellion" (Ph.D. thesis, Harvard University, 1958), p. 512; the rebels possessed "little centralized organization."

27. Unfortunately, no data have been located that list New Hampshire Regulators individually. For the towns, see William Plumer, "Letters of William Plumer," *Transactions of the Colonial Society of Massachusetts* 11, no. 7 (December 1907): 392.

28. Ibid., p. 391.

29. *Worcester Magazine,* 2d week, October 1786.

30. Cobb to Bowdoin, October 30, 1786, 190:295c, Massachusetts Archives.

31. Lyman to Samuel Breck, December 27, 1786, "Bowdoin-Temple Papers," pp. 122–23.

32. C. O. Parmenter, *The History of Pelham, Massachusetts* (Amherst, 1898), pp. 391–92; Feer, "Shays' Rebellion," p. 233; *Massachusetts Centinel,* January 20, 1787. For Shays' continued indebtedness, see Shays to James Hunter, September 17, 1794, Case 8, Box 17, Gratz Collection, Historical Society of Pennsylvania, Philadelphia.

33. Francis Blake, *The History of Princeton, Massachusetts,* 2 vols. (Princeton, 1915), 2:108; Hampshire County Court Records, Northampton, Mass.

34. Billings to Unknown, February 7, 1787, John Billings Folder, Jones Library, Amherst; Hampshire County Court Records.

35. Compiled by a comparison of lists of Shaysites in vol. 190, Massachusetts Archives, and the various county court files.

36. Two-in-One Book: Hampshire County House of Correction, Forbes Library, Northampton; E. P. Walton, ed., *Records of the Governor and Council of Vermont,* 8 vols. (Montpelier, 1875), 3:367.

37. *Worcester Magazine,* 2d week, October 1786.

38. *Hampshire Gazette,* October 25, 1786.

39. Ibid., October 18, 1786.

40. *Gentlemen's Magazine and Historical Chronicle* (London) 57 (January 1787): 80.

41. Michael Hatch Testimony, Shays' Rebellion Box, Robert Treat Paine Papers, Massachusetts Historical Society, Boston.

42. Lee Newcomer, *The Embattled Farmers: The Massachusetts Countryside in the American Revolution* (New York: King's Crown Press, 1953), p. 45.

43. Aaron Burr to Matthew Ogden, August 17, 1774, in Matthew Davis, *Memoirs of Aaron Burr,* 2 vols. (New York, 1838), 1:48; Unknown to Provincial Congress of Massachusetts, February 23, 1775, in Peter Force, *American Archives,* 4th ser. (Washington, D.C., 1837), 1: 1260–61.

44. Henry Van Schaack, *Memoirs of the Life of Henry Van Schaack* (Chicago, 1892), p. 226.

45. John Thompson, Asa Miller, Thomas Ansolen, Luke Day, Simeon Vaughan, and Joel Billings to the Justices of the Northampton Court, August 29, 1786, 189:111–13, Massachusetts Archives.

46. Quoted in Daniel Ricketson, *The History of New Bedford, Massachusetts* (New Bedford, 1858), pp. 224–25.

47. *Worcester Magazine,* 4th week, November 1786.

48. French to the General Court, September 20, 1786, in Plumer, "Letters," pp. 390–91.

49. Wheeler to the Public, November 7, 1786, in Ellery Crane, "Shays' Rebellion," *Proceedings of the Worcester Society of Antiquity* 5 (1881): 82 n.; Daniel Matthews Testimony, September 15, 1786, *Worcester Magazine,* 4th week, September 1786.

50. Whitney Smith, *The Flag Book of the United States* (New York: Morrow, 1970), pp. 28–29, 32–33, 38–39.

51. Francis Williams, *A Founding Family: The Pinckneys of South Carolina* (New York: Harcourt Brace, 1978), p. 91.

52. Judges Sawtell and Sargent to James Bowdoin, September 25, 1786, 190:294a–b, Massachusetts Archives; William Lyman to Ezra Badlam, April 14, 1787, Ezra Badlam Papers, Dorchester Historical Society, Dorchester, Mass. Government men in 1786 and 1787 wore a piece of white paper in their hats. Ibid.

53. George Richards Minot, *The History of the Insurrections in Massa-chusetts in the Year 1786 and the Rebellion Consequent Thereon* (Boston, 1788), p. 39.

Chapter 5

1. Bowdoin to the Council, February 1787, in "Bowdoin-Temple Papers," *Collections of the Massachusetts Historical Society,* 7th ser. (1907): 162.
2. Shepard to Henry Knox, December 17, 1786, Henry Knox Papers, Massachusetts Historical Society, Boston.
3. Bowdoin to General Court, September 2, 1786, in "Bowdoin-Temple Papers," p. 112; Lincoln to Officers of the Massachusetts Line, October 11, 1786, Benjamin Lincoln Papers, Massachusetts Historical Society, Boston.
4. Lyman to Samuel Breck, December 27, 1786, in "Bowdoin-Temple Papers," p. 122; Tyler to David Daggett, December 3, 1786, Box 11, David Daggett Papers, Sterling Library, Yale University, New Haven; Knox to George Washington, October 23, 1786, Knox Papers.
5. *Hampshire Gazette,* September 20, 1786.
6. *Worcester Magazine,* 4th week, November 1786.
7. Knox to Washington, October 23, 1786, Knox Papers; Lincoln to Washington, December 4, 1786, Lincoln Papers.
8. *New Hampshire Mercury,* November 15, 1786.
9. Flagg to Benjamin Franklin, September 12, 1786, fol. 142, vol. 34, Benjamin Franklin Papers, American Philosophical Society, Phila-delphia; Cutler to Winthrop Sargent, October 6, 1786, Winthrop Sargent Papers, Massachusetts Historical Society, Boston; King to Daniel Kilham, October 29, 1786, King-Kilham Papers, Butler Library, Columbia University, New York.
10. *Hampshire Gazette,* September 20, 1786.
11. Fisher Ames, *The Works of Fisher Ames,* ed. Seth Ames, 2 vols. (Boston, 1854), 2:97; Fisher Ames, *The Works of Fisher Ames* (Boston, 1809), p. 10.
12. Ames, *Works* (1854), 2:93.
13. *An Address from the General Court* (Boston, 1786), p. 28.
14. Abigail Adams to John Adams, November 28, 1786, Adams Family Papers, Massachusetts Historical Society, Boston; Shepard to the Militia, December 5, 1786, in Orasmus Turner, *History of the Pioneer Settlement of Phelps and Gorham's Purchase* (Rochester, 1851), p. 483.
15. Bernard Bailyn, *The Ideological Origins of the American Revolu-tion* (Cambridge: Harvard University Press, 1967), pp. ix, 150.

16. *Hampshire Gazette,* June 6, 1787.

17. *New Hampshire Mercury,* September 27, 1786.

18. Welch to Abigail Adams, October 27, 1786, Adams Family Papers; Shepard to Bowdoin, December 4, 1786, 318:202, Massachusetts Archives, Boston.

19. Williams, in Paul Ford, ed., *Essays on the Constitution of the United States* (New York, 1892), p. 157.

20. Clarke to Bowdoin, September 8, 1786, Ward to Bowdoin, September 12, 1786, 190:238, 252, Massachusetts Archives.

21. Osgood to John Adams, November 11, 1786, Adams Family Papers.

22. *Worcester Magazine,* last week, November 1786.

23. *Independent Chronicle,* August 31, 1786.

24. *Massachusetts Centinel,* April 2, 1785.

25. Dane to Samuel Phillips, January 29, 1786, Nathan Dane Papers, Library of Congress, Washington, D.C.

26. *Worcester Magazine,* 1st week, January 1786.

27. Gordon Wood, "A Note on Mobs in the American Revolution," *William and Mary Quarterly* 23, no. 4 (October 1966): 641.

28. Orina to Judges, May 24, 1787, Shays' Rebellion Box, Robert Treat Paine Papers, Massachusetts Historical Society, Boston.

29. James Kirby Martin, *Men in Rebellion: Higher Governmental Leaders and the Coming of the American Revolution* (New Brunswick, N.J.: Rutgers University Press, 1973), pp. 190, xi.

30. Pauline Maier, *From Resistance to Revolution* (New York: Vintage, 1972), p. xv.

31. Quoted in Bruce Merritt, "Loyalism and Social Conflict in Revolutionary Deerfield, Massachusetts," *Journal of American History* 57, no. 2 (September 1970): 281. Also see Gouverneur Morris to John Penn, May 20, 1774, in Peter Force, *American Archives,* 4th ser. (Washington, D.C., 1837), 1:342–43; and Maier, *From Resistance to Revolution,* pp. 28, 32.

32. *Boston and Country Gazette,* November 6, 1786.

33. E. P. Walton, ed., *Records of the Governor and Council of Vermont,* 8 vols. (Montpelier, 1875), 3:367.

34. Ibid., 3:366, for the Rutland incident. For the Vermont legislation, see John Williams, ed., *State Papers of Vermont: Laws of Vermont, 1785–1791,* 17 vols. (Montpelier, 1918–), 14:281–83, 266.

35. Plumer to John Hale, September 20, 1786, in William Plumer, "Letters of William Plumer," *Transactions of the Colonial Society of Massachusetts* 11, no. 7 (December 1907): 394, contains information on the social background of government supporters. Unfortunately, no lists of government supporters exist. For descriptions of the September 20, 1786, incident at Exeter, see ibid.; and Jeremy Belknap to Josiah Waters, September 24, 1786, in "The Belknap Papers," *Collections of the Massachusetts Historical Society,* 6th ser., 4 (1891): 315.

36. Plumer to John Hale, September 21, 1786, in Plumer, "Letters," pp. 393–94.
37. Jere Daniell, *Experiment in Republicanism: New Hampshire Politics and the American Revolution, 1741–1794* (Cambridge: Harvard University Press, 1970), p. 199.
38. Isaac Hammond, ed., *Documents Relating to Towns in New Hampshire,* 40 vols. (Concord, 1882–), 20:683.
39. Samuel Hobart to Jeremy Belknap, December 18, 1786, in "Belknap Papers," p. 321.
40. *Hampshire Gazette,* January 10, 1787.
41. George Richards Minot, *History of the Insurrections in Massachusetts in the Year 1786 and the Rebellion Consequent Thereon* (Boston, 1788), p. 39.
42. Warner to Bowdoin, n.d., 190: 230, Massachusetts Archives.
43. Greenleaf to Bowdoin, n.d., p. 235, ibid.
44. Ward to Bowdoin, September 5, 1786, p. 233, ibid.
45. Caleb Hyde to Bowdoin, September 13, 1786, 190:263–64, Massachusetts Archives.
46. Elisha Porter to Bowdoin, September 25, 1786, p. 265, William Shepard to Bowdoin, September 29, 1786, p. 291, Judges Sawtell and Sargent to Bowdoin, September 25, 1786, p. 294c, ibid.
47. Christopher Gore to Rufus King, November 7, 1786, Box 1, Rufus King Papers, New York Historical Society, New York. Also see List of General Brook's Forces, November 4, 1786, 190:296d, Massachusetts Archives, for a list of the troops.
48. Bowdoin to the General Court, September 28, 1786, 190: 275, Massachusetts Archives; Swan to Henry Knox, October 26, 1786, Knox Papers; Henry Lee to James Madison, October 25, 1786, in Edmund Burnett, ed., *Letters of Members of the Continental Congress,* 8 vols. (Washington, D.C.: Government Printing Office, 1931–36), 8:492.
49. Dexter to Bowdoin, October 3, 1786, in "Bowdoin-Temple Papers," p. 116.
50. Jonathan Judd Diary, vol. 3, Forbes Library, Northampton, Mass.
51. *Connecticut Courant,* November 20, 1786.
52. Joseph Gardner Swift, *Memoirs* (New York, 1890), p. 164; Rufus King, *The Life and Correspondence of Rufus King,* ed. Charles King, 6 vols. (New York, 1894), 6:643–44. For more material on the Prince Henry incident, see Richard Krauel, "Prince Henry and the Regency of the United States, 1786," *American Historical Review* 17, no. 1 (October 1911): 44–51; and Louise Dunbar, "A Study of 'Monarchial' Tendencies in the United States from 1766 to 1801," *University of Illinois Studies in the Social Sciences* 10 (1922): 54–58. Also see Mercy Otis Warren to John Adams, December 1786, Mercy Otis Warren Papers, Massachusetts Historical So-

ciety, Boston, for more material on the tendency toward monarchy in the Bay State during Shays' Rebellion.

53. Knox to Congress, October 18, 1786, in John Fitzpatrick, ed., *Journals of the Continental Congress,* 36 vols. (Washington, D.C., 1905–), 31:887. For Knox's preoccupation with a standing army before 1786, see Henry Knox, *Plan for the General Arrangement of the Militia* (New York, 1786).

54. For the pretext of Indian troubles, see Baron von Steuben in *New York Daily Advertiser,* November 1, 1786, as "Bellisarius"; Abraham Yates statement, in Staughton Lynd, *Class Conflict, Slavery, and the United States Constitution* (New York: Bobbs-Merrill, 1967), pp. 244–46; and *Secret Journals of the Acts and Proceedings of Congress,* 4 vols. (Washington, D.C., 1821), 1:269. This evidence calls into question the position of Joseph P. Warren, "The Confederation and Shays' Rebellion," *American Historical Review* 11, no. 1 (October 1905): 42–57.

55. *Records of the United States: Massachusetts, 1783–1787,* October 18, 1786, vol. 11, A 1*b*, p. 276.

56. *Address from the General Court,* pp. 33, 35.

57. *Acts and Laws of Massachusetts, 1786* (Boston, 1786), pp. 494–95, 497.

58. Ibid., pp. 502–3. For the many riot acts in colonial America, see Maier, *Resistance to Revolution,* pp. 24–25.

59. *Acts and Laws of Massachusetts, 1786,* p. 510. Benjamin Hichborn to John Adams, January 16, 1787, Adams Family Papers.

60. *Records: Massachusetts,* November 16, 1786, vol. 11, A 1*b*, pp. 356–57.

61. *Acts and Laws of Massachusetts, 1786,* p. 522; and Bowdoin to the General Court, February 3, 1787, *Records: Massachusetts,* vol. 12, A 1*b*, p. 369.

62. *Worcester Magazine,* last week, November 1786; Dane to Jonathan Choate, January 31, 1786, Dane Papers.

63. Jackson to Knox, November 12, December 11, 1786, Knox Papers.

64. Gore to Rufus King, November 7, 1786, Box 1, King Papers.

65. Jackson to Knox, January 9, 1787, Knox Papers.

66. *Litchfield Monitor,* November 21, 1786.

67. Henry Knox to Edmund Randolph, February 12, 1787, in William Palmer, ed., *Calendar of Virginia State Papers,* 4 vols. (Richmond, 1884), 1:236; Knox to the President of Congress, February 12, 1787, vol. 1, *m*247, pp. 243–44, Papers of the Continental Congress, National Archives, Washington, D.C.

68. Bowdoin to Lincoln, January 4, 1787, Lincoln Papers.

69. Bowdoin to Lincoln, January 19, 1787, in Minot, *History of the Insurrections,* pp. 99–100.

70. Lincoln to Washington, December 4–January 1787, George Washington Papers, Library of Congress, Washington, D.C., for the

mechanics of money raising. The aggregate figures can be found in Jackson to Henry Knox, January 7, 1787, Knox Papers; and Lists of Subscription, 189:65–66, Massachusetts Archives. The Jackson quote is in Jackson to Knox, January 28, 1787, Knox Papers.

71. Lincoln to Washington, December 4, 1786, Lincoln Papers.

72. Archer Butler Hulbert, *Records of the Original Proceedings of the Ohio Company,* 2 vols. (Marietta, 1917), 1:4; Sidney Kaplan, "Veteran Officers and Politics in Massachusetts, 1783–1787," *William and Mary Quarterly* 9, no. 1 (January 1952): 29–57.

73. Frederick Allis, Jr., "The Early Life of David Cobb," William Bingham Maine Lands, *Transactions of the Colonial Society of Massachusetts* 36 (1954): 386–499.

74. Thomas Egleston, *The Life of John Paterson* (New York, 1894), pp. 151–52; Chanango Land Subscribers, Box 2, Walker-Rockwell Papers, New York Historical Society, New York.

75. Benjamin Labaree, *Patriots and Partisans: The Merchants of Newburyport, 1764–1815* (Cambridge: Harvard University Press, 1962), pp. 208, 214, 218.

76. *Massachusetts Society of Cincinnati* (Boston, 1964), pp. 23, 8–11. Despite the many officers in their ranks, only Shaysites Luke and Elijah Day belonged to the Cincinnati; on July 13, 1787, they were expelled for their part in the Rebellion (p. 45). Also see Kaplan, "Veteran Officers and Politics," p. 51. For officer wartime protests, see his "Pay, Pension, and Power: Economic Grievances of the Massachusetts Officers of the Revolution," *Boston Public Library Quarterly* 3, nos. 1 and 2 (January-April 1951): 1–36.

77. Kaplan, "Veteran Officers and Politics," p. 32; Ronald Heaton, *Masonic Membership of the Founding Fathers* (Washington, D.C.: Masonic Service Association, 1965), pp. 41, 51–52, 54–55; and Sidney Kaplan, "Rank and Status among Massachusetts Continental Officers," *American Historical Review* 56, no. 2 (January 1951): 318–26.

78. James Winthrop to Mercy Otis Warren, February 26, 1787, in "Warren-Adams Letters," *Collections of the Massachusetts Historical Society,* 7th ser., 73 (1925): 282–83; Thomas Cushing to Unknown, February 5, 1787, Folder MSS no. 2, Shays' Rebellion Box, Jones Library, Amherst, Mass.; William Pynchon, *The Diary of William Pynchon,* ed. Fitch Oliver (Boston, 1890), pp. 257–58.

79. Pynchon, *Diary,* pp. 260, 267; Thompson Journal, March 22, 1787, Lloyd C. Stevens Collection, Morristown National Historic Park, Morristown, N.J.; Jonathan Jackson to Lincoln, January 4, 1788, Lincoln Papers; Harrison Gray Otis, *Life and Letters of Harrison Gray Otis,* ed. Samuel Eliot Morison, 2 vols. (New York, 1913), 1:30–31; Entry for January 18, 1787, in John Quincy Adams Diary, Adams Family Papers, Massachusetts Historical Society, Boston.

80. Webster to Hudson and Goodwin, September 10, 1786, Noah Web-

ster Papers, New York Public Library, New York. For wartime food shortages and the urban reaction against the farmers, see Ralph Harlow, "Economic Conditions in Massachusetts during the American Revolution," *Publications of the Colonial Society of Massachusetts* 20 (March 1918): 175–78.

81. Sullivan to Rufus King, February 25, 1787, in Thomas Amory, *The Life of James Sullivan*, 2 vols. (Boston, 1859), 1:390–91.

82. The coastal county troop enlistments can be found in List of Town Quotas for Suffolk and Essex Counties, January 20, 1787, Lincoln Papers. The quote on the composition of the Worcester regiment can be found in *Worcester Magazine*, 1st week, February 1787. Lists of the government troops do exist, but unfortunately the men are listed by regiment rather than town. This method of listing makes a close analysis of the composition of the government troops virtually impossible. For the government payrolls, see vols. 191–92, Massachusetts Archives. The few payroll lists that arrange the men by towns bear out the generalization that men from the inland regions fighting for government came from market towns. For Middlesex troops, see n. 47. The commercial orientation of government volunteers in Hampshire can be found in *Massachusetts Centinel*, January 20, 1787, where one observer reported only twelve Shaysites in the Hampshire market towns of Hadley and Northampton. For the poor turnout for government in Hampshire County, see William Shepard to Benjamin Lincoln, February 19, 1787, Addendum 1, Wetmore Collection, Sterling Library, Yale University, New Haven. For sentiment in Hopkinton, see Hopkinton to the General Court, February 1, 1787, Petitions Folder, Shays' Rebellion Box, American Antiquarian Society, Worcester.

83. Prince Hall to Bowdoin, November 26, 1786, in William Grimshaw, *Official History of Freemasonry among the Colored People of North America* (New York, 1903), p. 81; Sidney Kaplan, *The Black Presence in the Era of the American Revolution, 1770–1800* (Greenwich, Conn.: New York Graphic Society, 1973), pp. 185–86. Even though Bowdoin rejected Hall's offer, at least one black fought with Lincoln. On April 11, 1787, "a soldier, by the name of Elisha Green, five feet, six inches high, dark complexion, short curled black hair," deserted the government army. *Worcester Magazine*, 2d week, April 1787, p. 21.

84. Samuel Phillips Savage Diary, January 23, 1787, Massachusetts Historical Society, Boston. For Thomas Allen, see Clifford Shipton, *Sibley's Harvard Graduates: Biographical Sketches of Those Who Attended Harvard College*, 17 vols. (Boston, 1873–1975), 15:159. The progovernment attitude of Eleazer Storrs can be found in Thomas Robbins, *The Diary of Thomas Robbins*, ed. Increase Tarbox, 2 vols. (Boston, 1868), 1:33 n. The position of Alexander Steele, actually attacked by Shaysites, can be found in Timothy

Newell to John Hancock, June 10, 1787, 190:16, Massachusetts Archives. For other evidence on the progovernment stance of ministers, see Arthur Chase, *The History of Ware, Massachusetts* (Boston, 1911), p. 96; Samuel King Diary, September 17, 1786, Pocumtuck Valley Association Library, Deerfield, Mass.; and Elizabeth Porter Diary, January 7, 1787, Porter-Phelps-Huntington Foundation, Hadley, Mass.

85. Kaplan, "Veteran Officers and Politics," p. 43 n.

86. *A Summary View of the Millennial Church or United Society of Believers, Commonly Called Shakers* (Albany, 1848), p. 54.

87. Isaac Backus, *The History of Baptists in New England,* 2 vols. (Boston, 1796), 2:470. For the anti-Shaysite position of Backus himself, see his *An Address to the Inhabitants of New England* (Boston, 1787), p. 6. Bidwell to David Daggett, June 16, 1787, Box 1, David Daggett Papers, Sterling Library, Yale University, New Haven. I have found only one pro-Shaysite "preacher"—Silas Little of Newburyport. Nicholas Pike to James Bowdoin, February 12, 1787, Bowdoin-Temple Papers, Massachusetts Historical Society, Boston.

88. Avery to Oliver Prescott, January 11, 1787, Boston Public Library, Boston.

Chapter 6

1. William Perry, *The Royal Standard English Dictionary* (Worcester, 1788), p. 427; "rebellion" is equated with "insurrection," p. 304.

2. George Richards Minot, *The History of the Insurrections in Massachusetts in the Year 1786 and the Rebellion Consequent Thereon* (Boston, 1788), p. 135.

3. Eric Hobsbawm, *Primitive Rebels: Studies in Archaic Forms of Social Movements in the Nineteenth and Twentieth Centuries* (New York: Norton, 1959), p. 5. For some similarities between the Shaysites at this stage and bandits in South Carolina during the 1760s, see Rachel Klein, "Crime and Regulation in the South Carolina Backcountry, 1765–1769," paper presented at the Organization of American Historians, New Orleans, April 14, 1979.

4. Charles Tilly, Richard Tilly, and Louise Tilly, *The Rebellious Century, 1830–1930* (Cambridge: Harvard University Press, 1975), p. 256.

5. Abel Whitney to William Shepard, October 25, 1786, 318:168, Massachusetts Archives, Boston.

6. Forbes Testimony in the Aaron Broad Case, Insurgents Tried Folder, Shays' Rebellion Box, American Antiquarian Society, Worcester.

7. *Hampshire Gazette,* December 6, 1786.

8. Petition of Daniel Shays and Luke Day, December 9, 1786, in *New Hampshire Mercury,* December 20, 1786; Rebel Petition, in *Worcester Magazine,* 2d week, December 1786; Gray to the People, in John Lockwood, *Westfield and Its Historic Influences,* 2 vols. (Springfield, 1922), 2:87–88.

9. Mary Cranch to Abigail Adams, November 26–30, 1786, Adams Family Papers, Massachusetts Historical Society, Boston.

10. Joseph Henshaw to James Bowdoin, December 3, 1786, 318: 199, Massachusetts Archives; Shrewsbury Town Petition, January 15, 1787, Petitions Folder, Shays' Rebellion Box, American Antiquarian Society.

11. Gill Testimony in Isaac Chenery Case, Insurgents Tried Folder; and Town of Ashburnham, December 19, 1786, Petitions Folder, Shays' Rebellion Box, American Antiquarian Society.

12. John Holland, Jr., Testimony, May 5, 1787, 189: 401, Massachusetts Archives. Also see *Massachusetts Centinel,* February 3, 1787.

13. Man in Worcester to Boston, December 8, 1786, *Massachusetts Gazette,* December 12, 1786; *Times* (London), January 24, 1787. For the accuracy of these reports, see Unknown to Isaiah Thomas, December 8, 1786, Sweet Calendar, Shays' Rebellion Box, American Antiquarian Society.

14. Georges Lefebvre, *The Great Fear of 1789* (New York: Pantheon, 1973), p. 72. See Stanley Miligram and Hans Toch, "Collective Behavior," in *The Handbook of Social Psychology,* ed. Elliot Aaronson and Lindzey Reading, 5 vols. (New York: Scribners, 1969), 4:538, for a theoretical discussion of rumor.

15. Grover and Pownell to the People, December 2, 1786, in Ellery Crane, "Shays' Rebellion," *Proceedings of the Worcester Society of Antiquity* 5 (1881): 85; Billings to Joshua Stiles, December 2, 1786, no. 155325, Suffolk County Court Files, Suffolk County Courthouse, Boston.

16. Nathan Mann Testimony in Francis Wilson Case, Insurgents Tried Folder, Shays' Rebellion Box, American Antiquarian Society.

17. Fillebrown and Winthrop to Bowdoin, December 13, 1786, 318: 212, Massachusetts Archives.

18. Daniel Gray Petition in Minot, *History of the Insurrections,* pp. 82–83.

19. Daniel Shays, Luke Day, and Thomas Grover to the Court, December 26, 1786, Case 8, Box 17, Gratz Collection, Historical Society of Pennsylvania, Philadelphia.

20. Levi Shepard to James Bowdoin, December 28, 1786, in "Bowdoin-Temple Papers," *Collections of the Massachusetts Historical Society,* 7th ser., 6 (1907): 125.

21. Shays, Powers, Billings, and Bardwell to Luke Day, January 20, 1787, 3:11, Worcester Collection, American Antiquarian Society;

Town of Sutton to James Bowdoin, January 1787, 190:305, Massachusetts Archives.

22. Robert Holt Testimony, Shays' Rebellion Box, Robert Treat Paine Papers, Massachusetts Historical Society, Boston. Also see D. M. Wilcox, "An Episode of Shays' Rebellion," *Magazine of History* 22, no. 3 (March 1916): 102.

23. Rebel Petition, January 12, 1787, in Carpenter and Morehouse, *The History of the Town of Amherst, Massachusetts,* 2 vols. (Amherst, 1896), 2:106; Robert Holt Testimony, Shays' Rebellion Box, Paine Papers.

24. Bardwell et al. to Luke Day, January 20, 1787, 3:11, Worcester Collection.

25. Clark to James Bowdoin, January 11, 1787, 190:301, Massachusetts Archives; Day to William Shepard, January 25, 1787, Adams Family Papers.

26. Billings Petition, January 4, 1787, in *Worcester Magazine,* 3d week, January 1787; Stephen Riley, "Doctor William Whiting and Shays' Rebellion," *Proceedings of the American Antiquarian Society* 66, no. 3 (January 1956): 132.

27. Webb Testimony in Isaac Chenery Case, Insurgents Tried Folder, Shays' Rebellion Box, American Antiquarian Society; Bardwell et al. to Luke Day, January 20, 1787, 3:11, Worcester Collection; Rebel Enlistment Form, 1787, in C. O. Parmenter, *The History of Pelham, Massachusetts* (Amherst, 1898), p. 373; Shays Interview, *Massachusetts Centinel,* January 17, 1787.

28. Knox to Marquis de Lafayette, February 13, 1787, Henry Knox Papers, Massachusetts Historical Society, Boston; Fisher Ames, *The Works of Fisher Ames* (Boston, 1809), p. 11.

29. Mallet to Robert Watts, April 20, 1787, Robert Watts Papers, New York Historical Society, New York; *Bath Chronicle,* March 29, 1787.

30. John Powers to the General Court, December 9, 1786, 190:297*a*, Massachusetts Archives; Rufus Putnam to James Bowdoin, December 13, 1786, Boston Public Library, Boston. Also see Obed Foot to Deerfield, Mass., December 19, 1786, 190:297*b*, Massachusetts Archives. For the militia commands of Shays and Drury, see Return of Daniel Shays Militia Company, August 24, 1786, Elisha Porter Papers, Massachusetts Historical Society, Boston; and Simeon Bruce Testimony, April 26, 1787, Shays' Rebellion Box, Paine Papers.

31. Richard M. Brown, "Backcountry Rebellions and the Homestead Ethic," in *Tradition, Conflict, and Modernization: Perspectives on the American Revolution,* eds. Richard M. Brown and Don Fehrenbacher (New York: Academic Press, 1977), pp. 86–87, 91.

32. This long conversation has been reprinted in Parmenter, *History of Pelham,* p. 396. According to a government spy report, "Shays disclaims any other title but *captain* which he had in the army."

Spy Report, December 8, 1786, Daniel Shays Papers, Manuscript
Division, Library of Congress, Washington, D.C. For the role of
Captain Swing, see E. J. Hobsbawm and George Rudé, *Captain
Swing* (New York: Pantheon, 1969), p. 100.

33. Henry Knox Report, September 20, 1786, in John Fitzpatrick, ed.,
    Journals of the Continental Congress, 36 vols. (Washington, 1905–),
    31:675; Shepard to Knox, December 20, 1786, in *Springfield Repub-
    lican,* December 21, 1894.

34. Daniel Shays Interview, *Massachusetts Centinel,* January 20, 1787,
    quoted in Seth Chandler, *History of Shirley* (Shirley, 1883), pp.
    702–3; Daniel Shays Interview, *Massachusetts Centinel,* January 17,
    1787.

35. Dwight to Rufus King, February 1, 1787, Adams Family Papers.

36. Shepard to Wadsworth, January 24, 1787, Jeremiah Wadsworth
    Papers, Connecticut Historical Society, Hartford; Shepard to James
    Bowdoin, January 25, 1787, 318: 287, Massachusetts Archives.

37. Henry Knox to Jeremiah Wadsworth, January 24, 1787, vol. 1,
    *m*247, p. 180, and Unknown to Jeremiah Wadsworth, January 24,
    1787, vol. 1, *m*247, p. 184, Papers of the Continental Congress,
    National Archives, Washington, D.C.

38. Noah Warriner Testimony, April 1787, Shays' Rebellion Box, Paine
    Papers; Aaron Graves to Benjamin Lincoln, January 24, 1787, Lloyd
    C. Stevens Collection, Morristown National Historic Park, Morris-
    town, N.J.

39. Day to Shepard, January 25, 1787, Adams Family Papers; Henry
    Knox to Jeremiah Wadsworth, January 24, 1787, 1:179, Papers of
    the Continental Congress; Day to Daniel Shays, January 25, 1787,
    Adams Family Papers.

40. Jeremy Belknap to Ebenezer Hazard, February 2, 1787, in "The
    Belknap Papers," *Collections of the Massachusetts Historical So-
    ciety,* 5th ser., 2 (1877): 455.

41. Shepard to James Bowdoin, January 26, 1787, in "Documents Re-
    lating to Shays' Rebellion," *American Historical Review* 2, no. 3
    (July 1897): 694; Thomas Dwight to Rufus King, February 1, 1787,
    Adams Family Papers; William Lyman Narrative, February 6,
    1787, Caleb Strong Papers, Forbes Library, Northampton, Mass., for
    Shays quote.

42. Idem: Samuel Buffington Narrative, February 1, 1787, Caleb Strong
    Papers; and Henry Knox to Marquis de Lafayette, February 13,
    1787, Knox Papers. The dead rebels were Ezekiel Root, Ariel
    Webster, John Hunter, and Jabez Spicer. *Hampshire Gazette,*
    February 14, 1787. On the government side, John Chanoler was
    wounded by a misfired cannon. Thomas Dwight to Rufus King,
    February 1, 1787, Adams Family Papers. Haskell to Colonel Platt,
    January 30, 1787, Knox Papers.

43. Thomas Dwight to Rufus King, February 1, 1787, Adams Family Papers.
44. Sprague and Allen to Bowdoin, February 2, 1787, Bowdoin-Temple Papers, Massachusetts Historical Society, Boston. For the organization of rural forces after Springfield, see Matthew Clark Account, in Seth Chandler, "Shirley," in *The History of Middlesex County, Massachusetts,* ed. Samuel Drake, 2 vols. (Boston, 1880), 2:304.
45. Letter from Hadley to Boston, January 30, 1787, *American Herald,* February 5, 1787; Daniel Shays Interview, *Massachusetts Centinel,* January 20, 1787, quoted in Chandler, *History of Shirley,* p. 703. Recruiting efforts of the Shaysites after Springfield can be found in Spy Report, January 30, 1787, Paine Papers; and Samuel Phillips Savage Diary, February 2, 1787, Massachusetts Historical Society, Boston.
46. Nos. 159003–6, Suffolk County Court Files.
47. Justus Forward to Benjamin Lincoln, January 31, 1787, Stevens Collection; John Billings to the General Court, n.d., John Billings Folder, Jones Library, Amherst.
48. No. 133939, Suffolk County Court Files.
49. Thompson Journal, March 26, 1787, Stevens Collection; No. 71, September 20, 1973, *Charles Hamilton Auction Sheet,* New York; Government Soldier to Boston, February 4, 1787, in *American Herald,* February 12, 1787.
50. Minot, *History of the Insurrections,* p. 135. Also see William Sullivan, *Familiar Letters on Public Characters* (Boston, 1834), p. 10.
51. F. W. Minot Diary, February 3, 1787, Theodore Sedgwick Papers, Massachusetts Historical Society, Boston.
52. King to Elbridge Gerry, February 11, 1787, Rufus King Papers, New York Historical Society, New York.
53. Massachusetts Senate to Bowdoin, February 4, 1787, 189:105, Massachusetts Archives; Daniel Kilham to Rufus King, February, 1787, King-Kilham Papers, Butler Library, Columbia University, New York; Massachusetts General Court, February 4, 1787, p. 397, reel 88, Papers of the Continental Congress.
54. Van Beck Hall, *Politics without Parties: Massachusetts, 1780–1791* (Pittsburgh: University of Pittsburgh Press, 1972), p. 229.
55. *Acts and Laws of Massachusetts, 1787* (Boston, 1787), pp. 557–58.
56. Warner to Benjamin Lincoln, February 10, 1787, Benjamin Lincoln Papers, Massachusetts Historical Society, Boston; Warner to James Bowdoin, February 7, 1787, 189:143, Massachusetts Archives; Shepard to Bowdoin, February 18, 1787, in "Bowdoin-Temple Papers," p. 141; Man in Berkshire, February 21, 1787, in *Middletown Gazette,* March 12, 1787; Parsons to the People, February 13, 1787, in *New Hampshire Mercury,* February 28, 1787.
57. Royall Tyler to James Bowdoin, February 13, 1787, 318:335, Mas-

sachusetts Archives, for the movement of Shays and the Days. The migration of Billings, Dickinson, and Nash can be found in *Worcester Magazine,* 3d week, February 1787. Aggregate numbers were discovered in Sir George Yonge to the British government, April 5, 1787, 1: 77, America and England: 1783–1789, Bancroft Collection, New York Public Library, New York; and William Shepard to James Bowdoin, February 27, 1787, 190:379–80, Massachusetts Archives. The government decree can be found in the *Middlesex Gazette,* March 26, 1787.

58. Tyler to the Vermont legislature, n.d., Royall Tyler Papers, Vermont Historical Society, Montpelier; Prince and Ruggles to Richard Devens, February 19, 1787, 189:139, Massachusetts Archives.

59. *New Hampshire Mercury,* March 28, 1787; Nathaniel Bishop to Benjamin Lincoln, April 3, 1787, Lincoln Papers. For the Shaysites in Pittsford, a town prominent in Vermont court disruptions during November 1786, see Jeremy Belknap to Ebenezer Hazard, February 27, 1787, "Belknap Papers," p. 464. For the Shaysites in New York, see Nathan Dane to Caleb Davis, June 2, 1787, Addendum 1, Wetmore Collection, Sterling Library, Yale University, New Haven.

60. Lord Dorchester to Lord Sidney, February 28, 1787, 50: B-39, 135, Colonial Office 42, Public Archives of Canada, Ottawa, tells of the arrival of the Shaysites in Quebec. Timothy Newell to Benjamin Lincoln, April 30, 1787, Addendum 1, Wetmore Collection; and John Johnson to Joseph Brant, March 22, 1787, 5:80, Henry O'Reilly Papers, New York Historical Society, New York, tell of the outcome. This interpretation of British involvement in Shays' Rebellion differs from Robert Feer, "The Devil and Daniel Shays," *Cambridge Historical Society Publications* 40 (1967): 7–22.

61. Abigail Adams to Mary Cranch, April 28, 1787, Adams Family Papers.

62. Wiley to Colonel Clark and Captain Parcetor, April 23, 1787, *Hampshire Gazette,* June 6, 1787.

63. Joseph Raymond, Benjamin Pierson, William Barnes, et al. to Benjamin Lincoln, February 26, 1787, Shays' Rebellion MSS, Berkshire Athenaeum, Pittsfield, Mass. For the social composition of the farmers, see no. 160538, Suffolk County Court Files.

64. *Worcester Magazine,* 4th week, March 1787; Henry Van Schaack to Peter Van Schaack, March 3, 1787, in Henry Van Schaack, *Memoirs of the Life of Henry Van Schaack* (Chicago, 1892), p. 133.

65. Elisha Williams to Eliphalet Williams, March 12, 1787, Williams Papers, Connecticut Historical Society, Hartford; Sargeant to William Shepard, March 5, 1787, Folder 3, Box 1, Shays' Rebellion Box, Jones Library, Amherst.

66. For the various attacks, see Henry Van Schaack to Peter Van Schaack, in Van Schaack, *Memoirs,* p. 131; *Springfield Republican*

excerpt, Shays' Rebellion Box, Berkshire Athenaeum; and Electa Jones, *Stockbridge: Past and Present* (Springfield, 1854), pp. 191–94.

67. Lincoln to George Clinton, February 27, 1787, Lincoln Papers.

68. *Hampshire Gazette,* March 14, 1787.

69. Gentleman in Camp to Boston, February 27, 1787, *American Herald,* March 12, 1787.

70. *New Haven Gazette,* March 15, 1787; John Ashley to Benjamin Lincoln, February 27, 1787, Addendum 1, Wetmore Collection.

71. *Hampshire Gazette,* April 11, 1787.

72. Elisha Williams to Eliphalet Williams, March 12, 1787, Williams Papers; Little to Benjamin Lincoln, March 26, 1787, Lincoln Papers.

73. Roger Bagg and Noble Dewey to Loomis, April 5, 1787, in *Hampshire Gazette,* April 11, 1787; *Hampshire Gazette,* April 18, 1787.

74. Thomas Thompson Journal, April 2, 1787, Stevens Collection.

75. Mason Green, *Springfield, 1636–1886* (Springfield, 1888), p. 330.

76. *Hampshire Gazette,* April 11, 1787.

77. Shepard Testimony in Green, *Springfield,* p. 330; and Benjamin Lincoln to Colonel Murray, April 16, 1787, Paine Papers.

78. Shepard to Benjamin Lincoln, February 20, 1787, Lincoln Papers; *Hampshire Gazette,* May 30, 1787; Mattoon to Thomas Cushing, May 8, 1787, in Parmenter, *History of Pelham,* p. 388.

79. *New Hampshire Gazette,* June 2, 1787; Thomas Ives to Theodore Sedgwick, June 25, 1787, 190:21, Massachusetts Archives; *Hampshire Gazette,* June 27, 1787; no. 160536, Suffolk County Court Files.

80. Hall, *Politics without Parties,* pp. 246–48.

81. For commercial opinion see Hall, *Politics without Parties,* p. 239. For the Shaysite aversion to Bowdoin, see Benjamin Hichborn to John Adams, January 16, 1787, Adams Family Papers; J. R. Pole, "Suffrage and Representation in Massachusetts: A Statistical Note," *William and Mary Quarterly* 14, no. 4 (October 1957): 586; "A Springfield Farmer," *New Haven Gazette,* July 19, 1787; Levi Lincoln to James Bowdoin, March 9, 1787, 190:409a, Massachusetts Archives.

82. *Massachusetts Gazette,* June 26, 1787; Samuel Green, "Groton during Shays' Rebellion," *Proceedings of the Massachusetts Historical Society* 1, no. 3 (July 1884): 311–12; *Worcester Magazine,* 2d week, December 1787.

83. Hancock Proclamation, June 15, 1787, in John Noble, "A Few Notes on Shays' Rebellion," *Proceedings of the American Antiquarian Society* 15, no. 2 (March 1902): 224; Hancock to Bernard, January 22, 1766, in W. T. Baxter, *The House of Hancock: Business in Boston, 1724–1775* (Cambridge: Harvard University Press, 1945), p. 233; General Court, June 12, 1787, 190:13, Massachusetts Archives; Mercy Otis Warren, *History of the Rise, Progress, and Termination of the American Revolution,* 3 vols. (Boston, 1805),

3:354. For Hancock's tour, see Hall, *Politics without Parties,* p. 253.

84. See *New Haven Gazette,* April 5, 1787, for the vote. Information about the presence of Willard can be found in Jacob Richardson to Ebenezer Hazard, March 20, 1787, no. 307, item 61, Papers of the Continental Congress; John Brooks to Benjamin Lincoln, January 20, 1787, Stevens Collection.

85. Sullivan to Bowdoin, February 9, 1787, Shays' Rebellion Papers, Massachusetts Historical Society, Boston; Eleazear Wheelock to Sullivan, March 29, 1787, in John Sullivan, *The Letters and Papers of John Sullivan,* ed. Otis Hammond, 3 vols. (Concord: New Hampshire Historical Society, 1939), 3:514.

86. Huntington to Bowdoin, February 20, 1787, in "Bowdoin-Temple Papers," p. 146.

87. Heman Swift to Samuel Huntington, May 15, 1787, 3:252–3, 3d ser., Military Papers, Connecticut Archives, Hartford; Tapping Reeves to John Cotton Smith, May 22, 1787, no. 25, and Smith to Reeves, May 23, 1787, no. 37, Box 5, Helen Evertson Smith Collection, New York Historical Society, New York.

88. Leonard Labaree, ed., *Public Records of the State of Connecticut,* 10 vols. (Hartford, 1945), 6:294–95; Journal of the Lower House, May 16, 1787, *Records of the United States: Connecticut,* p. 250, A 1*b,* microfilm.

89. Tracy to Oliver Wolcott, May 21, 1787, Tracy MSS, New York Public Library, New York; John Sedgwick to Charles Burrall, May 6, 1788, 3:258, 3d ser., Military Papers, Connecticut Archives; Huntington to the Connecticut Delegates to the Constitutional Convention, June 22, 1787, Miscellaneous Bound, Massachusetts Historical Society, Boston.

90. *Middletown Gazette,* March 9, 1787; and McGregor, March 20, 1787, Colin McGregor Letterbook: 1783–1787, New York Public Library, New York.

91. Royall Tyler Report, February 1787, Tyler Papers.

92. Royall Tyler to Benjamin Lincoln, February 18, 1787, 318:366, Massachusetts Archives.

93. *Vermont Gazette,* May 7, July 30, 1787; Allen to Tyler, August 28, 1787, in Mary Cabot, ed., *Annals of Brattleborough,* 2 vols. (Brattleborough, 1921), 1:255.

94. Sidney to Dorchester, April 5, 1787, 50:78, B-39, Colonial Office 42, Public Archives of Canada.

95. Orasmus Turner, *History of the Pioneer Settlement of Phelps and Gorham's Purchase* (Rochester, 1851), p. 410; Sylvester Judd, *The History of Hadley* (Northampton, 1863), p. 78; Francis Blake, *The History of Princeton, Massachusetts,* 2 vols. (Princeton, 1915), 2:108–9; no. 1230, Brigham Collection, Vermont Historical Society, Montpelier.

96. Merrill Jensen, ed., *The Documentary History of the Ratification*

of the Constitution, 2 vols. (Madison: University of Wisconsin Press, 1976), 1:352–53. ,

97. Tudor to George Washington, July 26, 1788, George Washington Papers, Manuscript Division, Library of Congress, Washington, D.C.

98. Samuel Eliot Morison, *The Maritime History of Massachusetts, 1783–1860* (Boston: Houghton Mifflin, 1921), p. 38; *Acts and Laws of Massachusetts, 1787* (Boston, 1787).

Chapter 7

1. Van Beck Hall, *Politics without Parties: Massachusetts, 1780–1791* (Pittsburgh: University of Pittsburgh Press, 1972), p. 258. Robert Feer disagrees with this viewpoint. In his "Shays' Rebellion and the Constitution: A Study in Causation," *New England Quarterly* 42, no. 4 (September 1969): 410, he states that "Shays' Rebellion was not a cause of the Constitution.... In all likelihood, the Constitutional Convention would have met when it did, the same document would have been drawn up, and it would have been ratified even if Shays' Rebellion had not taken place."

2. Knox to Samuel Holden Parsons, March 29, 1785, Henry Knox Papers, Massachusetts Historical Society, Boston; Manning to Nathan Miller, June 12, 1785, in Edmund Burnett, ed., *Letters of Members of the Continental Congress,* 8 vols. (Washington, D.C.: Government Printing Office, 1931–36), 8:391.

3. Sparhawk to Benjamin Goodhue, December 27, 1785, Goodhue Collection, New York Society Library, New York.

4. Dane to King, October 8, 1785, Box 1, Rufus King Papers, New York Historical Society, New York; King to Dane, September 17, 1785, Nathan Dane Papers, Manuscript Division, Library of Congress, Washington, D.C.; King to Jonathan Jackson, June 11, 1786, in Rufus King, "The Letters of Rufus King," *Proceedings of the Massachusetts Historical Society* 49, no. 2 (November 1915): 86.

5. Address of the Annapolis Convention, September 14, 1786, in Alexander Hamilton, *The Papers of Alexander Hamilton,* ed. Harold Syrett, 24 vols. (New York: Columbia University Press, 1961–), 3:689.

6. Sedgwick to Caleb Strong, August 6, 1786, in Theodore Sedgwick, "Sedgwick Letters," *American Historical Review* 4, no. 2 (January 1899): 329.

7. Address of the Annapolis Convention, September 14, 1786, in Hamilton, *Papers* 3:687. King to James Bowdoin, September 17, 1786, no. 9446, Emmett Collection, New York Public Library, New York.

8. Washington to James Madison, November 5, 1786, in George Washington, *The Writings of George Washington,* ed. John Fitzpatrick,

39 vols. (Washington, D.C., 1931–44), 29:52; Stevens to John Stevens, Jr., February 6, 1787, Stevens Family Papers, New Jersey Historical Society, Trenton; Jay to William Carmichael, January 4, 1787, in John Jay, *The Correspondence and Public Papers of John Jay,* ed. Henry Johnston, 4 vols. (New York, 1890–91), 3:225.

9. Blount to Richard Caswell, December 7, 1786, and Grayson to James Monroe, November 22, 1786, in Burnett, *Letters,* 8:516, 510.

10. Pettit to Benjamin Franklin, October 18, 1786, ibid., p. 487; Rutledge to Unknown, October 21, 1786, Pratt Collection, Amherst College, Amherst, Mass.

11. Aubrey Land, ed., "Journals and Correspondence of the State Council of Maryland," *Archives of Maryland,* 72 vols. (Baltimore, 1970), 71:123. Phillip Crowl, "Maryland during and after the Revolution," *Johns Hopkins University Studies in Historical and Political Science* 61, no. 1 (1943): 93–94.

12. Ibid., pp. 92–93.

13. William Smallwood, a Proclamation, July 10, 1786, in *Maryland Gazette,* July 20, 1786. Also see the *New York Gazetteer and Country Journal,* June 27, 1786.

14. Timothy Ford, "The Diary of Timothy Ford," *South Carolina Historical and Genealogical Magazine* 13, no. 4 (October 1912): 193.

15. Thomas Pinckney to Harriot Pinckney, September 16, 1786, Thomas Pinckney Papers, Library of Congress, Washington, D.C.

16. John Adams Report, October 13, 1786, in John Fitzpatrick, ed., *Journals of the Continental Congress,* 36 vols. (Washington, 1905–), 31:788. Burke and Moultrie quoted in Robert Becker, *"Salus Populi Suprema Lex:* Public Peace and South Carolina Debtor Relief Laws, 1783–1788," *South Carolina Historical Magazine* 80, no. 1 (January 1979): 71. Also see *Maryland Journal,* October 11, 1786, for the riots in Camden and the elite response.

17. Joseph Lewis, "The Diary of Joseph Lewis," *Proceedings of the New Jersey Historical Society* 60, no. 1 (January 1942): 61.

18. David Bernstein, ed., "Minutes of the Governor's Privy Council," *New Jersey Archives* (Trenton: New Jersey State Library, 1974), 3d ser., 1:270–71; *Independent Chronicle,* April 30, 1786.

19. John Fiske, "The Paper Money Craze of 1786 and the Shays' Rebellion," *Atlantic Monthly* 58 (September 1886): 379.

20. Dawson to Madison, April 15, 1787, in James Madison, *The Papers of James Madison,* ed. Robert Rutland, 10 vols. (Chicago: University of Chicago Press, 1962–), 9:381; Dawson to Madison, June 12, 1787, James Madison Papers, Library of Congress, Washington, D.C.

21. James McClurg to Madison, August 22, 1787, Madison Papers; Beverly Randolph to Edmund Randolph, September 8, 1787, in Madison, *Papers,* 10:161 n.

22. Madison to Jefferson, September 6, 1787, in Jefferson, *Papers,* 2:103–4.

23. Richard Henry Lee to Henry Lee, September 13, 1787, Miscellaneous, New York Public Library, New York; Stuart to Madison, November 9, 1787, Madison Papers.

24. *Pennsylvania Mercury,* June 8, 1787.

25. Hahn to John Nicholson, December 15, 1786, in Samuel Hazard, ed., *Pennsylvania Archives,* 3d ser., 11 (1855): 98; entries of March 2, 1787, and February 3, 1787, in Henry Muhlenberg, *The Journals of Henry Melchior Muhlenberg,* trans. Theodore Tappert and John Doberstein, 3 vols. (Philadelphia: Evangelical Lutheran Ministerium, 1958), 3:730, 733.

26. Knox to George Washington, December 21, 1786, Knox Papers.

27. Wolcott to Oliver Wolcott, Jr., February 4, 1787, Oliver Wolcott, Jr. Papers, Connecticut Historical Society, Hartford.

28. Butler to Elbridge Gerry, March 3, 1788, Elbridge Gerry Papers, Library of Congress, Washington, D.C.

29. Washington to Marquis de Lafayette, March 25, 1787, and June 6, 1787, in Washington, *Writings,* 29:84, 229; Carrington to Thomas Jefferson, June 9, 1787, in George Bancroft, *The History of the Formation of the Constitution,* 2 vols. (New York, 1883), 2:427; Madison to George Muter, January 7, 1787, in Madison, *Papers,* 9:231.

30. For the connection between the appointment of delegates for Philadelphia and Shays' Rebellion, see Forrest McDonald, *The Formation of the American Republic, 1776–1790* (Baltimore: Johns Hopkins Press, 1968), pp. 151–54.

31. James Madison, *Notes of Debates in the Federal Convention of 1787 Reported by James Madison* (New York: Norton, 1969), p. 471.

32. Art. 1, sec. 10, of the Constitution, in John Jay, Alexander Hamilton, and James Madison, *The Federalist Papers,* ed. Clinton Rossiter (New York: New American Library, 1961), p. 532.

33. Rush to Jeremy Belknap, February 28, 1788, Jeremy Belknap Papers, Massachusetts Historical Society, Boston.

34. September 11, 1786, *Boston Town Records, 1786–1787* (Boston, 1903), p. 131.

35. Washington to Thomas Jefferson, November 12, 1786, in Washington, *Writings,* 29:61.

36. *Political Magazine,* November 1786, pp. 72–73.

37. Hamilton, in Gaillard Hunt and J. B. Scott, eds., *The Debates in the Federal Convention of 1787* (New York, 1920), p. 113.

38. Madison, *Notes of Debates,* p. 321.

39. Ibid., pp. 478, 515. See Richard Kohn, *The Eagle and the Sword: The Federalists and the Creation of a National Military Establishment in America, 1783–1802* (New York: Free Press, 1975), for the continuing debate over a standing army.

40. Madison, *Notes of Debates,* p. 484.

41. Ibid., p. 475.
42. Art. 1, sec. 8, of the Constitution, in Jay, Hamilton, and Madison, *Federalist Papers*, p. 533.
43. Art. 4, sec. 4, of the Constitution, ibid., p. 539.
44. Madison, *Notes of Debates*, p. 321. For a good analysis of the influence of Shays' Rebellion upon the guarantee clause, see William Wiecek, *The Guarantee Clause of the U.S. Constitution* (Ithaca: Cornell University Press, 1972), pp. 27–42.
45. Jonathan Elliot, ed., *Debates of the State Conventions on the Adoption of the Federal Constitution*, 5 vols. (New York: 1888), 2:521.
46. Art. 1, sec. 9, and Art. 4, sec. 2, of the Constitution, in Jay, Hamilton, and Madison, *Federalist Papers*, pp. 534, 539. As in the formulation of the Declaration of Independence, Southern fear of slave revolts also played an important part. See Sidney Kaplan, "The 'Domestic Insurrections' of the Declaration of Independence," *Journal of Negro History* 61, no. 3 (July 1976): 243–55.
47. Knox to George Washington, October 3, 1787, in United States, *Documentary History of the Constitution*, 5 vols. (Washington, D.C., 1894–1905), 4:311; Knox to Washington, January 14, 1788, in *Debates and Proceedings in the Convention of the Commonwealth of Massachusetts* (Boston, 1856), pp. 399–400.
48. Nathaniel Gorham to James Madison, January 27, 1788, in Madison, *Papers*, 10:436.
49. Jackson to Henry Knox, February 3, 1788, Henry Knox Papers, Massachusetts Historical Society, Boston; Knox to George Washington, January 14, 1788, in *Debates in Massachusetts*, pp. 399–400. On Maine farmers, see Christopher Gore to Jeremiah Wadsworth, January 9, 1788, no. 5047, Emmett Collection, New York Public Library, New York. Although Maine farmers opposed the new plan of government, the Maine seacoast backed the proposal. See Orin Libby, "Geographical Distribution of the Vote of the Thirteen States on the Federal Constitution," *Bulletin of the University of Wisconsin* 1 (1897): 14. For Quaker Nantucket, see Nathaniel Gorham to Henry Knox, January 6, 1788, Knox Papers. For the leadership of Bishop, see Jeremy Belknap, "Notes on the Massachusetts Ratifying Convention," *Proceedings of the Massachusetts Historical Society* 3, no. 3 (November 1858): 301. Other former insurgents in the Massachusetts convention included Gilbert Denck (Hopkinton), Benjamin Morse (Groton), Daniel Fisk (Pepperell), Benjamin Ely (West Springfield), John Williston (West Springfield), Consider Arms (Conway), Malachi Maynard (Conway), Asa Fisk (South Brimfield), Phineas Merrick (Monson), Timothy Blair (Blandford), Samuel Eddy (Colrain), Isaac Pepper (Ware), John Goldsbury (Warwick), Agrippa Wells (Bernardston), Ephraim Williams (Ashfield), Asa Powers (Shutesbury), Silas Fowler (Southwick), Elihu Cotton (Longmeadow), Caleb Curtis (Charlton),

John Black (Barre), Benjamin Josselyn (New Braintree), Isaac Harrington (Shrewsbury), Samuel Willard (Uxbridge), Josiah Whitney (Harvard), Moses Hale (Winchendon), Ephraim Fitch (Egremont), John Hurlburt (Alford), and Jesse Bradley (Lee). Data were gained from a comparison of rebels listed in various sources, primarily in Oaths of Allegiance, vol. 190, Massachusetts Archives, Boston, and lists of convention delegates in *Debates in Massachusetts.*

50. Gerry to Adams and Warren, October 18, 1787, and Gerry to Wendall, July 10, 1789, in George Billias, *Elbridge Gerry: Founding Father and Republican Statesman* (New York: McGraw-Hill, 1976), pp. 208, 396.

51. Sullivan to Unknown, September 23, 1787, in Clifford Shipton, *Sibley's Harvard Graduates: Biographical Sketches of Those Who Attended Harvard College,* 17 vols. (Boston, 1893–1975), 15:310. Also see Sullivan to Rufus King, n.d., in Thomas Amory, *The Life of James Sullivan,* 2 vols. (Boston, 1859), 2:203. The same lukewarm opposition can be found in other so-called prominent Antifederalists. "Altho' the names of Colonel Mason and myself are not subscribed, it is not, therefore, to be concluded that we are opposed to its adoption," Edmund Randolph wrote about the Constitution. Randolph to Beverly Randolph, September 18, 1787, in Max Farrand, ed., *The Records of the Federal Convention of 1787,* 3 vols. (New Haven: Yale University Press, 1911), 3:83. Similarly, James Madison believed that Edward Carrington and George Mason "did not object to the substance of the government but contend for a few additional guards in favor of the rights of the states." Madison to Thomas Jefferson, December 9, 1787, in Madison, *Papers,* 10:312.

52. "Cornelius," in Samuel Harding, *The Contest over the Federal Constitution in the State of Massachusetts* (New York, 1896), p. 124.

53. Singletary, in *Debates in Massachusetts,* p. 203; Bishop and Nasson, in Elliot, *Debates,* 2:23–24, 136–37.

54. Jackson Turner Main, *The Antifederalists: Critics of the Constitution, 1781–1788* (New York: Norton, 1961), p. 207 n.; also see pp. 208–9.

55. Ibid., p. 209. For the "well-managed" campaign of the nationalists, see Henry Jackson to Henry Knox, February 6, 1788, Knox Papers.

56. Gibbs to George Washington, February 9, 1788, in U.S., *Documentary History of the Constitution,* 4:492. For nationalist control of the newspapers, see Main, *Antifederalists,* p. 209 n.

57. Washington to Minot, August 28, 1788, in Washington, *Writings,* 30:65.

Index